CONTENTS

SECTION ONE   9
Language, Literacy, and Learning
in Elementary Classrooms

SECTION TWO   *119*

Language, Literacy, and Learning in Middle and Secondary School Classrooms

SECTION THREE *205*
Improving Teaching and Learning in Multilingual Classrooms

Julie Coppola is an assistant professor of education and co-ordinator of the bilingual education and teaching English as a second language (pre-K–12) programs at Boston University, Massachusetts, USA. Her teaching and research focus on two areas: (1) first and second language and literacy development with a particular focus on young English language learners (ELLs) and (2) preparing preservice and inservice teachers to meet the needs of this student population. She has published numerous book chapters and journal articles in these areas and is the author of *Teaching English Language Learners in Grades K–3: Promoting Language and Literacy Development*.

A former first-grade bilingual/English as a second language teacher, Julie is a frequent contributor at local, national, and international language and literacy conferences. She has conducted extensive site-based professional development programs in teaching ELLs for school districts throughout Massachusetts. She frequently consults with school districts on efforts to improve second language and literacy curricula.

Julie is an active member of the International Reading Association. She has held leadership roles in her local council and served on the Multilingual Classroom Committee and the Commission on Second Language Literacy and Learning.

Julie and her husband, Robert, a professor of environmental design, are the parents of two children: Ann, a business analyst, and Matt, a college student. Julie may be reached at jcoppola@bu.edu.

Elizabeth V. Primas is the director of advanced programs for the District of Columbia Public Schools, an adjunct professor of education at George Washington University, and the director of education and technology for the Prince George's County, Maryland, Housing Authority.

Previously, Elizabeth was director of literacy: reading and language arts for the District of Columbia Public Schools and teacher-in-residence at Educational Testing

Services, Princeton, New Jersey, USA, where she led the development of the National Board Certification requirements for elementary and middle school literacy: reading/English language arts teachers. A former reading specialist, Elizabeth has received numerous teaching awards, including the 2000 District of Columbia Teacher of the Year Award.

Elizabeth is an active member of International Reading Association and most recently cochaired the Urban Diversity Initiatives Commission. She is also a member of the National Council of Teachers of English and serves on the Commission on Children's Literature. Elizabeth was inducted into the Phi Delta Kappa Honor Society, George Washington University Chapter, and she is a member of the National Alliance of Black School Educators.

Elizabeth enjoys writing poetry, painting, skiing, and traveling abroad. She is married to Vincent V. Lewis and takes her greatest pleasure in her family, which spans five generations from her mother to her youngest offspring. Elizabeth may be reached at elizabeth.primas@dc.gov.

CONTRIBUTORS

Jennifer Battle
Literacy Professor
Texas State University—San Marcos
San Marcos, Texas, USA

Donald R. Bear
Professor and Director
E.L. Cord Foundation Center
    for Learning and Literacy
University of Nevada, Reno
Reno, Nevada, USA

Margarita Calderón
Senior Research Scientist
    and Professor
Johns Hopkins University
Baltimore, Maryland, USA

Catherine Carrison
English Language Learner Specialist
Evergreen Public Schools
Vancouver, Washington, USA

Gisela Ernst-Slavit
Professor of Education
Washington State University
Vancouver, Washington, USA

Jill Fitzgerald
Senior Associate Dean and Professor
    of Literacy
University of North Carolina
    at Chapel Hill
Chapel Hill, North Carolina, USA

Brenda Gangemi
Physical Education Teacher
Cathedral Academy at Pompei
Syracuse, New York, USA

Michael F. Graves
Professor of Literacy Education,
    Emeritus
University of Minnesota
Minneapolis, Minnesota, USA

Lori A. Helman
Assistant Professor
University of Minnesota
Minneapolis, Minnesota, USA

Grete O. Kelsey
Sixth-Grade Teacher
Cathedral Academy at Pompei
Syracuse, New York, USA

Youb Kim
Assistant Professor of English
    as a Second Language/English
    Language Learning
Pennsylvania State University
University Park, Pennsylvania, USA

Zachary A. Konett
Fourth-Grade Teacher
East Lansing Public Schools
East Lansing, Michigan, USA

Charles LaBarbera
Principal
Cathedral Academy at Pompei
Syracuse, New York, USA

Trini Lewis
Associate Professor and Coordinator
for Master of Arts in Education,
Dual Language Development
California State University—Long
Beach
Long Beach, California, USA

Hyo Jin Lim
Doctoral Candidate, School
of Education
University of Southern California
Los Angeles, California, USA

Sharlene McKenzie
Technology Teacher
Cathedral Academy at Pompei
Syracuse, New York, USA

Meredith McLellan
English as a Second Language
Teacher
East Lansing Public Schools
East Lansing, Michigan, USA

Andrea McPherson-Rumsey
Second-Grade Teacher
East Lansing Public Schools
East Lansing, Michigan, USA

Carol Melchior
Kindergarten Teacher
Cathedral Academy at Pompei
Syracuse, New York, USA

Barbara Merrick
First-Grade Teacher
Cathedral Academy at Pompei
Syracuse, New York, USA

Eric S. Mohr
English Teacher
Frisco High School
Frisco, Texas, USA

Kathleen A.J. Mohr
Associate Professor of Language,
Literacy, and Bilingual/ESL
Education
University of North Texas
Denton, Texas, USA

Julie Nora
Director
International Charter School
Pawtucket, Rhode Island, USA

P. David Pearson
Dean of the Graduate School
of Education and Professor
of Language and Literacy, Society
and Culture
University of California, Berkeley
Berkeley, California, USA

Esmeralda Ramos
First-Grade Teacher
Long Beach Unified School District
Long Beach, California, USA

Nancy Roser
Professor of Language and Literacy
Studies
University of Texas at Austin
Austin, Texas, USA

Robert Rueda
Professor of Psychology in Education
University of Southern California
Los Angeles, California, USA

Patricia Ruggiano Schmidt
Literacy Professor
Le Moyne College
Syracuse, New York, USA

Fay Shin
Professor of Teacher Education
California State University—Long
    Beach
Long Beach, California, USA

Christyn Simpkins
Sixth-Grade Teacher
Stockton Unified Schools
Stockton, California, USA

Jan Spiesman-Laughlin
Clinical Faculty, Field Supervisor
College of Education
Washington State University
Vancouver, Washington, USA

Roseann Sunser
Librarian
Cathedral Academy at Pompei
Syracuse, New York, USA

Russell Wasden
Literacy Coach
Academy for Language and
    Technology
New York, New York, USA

Meg Williams
Reading Specialist
Cathedral Academy at Pompei School
Syracuse, New York, USA

Linda Woessner
ELL Teacher
Saint Paul Public Schools
Saint Paul, Minnesota, USA

Julie E. Wollman
Vice President for Academic Affairs
Wheelock College
Boston, Massachusetts, USA

Melody Patterson Zoch
Third-Grade Teacher
Austin Public Schools
Austin, Texas, USA

ACKNOWLEDGMENTS

The steadily rising numbers of English language learners in U.S. schools indicate that all involved in literacy education must learn more about how students develop second language literacy skills and how to implement effective instructional practices that support second language learning. In addition, all involved in teaching and learning in today's multilingual classrooms must be cognizant of the role of student diversity in literacy learning. To ensure that its members are provided with resources to help them reach these goals, the International Reading Association established two commissions: the Commission on Second Language Literacy and Learning and the Commission on Urban Diversity Initiatives. Commission members—practitioners and scholars—work together to plan professional development opportunities, presentations, and publications devoted to promoting understanding about issues of diversity as they relate to literacy learning. *One Classroom, Many Learners: Best Literacy Practices for Today's Multilingual Classrooms* and the accompanying institute on teaching and learning in multilingual classrooms presented in Atlanta, Georgia, USA, in May 2008 are results of this collaboration.

We wish to thank the more than 50 members of the two commissions who gave of their time and expertise. In particular, we wish to acknowledge Paul Boyd-Batstone, California State University—Long Beach, USA, for chairing the Commission on Second Language Literacy and Learning and William T. Hammond, DeKalb County Schools, College Park, Georgia, USA, for serving as chair of the Commission on Urban Diversity Initiatives.

Julie Coppola
Commission on Second Language Literacy and Learning

Elizabeth V. Primas
Commission on Urban Diversity Initiatives

INTRODUCTION

Julie Coppola

Throughout the United States, the number of students identified as English language learners (ELLs) and who require specialized instruction to achieve in English has risen dramatically. Between 1989 and 2006, the number of ELLs in U.S. schools more than doubled—from 2 million to 5.1 million—and the rate at which ELLs enrolled in school increased at nearly seven times the rate of total student enrollment (National Clearinghouse for English Language Acquisition, 2008). For the purpose of this volume, we define ELLs as students whose primary language is a language other than English and who are in the process of acquiring the language and literacy skills necessary to participate successfully in an English language classroom. We, Julie, a teacher educator with a research and teaching focus on assessment and instruction of ELLs, and Elizabeth, a literacy leader in a large urban school district that enrolls many ELLs, felt a book on this topic was necessary for several reasons.

First, this unprecedented growth in the number of ELLs shows no signs of slowing. Current estimates are that by the year 2020, children of immigrants will likely account for all of the growth in the school-age population (Passel & Cohn, 2008). By the year 2050, the number of children from linguistically and culturally diverse backgrounds will make up 62% of the population of children in the United States (U.S. Census Bureau, 2008). Although at one time ELLs were more likely to live in large urban areas and thus attend urban schools, the presence of these students and their families is felt increasingly in suburban and rural schools and classrooms throughout the United States. For example, current census figures demonstrate the greatest gains in the number of students identified as ELLs are not in the historically high immigration states of California and New York but are found in states such as Georgia, Nebraska, Nevada, and North Carolina (U.S. Census Bureau, 2006). Many of these students live in homes where no adult speaks, reads, or writes English. These rapidly changing demographics indicate that all teachers must expect that they will teach a student who depends upon school to learn the English language knowledge and skills necessary for school and later life success.

We also focus on ELLs because a large portion of these students is expected to need extra services if they are to succeed in English (Passel & Cohn, 2008);

however, both new and experienced teachers continue to report that they are not prepared to meet these students' language and literacy learning needs (Gándara, Maxwell-Jolly, & Driscoll, 2005; National Comprehensive Center for Teacher Quality, 2008). Teachers state that they need to know more about how students develop as readers and writers in a second language and about effective strategies to promote second language and literacy development. Teachers want to learn about their students' languages and cultures, and they want to better understand how cultural differences influence students' and families' approaches to and expectations of schooling (Gunderson, 2009). Teachers also want to know how to better communicate with students and parents and how to tap into and build upon the background knowledge and skills that ELLs and their families bring to school. Yet most teachers have not had any formal training to help them reach these goals.

Finally, we have turned our attention to ELLs because of ongoing concerns about their pattern of limited academic achievement in U.S. schools. Although there are recent signs of increased achievement on national reading and writing assessments among ELLs, these gains have not resulted in any appreciable difference in the achievement gap between these students and their English-proficient peers (Lee, Grigg, & Donahue, 2007; Salahu-Din, Persky, & Miller, 2008). Hispanic students, the largest group of ELLs, continue to drop out of high school at rates that far exceed those of their black and white peers (National Center for Education Statistics, 2008). Much remains to be done, therefore, to ensure that all students receive the language and literacy learning opportunities they need to experience success during their school years and beyond. We must ensure also that all ELLs are enrolled in classrooms with teachers who have the knowledge and skills to provide these opportunities.

The Goal of This Volume

We planned this book to provide important and much-needed information about how best to teach ELLs. In each chapter, we demonstrate how current theory and research-based evidence in first and second language and literacy development inform teaching practice in classrooms that enroll ELLs. Each chapter includes a review of the relevant theory and research, a description of the instructional context, and classroom-based demonstrations of the connections among theory, research, and practice. We also share students' oral and written responses to and, in many cases, teachers' and parents' reflections on the implementations of the recommended practices. To underscore the need to connect theory, research, and practice, most of the chapters are coauthored by a researcher or a team of researchers and a practitioner or team of practitioners in whose school or classroom(s) the work took place. Although chapter authors may have chosen to focus their work in one instructional context and with one particular group of students, the relevant theory and research and the related recommended instructional practices are useful to teachers who work in a variety of instructional settings. Furthermore, the recommended practices may be used to teach students from a wide range of age, grade, and English proficiency levels.

How This Volume Is Organized

In this volume, contributors explore important topics such as the instruction of word-level and text-level skills, the role of engagement and motivation in student success, vibrant home–school connections, and ongoing teacher preparation. Consequently, we organized the chapters into three sections. In the first section, we explore language and literacy teaching and learning in the elementary grades. Next we turn our attention to teaching and learning in middle and secondary schools. In the final section, we demonstrate successful outcomes of teachers' efforts to improve their teaching practices as they relate to ELLs.

In Chapter 1, Donald R. Bear, Lori A. Helman, and Linda Woessner share their experiences implementing word study assessment and instruction with students in Linda's second-grade classroom. Here, the authors focus on students who are in the beginning stages of learning English, and they show how Linda assessed the students' English word knowledge using a developmental spelling inventory. Next, we follow Linda as she implements a series of small-group word study lessons informed by the assessment results. The authors conclude with guidelines to help teachers construct meaningful and developmentally appropriate word study programs in classrooms with students who are learning English.

In Chapter 2, Youb Kim, P. David Pearson, Meredith McLellan, Andrea McPherson-Rumsey, and Zachary A. Konett demonstrate the use of instructional strategies that support both language and literacy development among ELLs. The chapter begins with a brief overview of the major theoretical perspectives and research findings that shed light upon the connections between oral and written language development. This information is important for teachers to consider because of the conflicting recommendations in the research literature about when to begin formal literacy instruction with ELLs (e.g., Fitzgerald & Noblitt, 1999; Snow, Burns, & Griffin, 1998). Next, the authors describe the implementation of integrated language and literacy instruction in Andrea and Zachary's first- and second-grade general education classrooms and Meredith's English as a second language classroom. Mindful of the many factors that contribute to student success including first and second language and literacy skills, the authors conclude their chapter with recommendations for creating learning communities that support language and literacy development for ELLs.

Nancy Roser, Jennifer Battle, and Melody Patterson Zoch provide an evidentiary display of effective incorporation of children's literature in classrooms that enroll large numbers of ELLs. In Chapter 3, the authors argue that to replace children's literature with manageable texts in classrooms with ELLs is to withhold opportunities for language use, literacy learning, and the shared creation of ideas. The best works in children's literature are marked with some of the most exquisite uses of language—language that is poetic, metaphoric, and filled with allusions. Students who enter schools speaking languages other than English are working to become members of classrooms that may be filled with such books. Initially both the books and the discussions that surround them may seem impenetrable to students who enter schools speaking a language other than English. The authors illustrate the ways that kindergarten, first-, and third-grade classroom teachers provided their English-learning students with access to the world and words of children's literature.

In Chapter 4, Gisela Ernst-Slavit, Catherine Carrison, and Jan Spiesman-Laughlin present literature circles as an effective means of engaging ELLs in authentic conversations about quality literature. First, the authors review the research in second language proficiency and literacy development. They then highlight the benefits of literature circles for English-only as well as English-learning students. Next, the authors outline the planning and implementation of literature circles in Catherine's fourth-grade classroom with a focus on the efforts of ELLs as they learn to engage in meaningful literature discussion. The authors conclude with recommendations for teachers that will help guide the implementation of literature circles in classrooms with students with a wide range of oral language abilities.

In the second section, we turn our attention to ELLs in middle and secondary school classrooms. Michael F. Graves and Jill Fitzgerald begin this section with an in-depth examination of Scaffolded Reading Experiences (SREs), an instructional framework for planning prereading, during-reading, and postreading activities that assist English-only and English-learning students to successfully comprehend and learn from the variety of narrative and expository texts they encounter in school. Chapter 5 provides a brief overview of the theoretical base for and the major elements of SREs. Next, the authors examine the many decisions and challenges that teachers face as they seek to implement SREs in today's multilingual classrooms and suggest criteria for making these decisions and meeting these challenges. They conclude the chapter by addressing the place of SREs in a comprehensive literacy program for multilingual classrooms.

In Chapter 6, Fay Shin, Robert Rueda, Christyn Simpkins, and Hyo Jin Lim address the factors that must be considered relative to effective integration of literacy, language, and content area instruction. Drawing on research in second language acquisition, learning, cognition, and motivation, the authors first present a theoretical framework and key principles that inform the planning and implementation of successful integrated content area instruction with a particular focus on using science as the context for language and literacy development. The authors provide a detailed description of how Christyn implemented this approach in her sixth-grade language arts classroom with students with a wide range of language skills. They conclude with recommendations for future work in this area.

In Chapter 7, Julie Nora and Julie E. Wollman consider the role of student engagement in promoting oral language development among ELLs. First, the authors demonstrate the ways that teachers may unknowingly deny students access to the very learning opportunities they need in order to grow their language abilities. They do so through an analysis of the organization of instruction in a middle school social studies classroom that enrolled ELLs. They then provide research-based guidelines for organizing instruction that promotes student engagement and oral language development. They conclude their chapter with recommendations for improving ELLs' opportunities to learn at the middle school level.

In Chapter 8, Kathleen A.J. Mohr and Eric S. Mohr demonstrate the challenges and successes a teacher encounters as he strives to plan effective and meaningful writing instruction for older students who are in the process of learning English. The authors share the conception, planning, and implementation of the guided writing approach in Eric's 12th-grade Sheltered English classroom. The authors acknowledge their successes, yet they do not shy away from the special challenges of teaching writing in a sheltered context. The authors conclude their chapter with recommendations for teachers and administrators who seek to improve writing instruction for ELLs.

In the third and final section, we share outcomes of small-scale and large-scale efforts to improve teaching practices in multilingual classrooms. We take a look at individual efforts, whole-school efforts, and efforts across the United States to provide teachers with the knowledge, skills, and strategies they need to promote ELLs' success.

In Chapter 9, Trini Lewis and Esmeralda Ramos present strategies for improving collaborations between parents and teachers in immigrant communities. They begin with an overview of the research on promoting parental involvement and highlight the limitations of the parent–teacher conference, the most common format for parent–teacher interactions. Next, they share the strategies that Esmeralda used to improve communication with and thus opportunities to collaborate with parents of her first-grade students from low-income Latino families. The authors conclude the chapter with recommendations about how to support parents in their efforts to become involved in their children's literacy learning.

In Chapter 10, Patricia Ruggiano Schmidt, Brenda Gangemi, Grete O. Kelsey, Charles LaBarbera, Sharlene McKenzie, Carol Melchior, Barbara Merrick, Roseann Sunser, and Meg Williams describe an inservice program planned to help teachers make connections with students' homes and communities. The context for this work is an urban elementary school in a high-poverty area with a mission to assist students from a wide range of language and cultural backgrounds to achieve academically and socially in their school and communities. The chapter begins with a brief review of the research on culturally responsive teaching as it relates to the inservice program and a detailed description of inservice program components. The authors demonstrate how teachers used what they learned to make family and community connections to support students' English language learning. They conclude their chapter by sharing their plans for continuing their work in this area.

In Chapter 11, Margarita Calderón and Russell Wasden report teacher and student outcomes from two large-scale professional development programs designed to improve teaching practices and students' oral language and literacy skills. The authors demonstrate how teachers can meet the needs of a growing segment of the ELL population—students with interrupted formal education. The authors conclude with recommendations to support ongoing teacher development in meeting students' needs.

At the end of each chapter, authors have provided a series of reflection questions. These questions encourage both individual readers and those reading as part of a school-based professional development effort or a graduate or undergraduate college course to consider how the information presented in each chapter relates to daily teaching practice and contributes to better understanding of ELLs' strengths and needs.

Our Hope for You, the Reader

We hope that both preservice and inservice teachers and all others concerned with improving teaching and learning in classrooms that enroll ELLs will find many insights about how students develop as readers and writers in a language they are learning to speak and listen to. We are confident that teachers will find useful suggestions they can implement in their classrooms and schools in this book. As we planned and prepared this book we were mindful of Shirley Brice Heath's (1983) belief that "teachers could make school a place which allows... children to capitalize on the skills, value, and knowledge they brought there, and to add on the conceptual structures imparted by school" (p. 13). We offer our experiences teaching and learning alongside ELLs firm in the belief that teachers can provide their students with direct instruction of oral and written forms, skills, and strategies, along with opportunities to use oral and written language in meaningful ways as well as in ways that recognize, build upon, and extend their students' and families' linguistic, cultural, and social resources.

REFERENCES

Fitzgerald, J., & Noblitt, G. (1999). About hopes, aspirations, and uncertainty: First-grade English-language learners' emergent reading. *Journal of Literacy Research, 31*(2), 133–182.

Gándara, R., Maxwell-Jolly, J., & Driscoll, A. (2005). *Listening to teachers of English language learners: A survey of California teachers' challenges, experiences, and professional development needs.* Santa Cruz, CA: The Center for the Future of Teaching and Learning.

Gunderson, L. (2009). ESL (ELL) literacy instruction: A guidebook to theory and practice (2nd ed.). New York: Routledge

Heath, S.B. (1983). *Ways with words: Language, life, and work in communities and classrooms.* New York: Cambridge University Press.

Lee, J., Grigg, W., & Donahue, P. (2007). *The nation's report card: Reading 2007 (NCES 2007-496).* Washington, DC: National Center for Education Statistics.

National Center for Education Statistics. (2008). *Dropout and completion rates in the United States: 2006.* Washington, DC: Author.

National Clearinghouse for English Language Acquisition. (2008). *Elementary and secondary enrollment of ELL students in U.S. 1989–1990 to 2005–2006.* Washington, DC: Author.

National Comprehensive Center for Teacher Quality. (2008). *Lessons learned: New teachers talk about their jobs, challenges, and long range plans: Issue No.3 Teaching in changing times*. Washington, DC: Author.

Passel, J., & Cohn, D. (2008). *U.S. population projection 2005–2050*. Washington, DC: Pew Research Center.

Salahu-Din, D., Persky, H., & Miller, J. (2008). *The nation's report card: Writing 2007 (NCES 2008-468)*. Washington, DC: National Center for Education Statistics.

Snow, C.E., Burns, M.S., & Griffin, P. (Eds.). (1998). *Preventing reading difficulties in young children*. Washington, DC: National Academy Press.

U.S. Census Bureau. (2006). *American community survey*. Retrieved August 17, 2008, from factfinder. census.gov

U.S. Census Bureau. (2008). *An older and more diverse nation by mid-century*. Retrieved March 4, 2009, from www.census.gov

Language, Literacy, and Learning in Elementary Classrooms

Word Study Assessment and Instruction With ELLs in a Second-Grade Classroom: Bending With Students' Growth

Donald R. Bear, Lori A. Helman, and Linda Woessner

Linda's second-grade classroom is vibrant with the sounds of students trying out their new language—English—and using their home languages with peers or school assistants. One of the students, Sashitorn, finishes a piece of writing in which she demonstrates her awareness of the languages interacting in her classroom. Sashitorn speaks Karen, and her writing, seen in Figure 1.1, is titled "Karen Language." She writes, "Did you know there are many languages some of the languages are different. Some speak like Sashitorn and some like Eh Hser Nay Taw and some speak like other people you never know how many languages? Can you guess? how many. I am going to tell you how many languages now there are 20 languages."

Sashitorn's writing provides a window into many aspects of her development: her view of the languages experienced in the classroom, her oral language development, and her knowledge of how the English writing system works. Throughout this chapter, Sashitorn and the other students in Linda's classroom provide real-world cases of students learning to speak and read in English and help us describe how word study can be adapted to match their language and literacy backgrounds. We call this adaptation "bending," to suggest that, although many of the practices we use are relevant to all students, instruction with English language learners (ELLs) requires teachers to stretch their normal routine to encompass vocabulary study, oral language practice, and explicit phonological support. Teachers of ELLs make connections between oral and written language as they study the sounds, meanings, and spellings of English words with their students.

One Classroom, Many Learners: Best Literacy Practices for Today's Multilingual Classrooms edited by Julie Coppola and Elizabeth V. Primas. © 2009 by the International Reading Association.

Figure 1.1. Karen Language

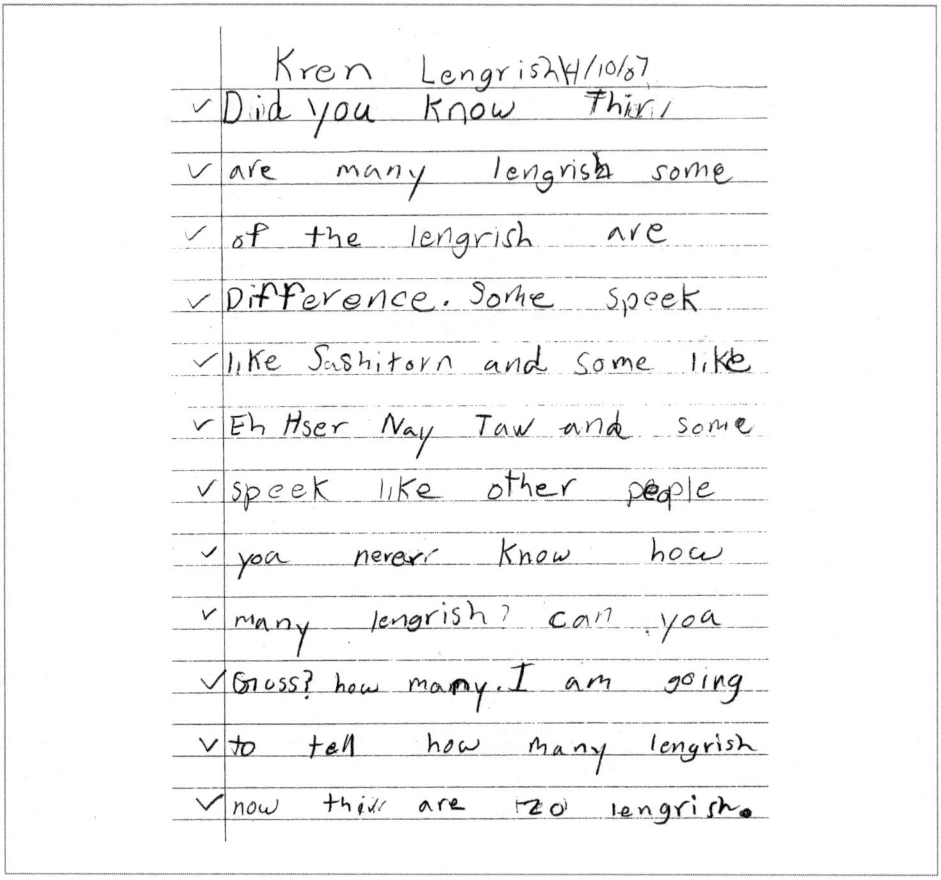

> Kren Lengrish 4/10/07
> ✓ Did you know Thir
> ✓ are many lengrish some
> ✓ of the lengrish are
> ✓ Difference. Some speek
> ✓ like Sashitorn and some like
> ✓ Eh Hser Nay Taw and some
> ✓ speek like other people
> ✓ you nerav Know how
> ✓ many lengrish? can you
> ✓ Gruss? how many. I am going
> ✓ to tell how many lengrish
> ✓ now thir are 120 lengrish.

In this chapter, we build on our earlier exploration of the phonics, vocabulary, and spelling instruction of ELLs in the beginning and transitional stages of development (Bear, Templeton, Helman, & Baren, 2003). From our studies of students' spelling samples, we have learned that ELLs progress through the same stages of literacy development as native English speakers but often take additional time and require explicit support to learn about the sounds of English and interlanguage interactions (Bear & Helman, 2004; Helman & Bear, 2007). Students' English learning builds on their knowledge of their primary languages. Teachers see these interlanguage interactions at all levels of language use, from the interaction of syntactic structures to the substitution of vowels from the primary language to spell the unfamiliar vowels of English.

The chapter shares our experiences implementing word study with ELLs over the course of a school year. The author–researchers include two university-based teacher educators, Donald and Lori, and a classroom teacher, Linda. Together we brought a range of teaching backgrounds and research knowledge to answer the following question: How do teachers construct meaningful and developmentally appropriate word study programs for ELLs in the primary grades? As we learn about students' resources in oral and written language, how do we bend our traditional instruction to promote their literacy development? We provide a detailed description of the word study assessment and instruction activities with one group of students learning English in Linda's classroom and offer examples of how to bend instruction to best support these students' growth. We look in depth at three students in this group—Khamtay, MaiKia, and Sashitorn (students' names are pseudonyms except for Sashitorn whose family has given consent to show her writing)—who have been learning English for less than two years, and share our analyses of their assessments and classroom work. We invite you to join us as we explore these students' learning during their second-grade experience.

A Multilingual Classroom

We first introduce you to the classroom we studied: a second-grade, self-contained support classroom for students learning English as a new language. Next, we provide information about our partnership. Then, we describe the languages heard in the classroom and provide background information for these languages.

The Classroom Context

The context for our word study implementation was a second-grade classroom designed specifically for ELLs who had attended less than two years of school in the United States. The school was situated in a large urban school district in the Midwest. Seventy-two percent of the school's population was learning English as a new language, and 79% received free or reduced lunch. The class consisted of 18 students—10 from a Hmong-speaking background, 3 from a Somali-speaking background, 3 from a Karen-speaking background, 1 from a Spanish-speaking background, and 1 from a Lao-speaking background. The teacher and coauthor on this chapter, Linda, is an experienced classroom teacher and ELL specialist who has taught in a variety of capacities over the past 25 years.

Linda runs the second-grade support classroom for a program called the Language Academy in her district. She teaches the second graders who are the most recent immigrants and who have the least proficiency in the English language; these students are clustered for the full morning in her classroom for their language and literacy instruction. Many of these students also come to Linda for their afternoon studies of math and other subjects. Students are not permitted to be in the Language Academy for more than two years.

Our Partnership

Throughout the 2006–2007 school year, we collaborated on a project to investigate word study with ELLs in Linda's classroom. Linda and Lori met each week to assess her students, discuss their development, plan lessons, provide word study instruction for the students, evaluate materials, and reflect on students' progress. At times, Linda taught the students and Lori observed and gave feedback. Other times, Lori taught and Linda was the observer. By January, we decided that an effective way to share what we were learning about word study with ELLs was to focus on one of the instructional-level reading groups in Linda's class. We chose the "purple" group because, although the students were newcomers to the United States, they represented the level of literacy development that would be most relevant to primary-grade teachers of ELLs.

There were five students in the purple group, including our three focal students. They were grouped together based on a combination of early literacy assessments, including their developmental spelling inventory and phonics and reading passage assessments. The students' assessments are discussed in great detail later in this chapter.

The Languages Heard in the Classroom

Before planning word study in English for the students, it was important for us to understand the language and literacy strengths students brought with them to the school setting. Knowing about students' background knowledge helps the teacher to make a bridge from the known—the home language—to the new—word study in English. Linda's classroom consisted of 18 students learning English from five distinct language backgrounds. A first step in knowing how to build on what students bring is to compare their oral languages to

English. The students on whom we chose to focus came from three language backgrounds—Lao, Hmong, and Karen. To understand the students we feature, we take a moment to share with you some brief notes about the languages they speak. To get this information, we spoke with teachers and community members who were involved with the school, and we also searched the Internet for information. We recommend Wikipedia (www.wikipedia.org) or an online reference source such as the National Virtual Translation Service (www.nvtc.gov/lotw/index.html) to get started.

The Lao language is the official language of Laos and is spoken by more than five million people, including approximately 206,000 Laotian Americans. Lao is a tonal language and has 21 consonant sounds and 24 vowel sounds. Some English sounds such as /sh/ or /f/ are not used in the Lao language. The Lao alphabet has curving, artistic letters that are based on an ancient Indian writing system.

The Hmong language is spoken by over four million Hmong people, including more than 200,000 Hmong Americans. The Hmong were traditionally a nomadic people who lived in several countries of Southeast Asia. Many Hmong Americans first waited in refugee camps before coming to the United States. Hmong is a tonal language and in general does not have consonants at the ends of words.

The Karen languages are spoken by people from lower Myanmar (Burma) and on the border of Thailand. Karen languages use tones to distinguish between words with the same consonant and vowel sounds. Many of the Karen words are monosyllabic; ending consonants are limited and often represent a suffix.

A Yearlong View of Assessments and Development

In this section, we present an overview of the assessment process, and our focal students' development over the course of the year. The assessments that led to our understanding of students' literacy development are foundational to a practical discussion of word study instruction in this classroom.

The Assessment Process

In Linda's classroom there were several required and optional literacy assessments. Among these were an informal reading inventory used with a series of leveled passages, a developmental spelling inventory, a check of the first

100 sight words, and assessments of phonics and phonemic awareness skills. Students were also assessed regularly using the DIBELS second-grade oral reading fluency measure (Good & Kaminski, 2002). In addition, the students were given the Language Assessment Scales-Oral to measure oral English proficiency (De Avila & Duncan, 1994). Across all measures, the three focal students made significant gains over the year. Ongoing portfolios of students' writing and creative efforts were also assembled. In concert with the structured measures just described, simply spending time with the students and their families provided insights into their lives and learning. Table 1.1 summarizes many of the measures that were collected as well as periodic, general ratings of students' reading and spelling development.

The spelling assessments were important guides in the selection of word study activities. Qualitative spelling assessments were administered three times over the year (Bear, Invernizzi, Templeton, & Johnston, 2008). These occurred in September/October, March, and May. Students' spelling errors on these assignments and in their writing helped us to understand what they knew about orthographic patterns, vocabulary, and the structure of English, and they provided a window into what word or orthographic knowledge students could draw upon as they read and wrote. Observing the change in spelling over the school year demonstrated the students' growth in word knowledge and also suggested the related reading and writing behaviors that we might expect (Bear & Templeton, 2000). Samples of the three students' spelling across the year are presented in the following sections. In the next section, we follow the three focal students' development over a year and investigate the relationships among reading, writing, and spelling.

Students' Growth Over the Year

Like all of the students in the Language Academy classroom, the three focal students in the purple group had spent less than two years in schools in the United States, and they were the students with the most limited oral proficiency in English.

The first student we present is Khamtay, who is a native speaker of Lao. We chose to focus on Khamtay to show how a new arrival with literacy in a language and orthography so different from English experienced a speeded or accelerated learning process.

Table 1.1. Summary of Assessments of Focal Children

	Language	Reading/spelling stages					100 words, Fry				DIBELS grade 2						Independent reading levels (teacher assessment)				
		Sept	Nov	Jan	Apr	May	Sept	Nov	Jan	Mar	Jan	Feb (A)	Feb (B)	Mar	Apr	May	Sept 6	Nov 6	Jan 31	Mar 6	May 25
Khamtay	Lao	Early emergent/early emergent	Middle beginning/middle letter name	Middle beginning/middle letter name	Early transitional/early within word pattern	Early transitional/early within word pattern	0	74	95	93	47	47	80	119	99	105	Pre- A	Mid D	H I	High J	Mid N
MaiKia	Hmong	Early beginning/early letter name	Early beginning/early letter name	Early beginning/early letter name	Middle beginning/middle letter name	Late beginning/late letter name	64	84	92	92	56	56	71	75	83	92	Low E	High G	Low I	Mid J	Low L
Sashitorn	Karen	Early beginning/early letter name	Early beginning/early letter name	Middle beginning/middle letter name	Early transitional/early within word pattern	Middle transitional/middle within word pattern	30	44	90	94	57	57	69	92	79	99	High A	High D	Low I	Mid J	Mid N

MaiKia is a native Hmong speaker, who followed a more average trajectory of learning and development that was quite evident in her grammar, and she even began to produce the short-vowel sound and the CVC pattern in English.

Sashitorn is a native Karen speaker, and her robust growth represents what we would like to see for all ELLs. She began the year as a beginning reader and ended second grade as a transitional reader, even as she was still internalizing the sounds of English. Sashitorn had amassed a knowledge of oral language that would serve her well as she moved into a third-grade classroom the following year.

In this overview, we examine the students' literacy development, in particular their knowledge of how words are spelled, pronounced, and what they mean.

Khamtay. Khamtay speaks Lao and understands Vietnamese, and this was the first year he was learning English. Khamtay had the good fortune of going to a formal school in Thailand as opposed to a refugee camp school, and he had some literacy in Lao.

Khamtay made phenomenal progress over the year—more than any other student—starting at the lowest level and ending at the highest level. He had entered second grade in the early emergent stage of reading and spelling, and he completed second grade in the transitional stage of reading and the within word pattern stage of spelling. Interestingly, his language testing at the end of the year placed him as a beginning speaker of English, and yet, in reading, Khamtay was a transitional reader, able to decode fairly complex texts.

As can be seen in Table 1.1, between September and November, Khamtay learned 74 words and went from being a nonreader to a level D in the Rigby PM Collection. Even then, his comprehension was not strong. Khamtay knew 93 words out of 100 of the sight words assessed at the end of the year. By March, Khamtay began to score above benchmark on the DIBELS's Oral Reading Fluency assessment for second grade (Good & Kaminski, 2002). In terms of instructional-level reading accuracy, and as noted in Table 1.1, he began as a nonreader in English, in November he was reading at level D, in January at level I, in March at level J, and in May at level N.

Khamtay's spelling during October, as seen in Figure 1.2, shows us that he used a letter-name strategy and substituted short vowels. Like many ELLs, he substituted /k/ for /g/ as in *cam* for *gum*. He also substituted *t* for /d/ and for /ch/

Figure 1.2. Spelling Development of Khamtay Over the Year

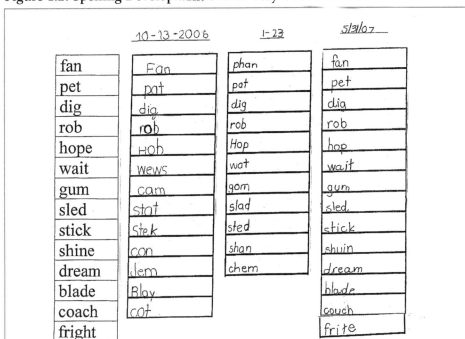

	10-13-2006	1-23	5/31/07
fan	Fan	phan	fan
pet	pat	pat	pet
dig	dig	dig	dig
rob	rob	rob	rob
hope	Hob	Hop	hop
wait	wews	wot	wait
gum	cam	gom	gum
sled	stat	slad	sled,
stick	Stek	sted	stick
shine	con	shan	shuin
dream	dem	chem	dream
blade	Blay		blade
coach	cot		couch
fright			frite

as in *stat* for *sled* and *cot* for *coach*. And, like many ELLs, he sometimes dropped final sounds.

By the time Khamtay reached the transitional stage of reading, his vocabulary knowledge and language development were beginning to lag behind the language and vocabulary demands of the texts he was reading and expected to comprehend. Reading materials at the transitional level were more complicated in vocabulary and syntax and required Khamtay to read many two-syllable words that were outside of his understanding of English.

In daily teaching, Khamtay's comprehension seemed stronger than it was. He was able to comprehend at a basic level using the partial cues he could gather, though his syntax and semantic bases were insufficient for full comprehension (Bear & Templeton, 2000). Reading with partial cues was sufficient for his comprehension of most first- and even second-grade texts, most of which were enhanced by pictures. In third grade, however, reading with partial cues will constrain Khamtay's success.

Over the year, Khamtay learned many written language conventions and wrote in phrases; terminal junctures were noted with punctuation or capitalization. In Figure 1.3, a writing sample from April 12, Khamtay developed a contingency for a broken computer and gave three examples of what games he would play on the computer.

Khamtay's writing was rich in tone and interest. At this point in the spring, he was able to spell many short-vowel words and some common long-vowel words; he was in the early part of the within word pattern stage of spelling. Khamtay's writing was precise in structure and design. Handwriting was emphasized in Laotian instruction with many exercises for correct stroke and character formation; this experience may have transferred to his writing in English. In his writing journal he placed a check mark in the margin of every other line prior to writing to remind him to skip a line for writing as instructed. His writing also demonstrated his knowledge of English syntax. Khamtay used the present tense and supported himself with a simple language pattern, "I can ___" (e.g., play, take another one, sing). He did not produce the expected verb form in "I wish I has..." and omitted an article in "...play math game" and "I can play game 123." He also substituted the word *went* for *when*. These are common errors for students learning English but point out the difference between the

Figure 1.3. Khamtay's Computer Story

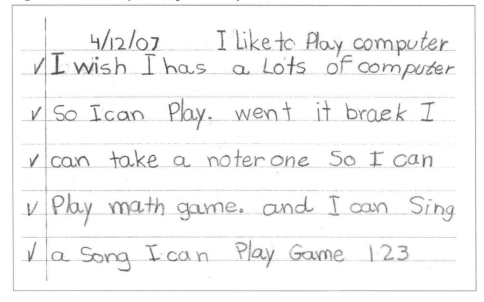

materials Khamtay was reading and the kind of language he produced on his own.

MaiKia. MaiKia speaks Hmong. In the fall she tried to spell as many sounds in words as she could, spelling some consonant sounds correctly, as seen in Figure 1.4. MaiKia was a very early letter-name speller—she spelled the beginning consonant sounds of most words correctly, especially at the beginning of the spelling inventory. Like many ELLs, MaiKia had difficulty with final nasal sounds (/n/, /ng/, and /m/). She spelled the endings of seven words with *ng*; in three instances the *ng* could have represented a final nasal sound (*fan, shine, dream*); and in four instances (*pet, sled, blade, coach*) there were no clear phonetic relationships between sound, articulation, and spelling. It is as if her strategy was, When in doubt, put *ng* at the end of a word.

Figure 1.4. Spelling Development of MaiKia Over the Year

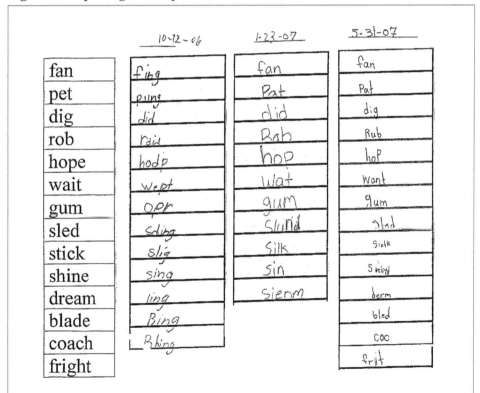

	10-12-06	1-23-07	5-31-07
fan	fing	fan	fan
pet	pung	Pat	Pat
dig	did	did	dig
rob	rad	Rab	Rub
hope	hodp	hop	hop
wait	wept	Wat	Want
gum	oer	gum	gum
sled	sding	slund	slad
stick	slig	silk	silk
shine	sing	sin	sriey
dream	ling	sienm	derm
blade	Bing		bled
coach	Bhing		coc
fright			frit

This yearlong look at MaiKia's spelling shows that she made solid progress throughout the year. She began as an early letter-name–alphabetic speller, and by the end of May, MaiKia had learned to spell many short-vowel words correctly and had a solid understanding of consonants; blends; digraphs; and the CVC, short-vowel pattern. Her spelling inventories contain many examples of spelling errors characteristic of ELLs, and like many Asian Americans, MaiKia worked over several months before she stabilized in her understanding of the spelling of final nasal sounds in English.

By late January, MaiKia was more accurate in spelling beginning and especially final sounds, and she also spelled two short-vowel words correctly (*fan*, *gum*). She used a letter-name strategy for long-vowel words (*hop* for *hope*). She made progress in spelling two nasal sounds correctly, yet confused the sounds in other words (*sin* for *shine*, *sland* for *sled*).

In mid-April, MaiKia wrote about a page a day during journal writing time, as seen in Figure 1.5. We see that MaiKia could spell many words correctly in a first draft writing activity. She described several activities playing with her cousins, and her command of English syntax was understandable and gaining a rhythm. Already, she was experimenting with ways to spell long vowels when she "used but confused" (Invernizzi, Abouzeid, & Gill, 1994) long-vowel markers by adding a final *e* (*catche* for *catch*) and vowel teams (*outseid* for *outside*, *behied* for *behind*).

At the end of May, MaiKia was considered a late letter-name–alphabetic speller. She had learned a tremendous amount about both the spelling and sounds of English. She spelled easy short-vowel words correctly (*fan*, *dig*, *rub*, *gum*, *sled*), and she spelled some consonant blends and digraphs correctly (*sl*, *bl*, *fr*). MaiKia used a letter-name strategy to spell some long vowels (*hop* for *hope*, *frit* for *fright*). Like other letter-name spellers, she was challenged by beginning and final consonant digraphs (*sniy* for <u>sh</u>*ine*, *coc* for *coa<u>ch</u>*). ELLs need extra time to learn the new vowel sounds of English, and this is reflected in atypical spelling errors as in *bled* for *blade* and *sniy* for *shine*. The former example may suggest how MaiKia pronounced the vowel in *blade* at this time. Characteristic of many ELLs, MaiKia substituted the known word *want* for *wait*, perhaps because the two words have the same beginning and ending sounds. At this point in the school year, MaiKia was reading level L reading materials, a slightly higher level than her spelling suggested.

Figure 1.5. MaiKia's Writing Sample

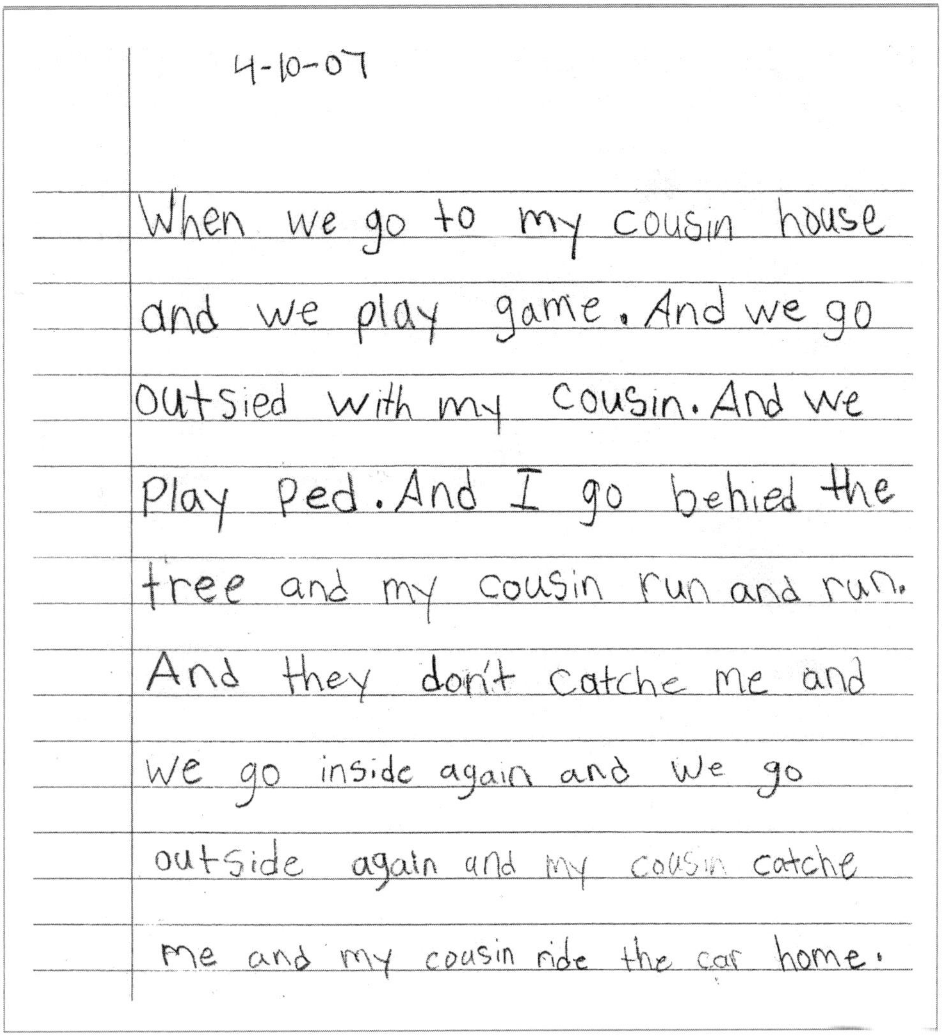

4-10-07

When we go to my cousin house
and we play game. And we go
outsied with my cousin. And we
play ped. And I go behied the
tree and my cousin run and run.
And they don't catche me and
we go inside again and we go
outside again and my cousin catche
me and my cousin ride the car home.

Sashitorn. Sashitorn speaks Karen, and throughout the year her oral English was at a beginning level. In reading, she started the year as a beginning reader recognizing 30 sight words and reading in level A materials. Figure 1.6 shows that in November's spelling on the primary spelling assessment, she was in the early part of the letter-name–alphabetic stage. Sashitorn spelled one short-vowel word correctly (*fan*) and included an incorrect vowel in 8 of 10 single-syllable

Figure 1.6. Spelling Development of Sashitorn Over the Year

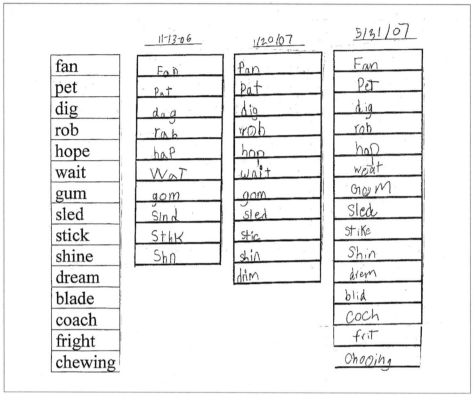

	11-13-06	1/20/07	5/31/07
fan	Fan	Pan	Fan
pet	Pat	Pat	Pet
dig	dag	dig	dig
rob	rab	rob	rob
hope	haP	hop	hop
wait	WaT	wait	weat
gum	gom	gom	Gom
sled	Sind	sled	Sled
stick	SthK	stic	stike
shine	Shn	shin	Shin
dream		drim	drem
blade			blid
coach			Coch
fright			frit
chewing			choping

words. She also spelled the beginning and ending sounds for all words, and she spelled two of the four beginning and ending consonant digraphs and blends correctly.

By January, Sashitorn was in the later part of the letter-name–alphabetic stage. As you can see in her spelling across the year, learning the vowels was particularly difficult for her, and some of the unusual vowel substitutions, like *drim*, not *drem*, for *dream*, may reflect the interactions between the vowels in Karen and English.

By March, she was reading at level J, which is comparable to the beginning of the transitional stage of reading. At the beginning of this stage, students are reading with an equal footing in oral and silent reading as they increase their sight vocabularies.

In the writing sample from April (see Figure 1.1 on page 12), Sashitorn was in the within word pattern of spelling. She spelled many single-syllable words correctly, and she was "using but confusing" long-vowel patterns (*speek* for *speak*). She was comfortable exercising her vocabulary through polysyllabic words the best she could (*lengrish* for *languages*).

Along with growth in word knowledge, Sashitorn showed fine growth in language development. The content of her writing was exceptional both for its awareness of language learning and for its grammatical and pragmatic structure. She wrote in long sentences and engaged the reader in a conversation throughout.

In May, Sashitorn had learned most of what she needed to know about short vowels and beginning consonant blends and digraphs. She continued to learn more about final consonant blends. As can be seen in Figure 1.6, she was still learning about the spelling of single-syllable words. Perhaps she marked the spelling of *stick* with a long-vowel marker (*stike*) as an overgeneralization of the silent *e* of the CVCe pattern. In this sample, she was still using a letter-name strategy to spell long vowels (*drem* for *dream*, *frit* for *fright*). Her misspelling of the long-vowel name for *blade* as *blid* is another error in perceiving long vowels of English.

The correspondences between Sashitorn's reading and spelling behaviors are worth investigating. It seems that her reading with comprehension was a bit ahead of her word knowledge. She read with good comprehension, answering all four questions correctly when she read level J material. We heard falling intonation and pauses at the end of sentences. Beginning in April, her spelling began to include long-vowel patterns, and yet, even in late May, there were letter-name–type spelling errors (*rob* for *rub*) mixed in with within word pattern spelling errors (*weat* for *wait*).

The descriptions of how these three students learned to read and write provide examples of how ELLs go through the developmental stages of spelling and orthographic knowledge with differences related to their previous language and literacy experiences. We saw the three students make rapid progress over the year. By the end of the year, reading with understanding became a greater concern as the content of what they read became more difficult. Many of the activities described in the next section aim to improve students' knowledge of the spelling and meanings of words so that both aspects of their development can progress.

Developmental Word Study and Language Activities With Emergent, Beginning, and Early Transitional Readers and Writers

Students in Linda's class are learning English at the same time they are learning to read. This dual focus presents an opportunity to use the pictures and words that are often used in phonics sorts and activities for concept and vocabulary sorts to expand students' knowledge of English. Vocabulary and language practice are built into every word study lesson; for example, before words are analyzed by sound, they are discussed as meaningful units. When the pictures and words are arranged in groups, they become springboards for discussions among students; for example, "Tell your partner why you sorted the way you did."

Each day, Linda aimed to meet with small, leveled-reading groups in her classroom. The groups rotated among different literacy tasks in the classroom, and one of their activities was to work at the teacher table. Linda organized her groups based on fall assessment data from students' passage reading and developmental spelling inventories. As needed, other early literacy assessments were reviewed as well, such as checklists of the number of sight words and phonics skills students had mastered. Oftentimes students' assessment results clearly clustered them into a specific instructional reading group with students working at the same level. In a few cases, however, students showed us on their spelling inventories that they were working at a level of word knowledge ahead of what they were able to show in their connected reading. This was due in some cases to the fact that these students had not memorized as many sight words. Instructional reading groups were formed by taking both orthographic understanding and reading proficiency into account. The groups were flexible, and as needed, students were changed to a more appropriate group based on their progress.

The small-group instructional reading time included guided and repeated reading activities, vocabulary instruction, and hands-on word study. Word study was a new activity for Linda, so integrating it into her small-group lessons was a learning process. She began by trying out a sorting activity one or two days a week and gradually included it more regularly. As Linda began to implement word study with her students, she followed a structured sequence over the course of a week:

1. She introduced a rhyme or short piece of text that had words with the feature of study, such as a rhyme about a frog when the word family –og was studied.

2. She introduced the sort cards—either pictures or words—and made sure that students knew what the words were. For the words that students didn't know, she conducted vocabulary minilessons. After the vocabulary was practiced, any words that were still unknown would be set to the side. It is important for students to work with words that they understand.

3. She demonstrated the sort, and students joined in as individual items were categorized.

4. Students practiced the sort on their own or with a partner.

5. Again, students returned to words in context by going on word hunts or finding words that followed the pattern in stories or rhymes.

6. Students applied the skill by playing a game or doing a writing activity. This sometimes served as an informal assessment (a brief "spell check" on paper or whiteboards can also be used to make sure students have mastered the feature studied that week).

An overview of this sequence is outlined in Table 1.2. Column 3 lists some of the language that we used when doing word study lessons.

Linda found it helpful to create a checksheet to keep track of where she was in the word study sequence with each small group in her class. At the end of each lesson, she checked off what she had accomplished, and that process guided her decision about where to begin the next time they met. The whole sequence with a given set of words took four or five lessons. Each time, students began by quickly repeating the sort to review the content.

The Introductory Lesson and Weekly Sequence for Word Study

In this section, we describe in greater depth the procedures and details of word study in Linda's multilingual second-grade class. Materials that were used are noted at the end of this section.

To begin a new lesson, Linda read a simple poem or story that had several examples of the word study feature embedded within. Before reading, students were encouraged to make a personal connection to the text. For example, if the poem was about a pet, students might be asked to share any pets they had or

Table 1.2. Sequence and Components of Word Study

Lesson component	What students do	Examples of teacher language
Present words in context: Introduce the word study feature within connected text. A reading selection is chosen with words that follow the pattern.	Listen along to a poem or story. Show thumbs-up or other signal when they hear or see the feature being studied.	"As I read, listen for words that have the sound /og/ at the end as in *frog*." "Great, you heard the sound of /og/ at the end of *log* and *fog*."
Introduce the sort and vocabulary: Read through the word or picture cards and teach new vocabulary in context.	"Read" the pictures or words. Share their background knowledge of the words. Put the words into sentences.	"What does *jog* mean? Can you show me?" "When we run slowly we *jog*." "That word *clog* is giving us some trouble. Let's put it to the side while we do this sort."
Demonstrate the sort: Introduce the key pictures or words and model the sort with the entire or most of the words or pictures.	Watch the teacher sort, and make suggestions for where each item belongs.	"I am going to put the word *fog* under the picture of a frog, because it has the same /og/ sound at the end." "Should I put *log* under *pig* or *frog*?"
Have students sort and check: Individually or with a partner, students sort and read through the words to check their sorts.	By themselves or with a partner, students repeat the sort independently. When finished, students read the words or pictures in each column to check for accuracy.	"Remember to say the word aloud as you sort it." "Read your sort to me." "Tell me about how you sorted your words or pictures."
Extend: Extend the sort by working with words in context.	Find words in books or environmental print. Write words on lists or in word study notebooks.	"Let's read another poem and listen for words that have the /og/ sound." "Find words in the book we read that have /og/ or /ig/ in them."
Apply and assess: Apply the skill in a game or other activity. Informally assess students' learning.	Play a board game or card game to reinforce the features they have been learning. Create a group or individual story using related words. Write words that represent the feature being studied as the teacher dictates them.	"Who has a word that ends like *frog*?" "How should we start our story about a big dog?" "I will say some of the words we have been learning, and I want you to write them on your whiteboards."

talk about familiar animals. The first time through, students simply listened to and enjoyed the story. Then, Linda pointed out the kinds of words to be studied next, for example, words that had the /og/ and /ig/ sounds like *frog* and *pig*. Students were asked to show a thumbs-up sign if they heard a word that included the word study features being studied as Linda reread the poem or story.

Next, the words or pictures of the sort were introduced. Linda's important work was to determine if students were familiar with the key vocabulary words needed to study the feature. She asked questions to find out what students knew about the words and explained new vocabulary in simple terms, using objects or visuals whenever possible. She asked students questions about the vocabulary and then clarified what they said, adding information if they seemed confused by a word. Words that could not easily be learned were set aside and saved to work on again another day. If there were many unknown words within a given sort, subsequent lessons began with a concept sort to review the words. In a concept sort, the teacher calls out semantic categories and asks students to find the pictures that fit; for example, "Put pictures of animals under the picture of the dog." Students are asked to say the names of the words or pictures aloud as they sort.

Once it was clear that students knew the names of the pictures, the sort focused on the orthographic features under investigation. For this part of the lesson, the sort was demonstrated on a pocket chart. Words and pictures for the sort were put on large cards for the group to use. First, Linda put the heading words or pictures at the top of the chart. Next, she picked up one of the sorting cards and thought aloud, "This is *dog*. Does *dog* sound like *frog* or *pig* at the end? I am going to put *dog* under the picture of the *frog*." Eventually she asked students to join in with their opinions, and students were invited to move the cards to where they belonged on the pocket chart. Figure 1.7 depicts a group of students working at the pocket chart. When the guided sort was completed, students chorally read through the columns of words or pictures. Individual students were encouraged to lead the group by pointing at the words with a pointer.

In the students sort component of the word study lesson, students first took out their own copies of the sorting sheets and cut out the words or pictures. While they cut, they read aloud the names of the pictures and words, setting to the side those they could not read or name. If students were doing this part of the activity independently, they placed the individual cards into an envelope or plastic baggie and brought it with them when they came to small-group time

Figure 1.7. Students at the Pocket Chart

with the teacher. When it was time to meet with the teacher, a brief period was spent exploring the vocabulary again and providing practice if needed. When Linda worked with the group, she held up a picture for group naming, and if students were even slightly familiar with the picture or had any previous experiences to call upon, they would try to make sentences.

Next, Linda guided students in establishing the key pictures or words for sorting. Students sorted individually or with a partner while Linda observed. Linda's role was to make sure students were saying the names of the words aloud and to assess their success at discriminating the features. After sorting, students checked their work by reading each column to see if they were accurate. If there was time, students talked about the sort and why they sorted the way they did. Linda checked off the activities completed that day in small group and knew just where to begin the sort the next day.

The next time the group met, Linda began by rereading the passage from the day before. Students listened for words with the related sounds, and then they went on word hunts for words that fit the pattern. For example, they searched for words that sounded like /t/ at the end as in *cat* or later words that rhymed with *cat* and had the /at/ sound. Again, students repeated the sort independently. A card or board game that used words from the sort was then introduced and played. Students sorted and played the games over several days in stations or centers. The students were ready to move on to a different sort when they sorted accurately and fluently, when they played the games with gusto, when they could think of words related to the word patterns studied, or when they spelled the word patterns correctly in their writing. On the other hand, if students did not understand the sort and did not grow in fluency, there was some "bending" to do by slowing down and finding and conducting additional sorts. One of the best assessments was the "whiteboard check." Linda called out words similar to the words in the sort to see if students could write them on their whiteboards. Accuracy and speed of writing the words on the whiteboards was an informal assessment to guide instruction.

Many materials are available to use in constructing word and picture sorts and games to apply the word study skills that are being learned. Linda used *Words Their Way: Word Study in Action* (Bear, Invernizzi, & Johnston, 2005), but teachers may also construct a word study scope and sequence that builds from the qualitative spelling inventories used in this chapter (Bear et al., 2008), word study activities tailored for ELLs (Bear, Helman, Templeton, Invernizzi, & Johnston, 2007), or other commercial word study programs on the market.

How Word Study Supported Oral Language Development

Word study through picture and word sorts facilitated an interplay and reciprocity of learning between oral and written language when students examined words by their meaning, sounds, and spelling. In this section, we describe how word sorts reinforced students' oral language learning when a clear focus was maintained during the word study lesson.

How Word Study Facilitates Vocabulary Learning. The transitional reading stage is a good time to present word and picture sorts to scaffold vocabulary learning. Concept sorts based on the meanings of words preceded each phonic, sound, or pattern sort. With the sorts in front of them, students had pictures and words as referents to scaffold their discussions; it was common for students to point to the pictures in a column as they talked. In concept sorts, Linda and Lori drew out students when they asked questions about the words, used words in different ways, and involved students in a variety of activities related to a word. Characterization is an active way to involve students; for example, "This is a picture of a slide, a slide like we see on the playground. We slide down the slide, whoosh. Pretend with me that you are sliding down the slide. Whoosh, down the slide we go. Let's watch MaiKia show us sliding."

Newcomers to English had so much to know that they often did not know what assistance to ask for. One way students got around their limited vocabulary knowledge was to use common demonstrative pronouns (e.g., *this* and *that one*) in place of the specific nouns. We were surprised sometimes by the common nouns, such as *comb*, *roof*, and *slide*, students did not know. When students were most verbal, their remarks helped us to bend conversations to their immediate areas of need and interest. To illustrate, one surprise occurred when after reading a book about water and ice; Linda realized that MaiKia did not know the words to describe *ice*. Linda took an ice cube tray out of the freezer to support the reading. MaiKia said, "Oh, we have one of those." "Oh, you mean ice?" Linda asked. "Yes, yes!" So Linda and the students had a group discussion about what an ice cube tray is, what you put into it, and what comes out—ice cubes. MaiKia liked to chew on ice, and that's why she was so drawn to it. We were glad that her curiosity opened up this discussion; Linda did not know until far into a content lesson that students were unfamiliar with the word *ice* and had not had experiences with ice cubes before immigrating to the United States.

While the study of long-vowel sounds and patterns continues in the transitional stage, vocabulary lessons might include the study of easy, inflected morphology (*–ed*, *–ing*) in "take apart" activities to identify base words and suffixes. For example, a word like *combed* is a verb that is easy to support nonverbally with a combing motion. In a variety of activities, students examine the grammar of past tense endings in meaningful contexts at the sentence level. In a word hunt in familiar texts, students look for words that end with *–ed* and determine if they represent past tense verbs. As an example, while pointing to a calendar, the teacher might say, "Yesterday, Monday, I combed my hair. Today, Tuesday, I comb my hair." As keywords for the hunt, the words *combed* and *comb* would be written on the board, and students would hunt for words that end in *–ed*, first writing the inflected verb (e.g., *rested*) and then the base word (e.g., *rest*) in the appropriate column. Students continue to explore the *–ed* past tense ending, including collecting examples from their reading. When students have a rather extensive collection of sight words that end in *–ed*, they may be ready for lessons that use word sorts to explore the three sounds of *–ed* (/t/, /id/, /d/); in this example, the /d/ sound in *combed*. The students in this group found it difficult to perceive the final /d/ sound, particularly with preconsonantal nasals. Sorting activities and word hunts like the one described previously can help them with these tricky parts of words.

How Word Study Facilitates Phonological Learning. It takes time to learn the sounds of a new language. The spelling stages and the feature analyses from the qualitative spelling assessments guided us directly to sounds and spelling features that students needed to learn. Here we look developmentally at some of the examples that arose in our work.

When students are in the emergent stage, the emphasis is at the word level and on enjoying listening to rich language in stories. To learn explicitly about words in English, students read easy, leveled readers and two-line rhymes, and then in numerous activities, they match what they have memorized with the written words. They learn to segment English at the word level. Matching words of a two-line poem, they fingerpoint read to acquire concept of word in print (Flanigan, 2007; Morris, Bloodgood, Lomax, & Perney, 2003). Once concept of word is acquired, students begin to analyze sounds in more formal exercises. Letter recognition is also a skill that is mastered during the emergent stage.

We were patient with students who were learning about English rhyming and alliteration. There were many rhymes that students did not perceive initially, and this was because the vowels of English may be quite different from the vowel sounds students are used to hearing, and some of the final consonant sounds are unfamiliar or easily confused with similar sounds. We did not expect students from open-syllable languages to easily perceive the closed-syllable, word family rhyming (e.g., –at, –ed, –it, –ot, –un) as a unit. We bent in our instruction with students, giving them time to learn about rhyming while they continued to learn more about the vocabulary, structure, and sounds of English. When students showed excitement in recognizing English rhymes and alliteration we knew they were advancing, and in turn we could gear instruction toward word-family rhyming. Students returned to rhyming and word families when they had enough sight words to draw on to make the generalization for the sounds of the closed syllable. This is a time when the CVC written pattern for short vowels became a unit lodged deeply and tacitly in their perceptual systems.

When students were in the early letter-name stage of spelling, they studied beginning consonant sounds. Beginning with obvious contrasts, students sorted pictures by the way they sounded at the beginning (e.g., /b/, /m/; /r/, /s/).

With pictures and words that they could read easily, students recognized and discriminated the sounds of English that they already knew. After mastering obvious contrasts, they examined contrasts that were subtler, like /t/. /d/; /g/, /k/; /m/, /n/, /ng/ in both beginning and final positions.

Tapping Down the Arm was a segmentation activity that students enjoyed. In this activity, students segmented single-syllable words by tapping out sounds along the arm: first sound on the shoulder, next sound on the elbow, and final sound at the wrist. For example, to segment the word *sun*, a student started by tapping his shoulder for the /s/, his elbow for the /u/, and wrist for the /n/. Teachers modeled this procedure several times, and students soon used it regularly.

For words with two sounds like *at* or *go*, students benefited from additional modeling and support. The teacher explained to students, "Not all words have three sounds. Sometimes you just sound out two sounds. We still start from the shoulder when there are just two sounds, but we don't have a sound at the wrist."

This activity was also used for blending words. Starting back at the shoulder, the sequence was repeated, and this time the movement was a sweeping motion down the arm to blend the word. Early and middle letter-name–alphabetic spellers used this practice spontaneously in class when they wrote or completed a segmentation task in an assessment.

When the three focal students were in the letter-name stage of spelling, they were taught the sounds of short vowels; first perceiving them and then contrasting short *a* and short *e*. Through multiple opportunities to read and sort the pictures and words in word study activities and then in rereading the sorts to check their work, students practiced the pronunciation of the vowels and attached the pronunciation to a letter.

During the within word pattern stage of spelling, students became familiar with long-vowel patterns. When students were ready to differentiate among the vowel sounds, they first sorted with pictures and then with words; the pictures ensured that the students were sorting by sound. After sorting, students checked their work by reading each column aloud. Students sorted to make orthographic or phonic generalizations, and then they read through the list of words in each column and listened, felt, and looked to check if the words or pictures fit the category that had been established. Over the course of the lesson, students said the words with the targeted sounds 15–24 times. Teachers of ELLs use word sorts and other word study activities to have students notice and distinguish the articulation of particular sounds. The sorts are the hands-on tasks that guide students to generalizations about how words are pronounced, spelled, and what they mean.

Using Personal Readers for Repeated Reading and Word Hunts

For a store of meaningful, readable materials for rereading and support in word study, we have Personal Readers. These binders contain collections of familiar materials students reread during the early developmental stages (Bear, Caserta-Henry, & Venner, 2004). ELLs acquire new vocabulary and language structures in their practice rereading the passages in the Personal Readers.

The materials in Personal Readers include rhymes, student-created dictations, and, for transitional readers, passages to practice rereading for fluency and expression. Students house familiar passages in their Personal Readers and reread passages over a few weeks. Leveled and skilled readers are placed in the pockets of the Personal Readers and are used for repeated reading and word study activities like word hunts. In Linda's classroom, there was a bin in which each student had a bag of books that had been read together in the small group. During independent reading time, students practiced rereading these poems and books.

Personal Readers are extensions of the Language Experience Approach (Nelson & Linek, 1998). Stauffer (1980), one of the first advocates of this approach, was fond of saying that his primary goal was for students to experience language, a principle that is crucial in teaching ELLs. The student-dictated accounts are usually based on a physical activity, like a science experiment. After having and then talking about the experience, students dictate to the teacher a few sentences about the experience, and this becomes the students' reading material. When it is comfortable interpersonally, the teacher can work with the students to make minor modifications in their dictations so the writing conforms to Standard English and referents are clear (i.e., changing a pronoun, like *he,* to the particular noun, *the turtle*). The governing feature in making changes in students' dictations is having to reread the texts. Dictations may be saved on word processors and printed in a 26-point font for easy reading. Students' dictations range from one sentence to three paragraphs, depending on their reading proficiency. Teachers may make several copies of the dictations: one for the Personal Reader, one for marking for sight words, perhaps a copy for a class book, and another copy for the student to take home. Students reread the three or four passages in their Personal Readers at least two times a day. When working with older students on content materials, we read parts of a text to them, and the students provide a content dictation based on what they remember (Bear et al., 2007).

Alternate Ways to Assess Spelling

A developmental spelling assessment is helpful at the beginning of the new school year. Periodic assessments can be conducted on a regular basis throughout the year, with perhaps the last assessment conducted in April to guide instruction for the last eight weeks of school (Bear et al., 2007).

To gather more information about students' knowledge of word meanings, an optional step can be considered. After administering the spelling inventory the first time, ask students to review their papers to see if the teacher can read their handwriting. As they look at handwriting, see if they know the meaning of the words. As they review the words independently, students write a question mark beside words that they do not know. A teacher demonstration offers the support needed to understand this step.

Sometimes we are not sure if students know the meaning of the words we are calling out. The picture spelling inventory assesses students' word knowledge through the within word pattern stage. The hardest word on this inventory is *whistle* (Bear et al., 2007).

A writing sample can also be used to analyze students' word knowledge, much as we have done in this chapter. It is assumed that students have not copied the words in this first draft writing. A developmental scoring guide helps teachers look for what types of errors students are making and align these errors with a spelling stage (Bear et al., 2008).

The sorts we have described are themselves informal assessments. For example, the speed and accuracy of students' sorting speaks to the depth of their knowledge. In an assessment we refer to as "The Elbow Test," teachers observe students sorting independently and notice the rapidity in the back-and-forth movement of their elbows. Those students who sort accurately and whose elbows move fluently are probably ready to move on to the next level sort.

Teachers can assess students' word study knowledge by observing students as they play games with words from the sorts. Students who sort or play the games accurately and quickly—and who can explain why they made the decisions they did—demonstrate that they have an understanding of the principle or generalization underlying the sort.

There are a few students who benefit by having teachers write for them. For these students, the multitasking involved in finding the letter-sounds or patterns in spelling and coordinating the writing is a bit too much, and the teacher's writing is a relief and a release for better production in the assessment. If you think that your student may understand the word study principle but cannot get it down on paper, ask the student to spell aloud for you first.

An indicator of learning is the words students spell correctly. Students often do not make the automatic transfer to writing until a word study principle is fully stable. We ask students solidly in the within word pattern to take a little time in their editing to look for the types of words that they are working on in their word study lessons. This type of writing activity will certainly be appropriate for the three focal students when they move to third grade.

Learning to Bend as Students Grow

We bring a combined 87 years of experience teaching students as they develop literacy, and we continue to learn from new approaches to instruction and, most important, from what we observe with the students who enter our classrooms. Our study of the second-grade students in Linda's classroom who were just beginning to learn English reinforced much of what we already knew about word study, but it also helped us see how new ELLs like Khamtay, MaiKia, and Sashitorn progressed through the same stages of literacy development as students who learn to read in only one language. Though these ELLs followed the same developmental sequence, our instruction needed to bend to navigate the interaction of English with students' primary languages and their literacy experiences.

Khamtay reminded us that students who bring background literacy to school in a language other than English often quickly transfer many of their literacy skills to a new language. He also demonstrated the huge importance of vocabulary development: Just because you can read a word doesn't mean you understand it, and it will take improvement in language development before writing and reading levels go beyond the basic level.

The case of MaiKia reinforced what we have seen in previous research: Students learning English make progress, but their development may take longer. It was tempting for Linda to look at students like MaiKia and think of all the things they needed to know; she would often feel herself start trying to give and push, give and push because there was so much her students needed. In our collaborative conversations in this project, we discussed how important it is to check for what a student has internalized and understood; if this is not done, a teacher ends up giving too much, the instruction goes over students' heads, and they end up not really "getting it." MaiKia will need a third-grade teacher who is able to meet her where she is at the letter-name–alphabetic stage and work with her on the short-vowel sounds and consonant digraphs.

Sashitorn showed many of the same characteristics of development that we saw with Khamtay and MaiKia. She developed from an early letter-name–alphabetic speller to a functioning speller at the later part of this stage. Her specific errors guided us to focus on phonics features that were difficult to contrast between English and her background language. For example, deliberate word study to transition from later letter-name spelling strategies included final blends and *n*-, *r*-, and *l*-influenced word sorts (*bend*, *bark*, *well*, respectively).

Because of the gap between Sashitorn's reading and word study levels, it would be a goal for her to have plenty of practice reading independent level materials to increase familiarity with single-syllable words and basic sentence structures. We learned a lot from her by reviewing her unedited writing samples and are grateful for getting her insights into how a young student thinks about learning languages in a multilingual classroom.

In our conversations together, Linda reflected on her growing understanding of orthographic development. She realized how spelling could tell her about students' development, and suddenly a new way of observing students' growth emerged. She described a big "Ah ha!" moment when she realized that she was going from leveled book to leveled book using the evidence of reading miscues, but she was not paying attention to what could be learned from students' writing. Linda gained a greater understanding of how the features of word study could be organized developmentally to provide a cohesive program for students. She saw many overlaps between what students showed in their reading and what they could do in their writing. She learned to take both things into account as she planned for small-group literacy instruction.

Working together in word study in Linda's multilingual classroom has provided a wonderful laboratory to investigate the interplay among word knowledge, reading development, and learning the sounds, structures, and meanings of the English language. As we worked to unravel how each of these strands interacted and we observed each other in the instructional moment of helping students learn about words in English, it became clear how much goes into effective word study instruction with ELLs. Key among the skills a teacher needs is the ability to bend teaching to the language and literacy foundations that students have. What students already understand is our platform to jump into the deep, rich pools of written and oral English.

REFLECTION QUESTIONS

1. What languages do you hear in your classroom? As you work with word study activities what do you notice about how these languages interact with sounds and spellings in English?

2. What information would help you to find out more about the linguistic backgrounds of English learners who enter your classroom? Where might you go for that information?

3. Observe the synchrony among reading, writing, and spelling with your students. Are there exceptions to this synchrony in some of your students? To what do you attribute these exceptions in the synchrony among reading, writing, and spelling?

4. After reading this chapter, how will you adapt your instruction to better meet the needs of English learners?

REFERENCES

Bear, D.R., Caserta-Henry, C., & Venner, D. (2004). *Personal readers for emergent and beginning readers*. Beaverton, OR: Teaching Resource Center.

Bear, D.R., & Helman, L.A. (2004). Word study for vocabulary development in the early stages of literacy learning: Ecological perspectives and learning English. In J. Baumann & E. Kame'enui (Eds.), *Vocabulary instruction: Research to practice* (pp. 139–158). New York: Guilford.

Bear, D.R., Helman, L.A., Templeton, S., Invernizzi, M., & Johnston, F.R. (2007). *Words their way with English language learners: Word study for phonics, vocabulary and spelling instruction*. Upper Saddle River, NJ: Pearson/Merrill Prentice Hall.

Bear, D.R., Invernizzi, M., & Johnston, F.R. (2005). *Words their way: Word study in action*. Parsippany, NJ: Pearson.

Bear, D.R., Invernizzi, M., Templeton, S., & Johnston, F. (2008). *Words their way: Word study for phonics, vocabulary, and spelling instruction* (4th ed.). Upper Saddle River, NJ: Prentice Hall.

Bear, D.R., & Templeton, S. (2000). Matching development and instruction. In N.D. Padak, T.V. Rasinski, J.K. Peck, B. Weible Church, G. Fawcett, J. Hendershot et al. (Eds.), *Distinguished educators on reading: Contributions that have shaped effective literacy instruction* (pp. 334–376). Newark, DE: International Reading Association.

Bear, D.R., Templeton, S., Helman, L.A., & Baren, T. (2003). Orthographic development and learning to read in different languages. In G.G. Garcia (Ed.), *English language learners: Reaching the highest level of English literacy* (pp. 71–95). Newark, DE: International Reading Association.

De Avila, E.A., & Duncan, S.E. (1994). *Language assessment scales.* Monterey, CA: CTB Macmillan/McGraw-Hill.

Flanigan, K. (2007). A concept of word in text: A pivotal event in early reading acquisition. *Journal of Literacy Research, 39*(1), 37–70.

Good, R.H., III, & Kaminski, R. (2002). *Dynamic indicators of basic early literacy skills (DIBELS).* Longmont, CO: Sopris West Educational Services.

Helman, L.A., & Bear, D.R. (2007). Does an established model of orthographic development hold true for English language learners? In D.W. Rowe, R. Jimenez, D.L. Compton, D.K. Dickinson, Y. Kim, K.M. Leander et al. (Eds.), *56th yearbook of the National Reading Conference* (pp. 266–280). Chicago: National Reading Conference.

Invernizzi, M., Abouzeid, M., & Gill, J.T. (1994). Using students' invented spellings as a guide for spelling instruction that emphasizes word study. *The Elementary School Journal, 95*(2), 155–167. doi:10.1086/461796

Morris, D., Bloodgood, J.W., Lomax, R.G., & Perney, J. (2003). Developmental steps in learning to read: A longitudinal study in kindergarten and first grade. *Reading Research Quarterly, 38*(3), 302–328. doi:10.1598/RRQ.38.3.1

Nelson, O.G., & Linek, W.M. (1998). *Practical classroom applications of language experience: Looking back, looking forward.* Boston: Allyn & Bacon.

Stauffer, R. (1980). *The language-experience approach to the teaching of reading* (2nd ed.). New York: Harper & Row.

CHAPTER 2

Connecting Language and Literacy Development in Elementary Classrooms

Youb Kim, P. David Pearson, Meredith McLellan, Andrea McPherson-Rumsey, and Zachary A. Konett

There is a dire need to understand effective instruction for English language learners (ELLs), as a growing number of U.S. classrooms are experiencing an influx of ELLs. According to the National Center for Education Statistics, "Sixty-three percent of public schools had students who were designated as limited-English-proficient" (Strizek et al., 2006, p. 3). The current educational context, which highlights the importance of leaving no child behind, puts additional pressure on teachers in these circumstances because they are expected to teach all students effectively, including ELLs. The focus of this chapter is how to adequately support English oral language and literacy development among beginning ELLs in the elementary grades, especially those students who come to U.S. schools with language and literacy skills in their native language.

For ELLs with native language and literacy skills, we recommend that teachers use English literacy (e.g., reading, writing, and drawing) to help these students participate in classroom activities (e.g., oral sharing) and to support their oral language development. This recommendation is drawn from our work in the Center for the Improvement of Early Reading Achievement, in particular from a research study we conducted between 1999 and 2001 to document the written to oral language connection in English as a second language (ESL) learning. We reported our initial research findings in 2001 (Kim, Lowenstein, Pearson, & McLellan, 2001). In this chapter, we will expand on those findings and provide more information about the integrated language activities and coordinated efforts at implementation in general education and ESL classrooms. We will begin with a brief review of relevant research in second language learning.

One Classroom, Many Learners: Best Literacy Practices for Today's Multilingual Classrooms edited by Julie Coppola and Elizabeth V. Primas. © 2009 by the International Reading Association.

Theory and Research Basis in Second Language Learning

A key to crafting effective instruction for ELLs is to understand their strengths and build upon them (Kim, Roehler, & Pearson, 2009). Research suggests that beginning ELLs possess metalinguistic strengths that derive from native language and literacy knowledge, and as a result they benefit from written language activities. According to Cummins's (1979) linguistic interdependency theory, ELLs who have already developed literacy skills in their native language possess the cognitive facility to learn a second language successfully. That is, although ELLs may not be able to verbalize their thoughts in English, they possess vocabulary-concept knowledge, metalinguistic insights (e.g., written language is meaningful), and the ability to process decontextualized language (e.g., classroom discourse).

Although it is logical to assume that this cognitive facility can be the basis for using written language as a scaffolding tool to effectively teach beginning ELLs in classroom contexts, researchers do not agree on whether written language activities should be used for beginning ELLs. A dominant view in second language research is that oral language has primacy in language development. Therefore, English reading and writing instruction should be postponed until ELLs possess an adequate level of oral language in English, partly because reading and writing are cognitively more challenging than speaking and listening (for a fuller discussion, see Kim et al., 2001). Only a handful of researchers suggest the possibility of using literacy for scaffolding lower elementary students' oral language development. For example, Weber and Longhi-Chirlin (2001) studied two first-grade, Spanish-speaking students of Puerto Rican origin: Ramón, who possessed knowledge about print in Spanish, and Nora, who did not. The authors found that the two beginning ELLs developed English literacy skills without "a strong oral foundation" (p. 45). Similar observations were made in Fitzgerald and Noblit's (1999) study on literacy teaching and learning in a first-grade classroom. In their report of two Spanish-speaking students from Mexico, these researchers noted that the students' English reading and writing development surpassed their English oral language development.

Understanding how to support oral and written language development for beginning ELLs is a complex issue. Despite the existence of empirical evidence that suggests the benefit of integrated language-based instruction on young

ELLs, disagreement among researchers regarding the utility of written language activities for beginning ESL instruction indicates that written language may be useful to support the oral language development of beginning ELLs under certain conditions. Thus, we need to understand effective ESL practice focusing on the classroom contexts in which successful English language learning took place and then carefully examine the connections between language and literacy development in that context.

Armed with these ideas, we focused our analysis on the instructional practices of three teachers and the learning practices of three students. From the teachers, we wanted to find out how they used written language activities to support both written and oral language development, especially in English. From the students, we wanted to examine the ways in which they responded to the teachers' practices and to discover any idiosyncratic written language practices they brought to the classroom as they approached the task of learning both written and oral English. The three learners, Yonsu, Tayl, and Hojun, were first and second graders in the early phases of communicating in English (student names are pseudonyms). Meredith, a coauthor of this chapter, was the ESL teacher for all the students. Andrea and Zachary, also coauthors, taught the students in their general education classrooms. Andrea was Hojun's second-grade teacher, and Zachary was Tayl's first-grade and Yonsu's second-grade teacher.

Classroom Portraits

The School

Spring Valley Elementary School, a public school located in the upper Midwest with a population of 240 K–5 students, served as our research site. During our research period, the majority of students were children of international graduate students or of visiting scholars at the neighboring university, and they represented over 20 different languages and cultures. Twenty-seven percent of the school's ELLs, who constituted approximately 80% of the student population, possessed limited English skills and were qualified for additional ESL support. To accommodate the diverse cultural and linguistic needs of these students, especially those who spoke minimal English when they first entered school, two ESL teachers coordinated and implemented a pull-out ESL program to complement general classroom instruction.

General Education Classrooms

Teachers in the general education classrooms implemented a literacy program requiring the use of all language skills (i.e., speaking, listening, reading, and writing) in classroom activities. For example, first- and second-grade students used both oral and written language skills as they engaged in whole-group, small-group, and independent activities. Students were exposed to a wide variety of reading materials including children's literature, newspapers, children's magazines, dictionaries, their own writing journals, and environmental print such as posters and word walls. The classrooms' daily routines included extensive written language use; students were exposed to a wide variety of reading and writing activities (e.g., read-alouds, shared reading, guided reading, and shared writing) throughout the day.

Zachary and Andrea, the two classroom teachers on whose instruction we focus, read aloud during transition times such as morning or afternoon recess or after lunch; guided reading instruction in small groups was also provided, and students had silent reading time at least once a day. During class activities that were designed to provide students with opportunities to use and practice their oral language skills, written language or objects facilitated the process. For example, during whole-group discussions on annoying behaviors and a follow-up small-group role play in the second-grade classroom, Zachary wrote directions for the activity on the board to remind students what they were expected to accomplish. During a science lesson in her second-grade classroom, Andrea gave magnets and various classroom objects to each small group of students to support their participation in a whole-group discussion on magnetism.

The ESL Program

The ESL program provided a supportive, small-group learning environment and featured English language learning opportunities within an integrated language arts program, where both oral and written language were used for instruction and class participation. ELLs were given abundant opportunities to develop both English oral and written language skills that would enable them to participate at grade level in their general education classroom. ESL instruction took place in small groups outside of the general education classrooms, and usually students from the same grade levels were instructed together. These sessions lasted for less than one hour per day, although there were some variations based upon the needs of each group. During the rest of the day, ELLs received instruction in their grade-level classrooms. Meredith, the ESL teacher, focused on helping ELLs develop English knowledge, skills, and a disposition for learning (e.g., democratic turn taking) through English language and literacy activities. She worked closely with the general education classroom teachers to ensure that language learning flowed seamlessly from one setting to the other. Meredith used various conversational opportunities such as classroom visits, hallway encounters, recess, or lunch to talk with general education teachers about instructional plans and activities to support her students' language learning. Students were supported to learn content knowledge and make connections among subject areas; develop feelings of empowerment in English; increase strategic reasoning for problem solving; and form appropriate constructs for authoring, reading, and learning conversations. Because her students possessed a wide variety of English skills, knowledge, and experience with U.S. culture, Meredith varied the support she provided while students developed English language skills. For example, she modeled questioning (e.g., May I have a pencil, Mrs. McLellan?) that would allow beginning ELLs to take the initiative in learning. She also used questions to introduce basic vocabulary, concepts, and classroom routines.

The Learners

Our three focal students, Yonsu, Tayl, and Hojun, came from Korea with their families. Their fathers were visiting scholars at a Midwestern university. During their stay in the United States, which spanned between one and two years, all families supported their children's English language learning in school and at home. The students played with Korean friends at the beginning of the school year and gradually made English-speaking friends as the year progressed. All three made advancements in both English oral and written language skills.

Yonsu was a female, second-grade student. She made positive gains in English oral and written language development. Between November and May, her oral English skills improved by two levels, and her written English skills by three levels on the Woodcock-Muñoz Language Survey (Woodcock & Muñoz-Sandoval, 1993). She made impressive reading gains in less than a year, moving from below preprimer to the fourth-grade level on the Qualitative Reading Inventory (Leslie & Caldwell, 1995) between January and September of her second-grade year.

Yonsu had previously attended a public elementary school in Korea for one year and had advanced literacy skills in her native language. At the beginning of the school year, she spoke Korean with her friends and family, and she spent her playtime outside of school with mostly Korean friends. Although Yonsu's use of English increased as the year progressed, she continued to speak Korean with her parents, who described her as quiet, sensitive, and shy with a keen memory. They felt that she could, however, sometimes be assertive—for example, in Korea she had volunteered to be the student representative in her homeroom.

Yonsu was an avid reader and writer. While in Korea, she sometimes skipped a meal to read through a new book her father had just bought for her. Her predilection for reading persisted in the United States. Though she mostly read Korean books in the beginning, she gradually came to read more material in English. Her English reading began with primer-level books that were sent home as reading assignments. Yonsu also read English at home during study sessions with an English tutor. Gradually, she began to read independently. By March, Yonsu was listening to books on tape from the local library at bedtime. By May, she read chapter books, including science fiction. Yonsu's parents also encouraged her to write regularly at home, and she kept a home journal throughout the year. Entries in her home journal were written in Korean in the beginning and gradually came to include English writing as the year progressed.

Tayl was enrolled in the first grade. Between October and May, his English oral language skills improved by one level, and his written English skills improved by two levels on the Pre-Las Oral (Duncan & De Avila, 1998). He also made gains in reading, moving from a nonreader in the beginning to become a primer-level reader by the end of the year on the Qualitative Reading Inventory (Leslie & Caldwell, 1995). Tayl read and wrote in Korean at his grade level. At the beginning of the school year, he was perceived as shy by Zachary, his first-grade teacher, who identified the need for him to be more vocal based upon his classroom interactions.

Tayl's family supported his English language learning. To encourage reading, Tayl's parents consulted with his teacher and purchased 50 used children's books, including titles by Dr. Seuss and from the Berenstain Bears series. His parents also tried to teach Tayl and his sister English at home for a few hours a day, using dictation to develop their children's English skills. During this time, they also tried to speak some English to encourage their children's use of conversational English at home. By January, Tayl was capable of reading English books independently. His parents continued to ask him to read books at home and also provided an English tutor who attended college in the area. The tutor came twice a week during the first four months, and later three times a week. With the tutor, Tayl read books, played Hangman, and studied workbooks that focused on phonics skills and reading comprehension.

Tayl's progress in English oral skills was evident in his social interactions and ESL assessment results. In the beginning, he had only one English-speaking friend from his class. At the end of the school year, he had made more English-speaking friends, and he used more English than Korean at home. Tayl's parents were proud of Tayl's development in English oral language, saying "Tayl speaks like foreign [American] students."

Hojun was enrolled in the second grade. He stayed in the United States for two years and participated in another second language research project during the first year. Although he was not one of the focal students in the study that examined written to oral language connection in second language learning, he is included in this report because his data show how written language can make oral language stand still, thus providing a critical insight into understanding the connection between the oral and literacy development of beginning ELLs in the elementary grades. Like Yonsu and Tayl, Hojun made positive gains in English. During his first year, his oral language skills improved by two levels on the IDEA Language Proficiency Test (Tighe & Ballard, 1991), and his reading improved from preprimer to third-grade reading level on the Qualitative Reading Inventory (Leslie & Caldwell, 1995) during the second year.

Unlike Yonsu and Tayl, however, Hojun was vocal. His mother described his personality as "outgoing, cheerful, playful, and good with friends, even with girls." Before he came to the United States, Hojun was exposed to English for six months while he attended a Montessori preschool in his home country. There, he learned English songs once or twice a week. Despite his outgoing and positive nature and his prior experience with English, he had a difficult time in the beginning. Hojun was frustrated by his inability to communicate in English, and initially he did not want to go to school. For example, he felt uncomfortable during a whole-class sharing time when he was not able to explain to his ESL teacher and peers that he went to a Korean church on the weekends. By late October, however, his mother noticed a positive change in his attitude toward school. This change coincided with Halloween, which Hojun found to be a new and fascinating cultural experience. Shortly after Halloween, he began to share positive classroom experiences with his mother, and he reported to her that he enjoyed going to school.

Connecting Oral and Literacy Development in Elementary Classrooms

In this section, we describe instructional strategies to support both oral language and literacy development among beginning ELLs in the elementary grades. We focus on how general education and ESL teachers used written language activities to scaffold students' oral language development. Although all language skills were emphasized during instruction, we pay particular attention to the role of written language (i.e., reading, writing, and drawing). With that in mind, we use the heading of each section to indicate a function of written language that contributed to the oral language development of the focus students, Yonsu, Tayl, and Hojun. We describe the classroom activities and explain how teachers connected oral language and literacy development among the students.

Making Language Material

Vocabulary instruction was a typical example of teachers using written language to scaffold the development of ELLs' oral vocabulary. There were several ways in which this occurred in classrooms: (a) writing to label an object (e.g., labeling objects in a classroom), (b) writing to describe a picture (e.g., writing picture word cards or sentences describing pictures), (c) writing to prompt speech (e.g., seeing and saying the word), and (d) combinations of the above. In these cases, written language was used to connect language to its base in the everyday world; thus, the role of written language seemed to be "making language material" (Kim et al., 2001).

Zachary encouraged his first-grade students, including Tayl and the other ELLs in his general education classroom, to explain their understanding of words through pictures when they wrote in their journals. After reading a book, he asked the students to share which words from the book they wanted to include in their journals. He then gave an example of how the students could demonstrate their understanding of words. Zachary drew a big rectangle on a piece of chart paper and divided it into two parts with a horizontal line in the middle. Then, he drew a picture of the sun in the top half of the rectangle and wrote the English word *sun* in the bottom half. Zachary asked the students to do the same in their journals. By modeling the drawing of a picture to represent the meaning of a word, the teacher encouraged students to make oral language material in their journal writing so that they could understand the semantic relationship between an object in the everyday world and its written English symbol, and their enhanced semantic understanding could become part of their active English vocabulary.

In the ESL classroom, Meredith also used pictures to build the basic English oral vocabulary that beginning ELLs needed to meaningfully participate in their general education classrooms, especially at the start of a school year. Individual ELLs were given a word bank consisting of small picture word cards—each featuring a picture of a real-world object—that were used to develop ELLs' vocabulary. Meredith also used bingo games to build basic shape and color vocabulary. For example, students and the teacher held bingo cards of different shapes and colors. The teacher called out the English names of the color and the shape on her card, and a student called "Bingo!" if he or she had a card with the same shape and color. Students' word banks were used to develop their knowledge about English language concepts such as plurals. For example, Meredith asked students to look at a picture of buttons in their word bank and say the English word. She then asked students to look at the number of buttons in the picture while the class discussed the plural marker s. In doing so, Meredith used written language (i.e., drawing) to make oral language material so that students could understand the meaning of a plural marker (i.e., s).

The teachers' vocabulary instruction through making language material seemed successful based upon students' performance in oral language assessments. For example, Yonsu made positive gains in vocabulary learning. Based on the Peabody Picture Vocabulary Test-Form 3B (Dunn & Dunn, 1997), she made substantial progress moving from an age equivalence of 3 years, 2 months in receptive vocabulary in November to an age equivalence of 5 years by the end of May. Although we do not have vocabulary assessment data from the other two students, we can infer the contribution of written language in students' vocabulary development because all three students made gains on oral language assessments of standardized ESL tests used for the study.

Making Language Stand Still

"Making language stand still" refers to how the teachers used written language to highlight specific aspects of oral or written language use so that it could be inspected closely, carefully, and deliberately. This is what Olson (1996) calls the metalinguistic advantage of written language. He claims that this advantage facilitates meta-awareness of both oral and written language—what we would typically label "linguistic analysis." According to Olson, it is this metalinguistic feature of written language that accounts for many of the differences in cognitive reflection that we discuss when we compare literate to preliterate societies (Kim et al., 2001). Considering that such differences also seem evident between readers and prereaders, it appears quite logical for teachers to use written language activities for ELLs who come to school with language and literacy skills.

In her second-grade classroom, Andrea implemented a written language activity to offer explicit instruction on the forms and functions of the past tense. She used chart paper with three columns to delineate past, present progressive, and root words with example sentences for each. Then she explained what the past tense meant. She said, "I stopped at the light. When did it happen? Past. If it is right now, I say that I am stopping." She wrote *stop* in the root word column. She then asked the students to think of root words. Students offered *park*, *cook*, *row*, *watch*, *smile*, and *play*. After Andrea finished writing these root words, she asked the students to explain what the words were to help them think of the lexical category (i.e., verb) of the words. A female intermediate ELL answered that the words meant things that they did. Andrea confirmed her answer and said, "Yes, these are words that describe what we do. They are called verbs." After Andrea's explanation, students individually found root words and wrote the past tense for each word. During this time, Hojun copied words from a female student who sat next to him.

In the ESL class the following week, we observed Hojun articulating the meaning of past tense during a weekend-activity sharing time. The students were given an opportunity to describe their weekend experiences orally in a whole group. While students took turns and explained what they did, Meredith occasionally chimed in to highlight the forms and functions of the past tense. For example, when a student said that he played with friends, Meredith asked the students if they noticed *played*, and she explained that they were talking about the weekend, something that was finished. Hojun used the lesson he learned from Meredith's "making language stand still" while he described his weekend activity:

Hojun: I played computer.

Meredith: Why did I say *played*? [Meredith intentionally uses "I" here so as not to confuse this beginning student.]

Hojun: Because you did it...like yesterday. [Hojun uses "you" in response to Meredith's use of "I."]

These two examples demonstrate consistent written language use in both general education and ESL classrooms. The teachers wrote the verb forms on chart paper and directed students to the appropriate contrast (e.g., *play* vs. *played*). During this process, students were supported to understand and orally demonstrate their understanding of the form and meaning of the past tense.

Reinforcing Natural Language

When teachers read stories aloud, ELLs have the opportunity to hear language they understand. This process of hearing language through a teacher read-aloud seems to serve as a reinforcement of students' natural language. By "natural language," we mean language structures and vocabulary that the student has internalized and made a part of the language repertoire but that may not have appeared yet in the student's oral and written language production. In an ESL context, natural language does not necessarily mean a student's home language only, although natural language certainly begins with home language knowledge and skills. As ELLs develop English proficiency and become more comfortable with using English for communication, both English and the home language become natural language for the student. An example comes from Tayl's engagement in teacher read-alouds.

In Tayl's general education classroom, story reading was prevalent. Zachary, his teacher, read stories aloud to the whole class at least twice a day during morning and afternoon snack and story time. Students usually sat on a carpet area and listened to the stories read by the teacher while eating their snacks. Most of the time, Tayl seemed to be more interested in eating his snack than listening to the story. His engagement in teacher read-alouds changed as the year progressed. In early February, we asked him if he enjoyed listening to the stories during snack and story time. He said that he enjoyed it because he could hear some words in the book that he already knew in Korean. He seemed to refer to borrowed words such as *cookies* or *snack* that originated from English but became part of Korean vocabulary when the products were introduced to the Korean culture. Two weeks later, when Meredith read *The Very Hungry Caterpillar* by Eric Carle in the ESL classroom, Tayl stood up to look at the book and quietly read the words he knew along with the teacher. Almost two months later in mid April, Tayl for the first time seemed to be engaged in listening to a story titled *Bear's Bargain* by Frank Asch during a snack and story time in his general education classroom. When we asked him about it after the teacher read-aloud, he said he enjoyed listening to the story because he knew all the words.

These three observations suggest that teacher read-alouds served as natural language reinforcement for Tayl. In the beginning, he was able to hear words he knew in Korean (e.g., *cookies* and *snack*) although he was not able to comprehend the text his teacher read to the class. At mid-year when he knew more English and when he was more comfortable with using English, he was engaged enough to enjoy the story his teachers read. In this sense, the teacher read-aloud was not a direct source of Tayl's knowledge in learning English, but it strengthened the knowledge he already possessed, either in Korean or English. In this way, the read-alouds reinforced Tayl's tacit knowledge of English language structure and vocabulary that was internalized and became part of his language repertoire but may not have appeared yet in his oral and written language production. Because it is often difficult to tap into ELLs' tacit knowledge, we recommend that teachers choose a wide variety of good children's literature, in addition to choosing books that ELLs demonstrate they understand during read-alouds.

Elaborating Language

A student's written text provides an opportunity for the teacher and other students to expand on oral language as a response to what the student has written. Teachers often encourage other students to ask questions that demand further elaboration on a story a student has read. When a student reads his or her own journal to the class, a teacher can ask questions to help the student clarify or expand on ideas in the written text. The teacher can also expand on and clarify the idea for the student. Sometimes another student in the audience can elaborate for the author. ELLs can benefit from the language input prompted by a student's text and ensuing oral discussions. An example comes from Hojun's reading of his journal in his ESL class.

In early December, students shared their ESL journal with the whole class. Hojun read his story:

> In the beach, there was one big tree and the one road that end come to far and water will waving very hard and Tom was in the tree. And he fell into the water and he said help help. That Faye rescued Tom and give a little Pokemon card and was...[the last part of his speech was inaudible].

When Hojun finished the reading of his story, students clapped and commented that the story was "super duper." Meredith raised a hand to ask what time of the year the story took place:

Hojun:	[looking at Meredith who raised a hand] Ms. McLellan.
Meredith:	Thank you for calling my name. Was it summer time or autumn?
Hojun:	End of summer.
	[Meredith repeats Hojun's response.]
Intern teacher:	Was it in a particular country? Which country was it in?
	[Hojun pauses.]
Meredith:	[to the intern teacher] He may have not thought about that.
Meredith:	[to Hojun] Hojun, do you want to decide now?
Hojun:	It was Japan.
	[The students and the teachers give a round of applause.]

In February, a couple of months later, we observed elaboration of language by fellow students. Meredith had brought her own leopard gecko to school and gave students a chance to hold the gecko and write about it. When students finished writing, the teacher organized a sharing time in which students shared their writing with the whole group. Hojun shared his writing, as shown in Figure 2.1.

Lu, a student from China, commented that he liked the part that said, "I smell stinky. And take shower and kills crickets." Zulu, another ELL in the class, said that Hojun acted like a gecko and that he found it strange. Meredith said that Hojun's story was wonderful.

Meredith provided students with opportunities to write their ideas in their journals and to share their writing with the class. Her use of student journals as a platform for discussion encouraged students to think about English language in a new way and to elaborate on their ideas. This process resembles peer-editing discussions in a writers' workshop. As the year progressed, other students also seemed to be able to ask questions to help one another think deeply about English language while validating their increased facility in language use.

Figure 2.1. Hojun's Writing About a Leopard Gecko

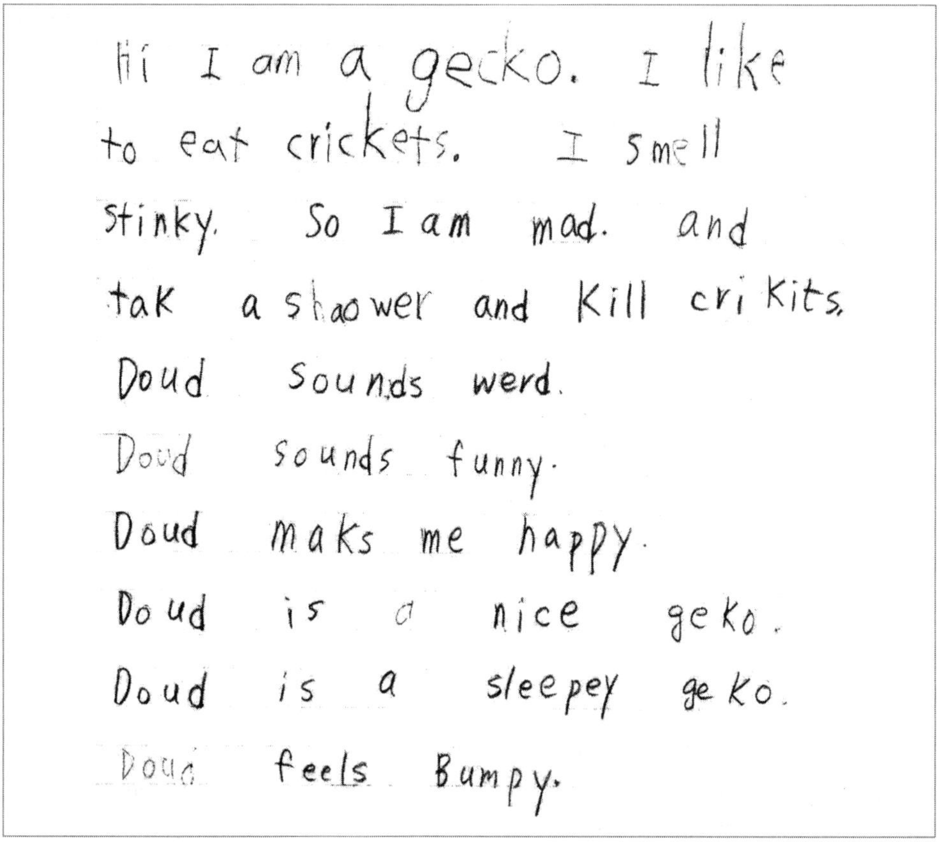

Hi I am a gecko. I like
to eat crickets.   I smell
Stinky.   So I am   mad.   and
tak   a shaower and Kill cri Kits.
Doud   Sounds   werd.
Doud   sounds   funny.
Doud   maks   me   happy.
Doud   is   a   nice   geko.
Doud   is   a   sleepey   geKo.
Doud   feels   Bumpy.

Rehearsing Language

"Rehearsing language" refers to using written language to practice emerging English skills, in much the same way a person would rehearse for a play. The rehearsal can be either overt, as in repeated readings or rehearsing for participating in a Readers Theatre reading. It can also be covert, as when a student uses a journal as a way of practicing or rehearsing a specific language pattern for later use in an informal conversational setting. Both overt and covert rehearsal focuses on the process of repeated practice of one or more language forms over an extended period of time; thus, repeated practice contributes to the development of both written and oral English proficiency.

Repeated readings seemed to have played a role in Tayl's learning of *caught*. On April 10, Meredith taught her students how to describe "things I did yesterday" as a way to teach past tense verb forms. Students were taught both regular and irregular forms. During the review of the day's lesson, Meredith gave a sentence and expected students to say the past tense form of a verb in the sentence. Tayl did not know the correct tense form of *catch* that day:

Meredith: [looking at Tayl] Can you catch that big ball?

Tayl: Catched.

Meredith: Close.

Tayl: Ca...

Meredith: Caught.

[Meredith writes the word on the board.]

After this conversation, Meredith asked her students to read their small books, which included past tense verb forms that they studied that day, to a partner or another adult in the room. She told Tayl to go to the principal's office and read to him. Because the school principal served as a listening partner to all students, going to the principal's office was a "cool" thing for the student. Tayl went to the principal's office and read his small book. Every time he encountered the word *caught*, he hesitated and the principal pronounced it for him. When Tayl was finished reading, the principal gave him a special pencil with compliments for his good work.

About a month later, Meredith read a text with the students and asked questions to check their comprehension. The text consisted of an illustration of a farmer and a truck at the top and a two-paragraph story at the bottom, describing a farmer whose pig jumped out of the truck and went into a nearby store when the farmer stopped at a red light. When Meredith asked a question in which the response required the use of a past tense verb, Tayl used the word *caught* accurately as seen in the following example:

Meredith: What did he take to his farm?

Anna: The pig.

Meredith: The pig. How did he get the pig?

Anna: Catch.

Tayl: No. Caught.

In this exchange, Tayl corrected his friend and provided an accurate past tense form for *catch*, which seemed to exhibit his solid understanding of the word. Although Meredith's comprehension question might be considered a low-level recall question, it served an important instructional purpose for beginning ELLs. Responding to the question required ELLs' understanding of the text, the teacher's question, and the semantic relationship between *get* and *catch* in the linguistic context. Repeated readings provided Tayl with opportunities to participate in overt rehearsal and may have played a role in Tayl's acquisition and accurate use of *caught*.

The following example shows the process of how writing may have helped Yonsu acquire a specific sentence structure ("I went to") and produce it orally in the ESL class. Data show that Yonsu used written language to practice emerging English skills for over four weeks. Understanding that her ESL class would have weekly whole-group sharing about weekend experiences, she used a journal to practice, or rehearse, a specific language pattern for later use in an informal conversational setting. In this sense, her rehearsal was covert rather than overt. The purpose of rehearsing a language form in covert rehearsal is for personal reflection rather than immediate public sharing, and the rehearsal process is not likely to be available to researchers. Understanding this function of written language would not have been possible had Yonsu's family not informed the first author that the home journal existed and given researchers permission to use it.

After Yonsu's ESL class discussed places the students visited during the winter break, Yonsu copied what the teacher wrote on the chalkboard into a journal entry on January 6. Yonsu, however wrote the title and one word in Korean as shown in Figure 2.2.

Practicing these sentences through writing in her home journal seemed to help Yonsu acquire the sentence structure. She appeared to understand that names of places could come after the preposition *to*. Her understanding of this sentence structure seems evident in her continued rehearsal, observed between January 24 and February 6 in her home journal:

Today, I went to MGM studio. (January 24)

Today, I went to Animal Kingdom. (January 25)

Today, I went to Daytona Beach. (January 26)

Today, I went to MGM studio, Animal Kingdom, Magic Kingdom. (January 28)

Today, my family went to swimming pool (no father). (February 6)

Figure 2.2. Yonsu's Journal Entry

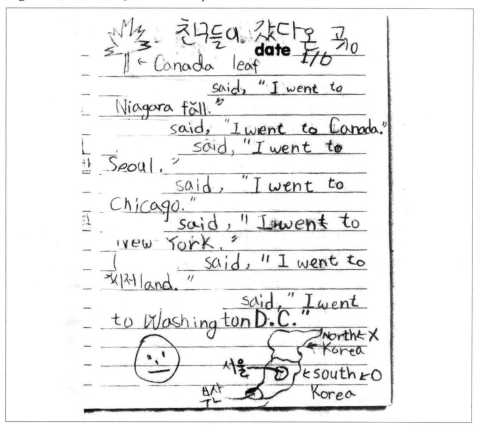

During these times, Yonsu added *today* in the beginning of the sentences. On February 6, she appropriately changed the subject of the sentence to "my family" instead of "I" and the names of places after the preposition, exhibiting her deeper understanding of the sentence structure.

The form "I went to" that Yonsu rehearsed over and over again in her home journal seemed to become readily available for oral language production, enabling her to answer in a complete sentence on February 22 during sharing time. When Meredith asked the students to share their experiences during the weekend, Yonsu answered, "I went to Frankenmuth" after the teacher's second prompting:

Meredith: [looking at Yonsu] Did you do something for the weekend?
           [Yonsu gives no answer.]
Meredith: [with a smile] Can you tell me one thing?
Yonsu: [in a soft voice] Franken...
Meredith: You went to Pokemon? I am sorry?
Yonsu: I went to Frankenmuth.

Repeated reading and journal writing provided Tayl and Yonsu with opportunities to rehearse a language form publicly or privately. In turn, the overt and covert rehearsal contributed to their learning of a language form.

The Significance of Thoughtful Written Language Activities for ELLs

By using written language activities in thoughtful ways, teachers can connect oral language and literacy development among beginning ELLs in the elementary grades who come to U.S. schools with native language and literacy skills. When used in meaningful communicative contexts (e.g., classrooms where all language skills are used for learning), written language can make oral language material and the meaning of words tangible to students in the early stages of English language learning. Written language can also make oral language explicit (i.e., "stand still") so that teachers and students can inspect its form and function more carefully. As we found in an example of Tayl's engagement in his teacher's storybook reading, written language can serve as natural language reinforcement. It can also provide ELLs with opportunities to elaborate on their language, as we saw in the class discussion followed by Hojun's oral sharing of the journal entry he composed in his ESL classroom. Last, written language can be used to help ELLs rehearse their emerging English language skills.

In implementing written language activities to support students' oral language and literacy development, it is important for teachers to understand the value of building a pro-social classroom community (Au, Mason, & Scheu, 1995; Kim & Turner, 2006). Examples from the classrooms we studied show that teachers established a learning community in which everyone supported and respected one another. The teachers saw their students' strengths as learners and fostered the students' ownership of their language learning. For example, Meredith welcomed student participation, encouraging Tayl to follow along while she read a story aloud. General education teachers also valued student participation in their instruction. Zachary asked students to choose their favorite words to include in their journals after teacher read-alouds. Andrea invited students to offer root words when they studied past tense verbs. These examples highlight the importance of creating a supportive learning environment— through encouragement and respect for individual students—to successfully craft effective language and literacy instruction for ELLs.

Collaboration seems to be another central piece in connecting oral language and literacy development among ELLs. For example, Andrea and Meredith consecutively implemented a lesson on the form and function of past tense verbs. This gave students opportunities to learn the concept for the first time in their general education classroom, and then they were able to use the form and share their understanding of the function explicitly in their ESL classroom. Considering that Hojun learned to explain the function of past tense verbs, such repeated exposure and use in two different contexts seems to be effective with ELLs. We believe this type of instructional collaboration is a genuine form of professional development among teachers. As a veteran teacher, Meredith served as a mentor for new teachers in the school, and Andrea and Zachary frequently visited Meredith's classroom and had conversations with her about individual ELLs in their classrooms. Because ESL and classroom teachers develop insights about individual students, it seems important for teachers to have an opportunity to share their thoughts and collaborate on their instruction so that they can be more effective.

Assessment seems to be another important aspect of effectively connecting oral language and literacy development for ELLs. In all three classrooms, assessment and instruction went hand in hand. Zachary used students' journal entries as a way to assess vocabulary knowledge. When his students showed him that they had written in their journals before they moved to free-choice activities, he asked the students to say the English names of objects in their entries. During the process, he checked whether the student understood the meaning of a word. Andrea kept students' work samples from classroom activities and included them in students' portfolios. Gleaning from student work samples she collected, she assessed students' understanding of the focus of a lesson. Meredith implemented student portfolio interviews to understand students' view of learning. During the interview, she showed the students their work samples from the classroom activities and asked them to choose and explain which piece they liked the most, which piece demonstrated the most progress they had made, and which piece showed what they could do better. From these interviews, she learned how students made sense of her instruction. In these ways, the teachers also used assessment to inform their instruction.

As we conclude our chapter, we earnestly hope to inspire teachers' thoughtful use of written language. In effective classrooms, language skills cannot be separated in classroom instruction (Hudelson, 1986). However, there seem to be classrooms in which written language is used to give students busy work, as documented in Garden School, California (Valdés, 2001). In that school, ELLs were given worksheets without opportunities for interaction and communication. We certainly do not propose such types of written language use in classrooms. We argue for the contrary, as our examples show the other end of the spectrum—written language was used to connect oral language and literacy development, leading to successful learning outcomes. We hope our work encourages teachers to explore how to use written language in a purposeful and meaningful way that brings school success for each and every ELL.

REFLECTION QUESTIONS

1. What types of language skills (i.e., speaking, listening, reading, and writing) do your students need to meaningfully participate in your classroom activities?

2. How do you help ELLs feel comfortable in your classroom?

3. How do you help ELLs develop English vocabulary?

4. How do you use reading, writing, and viewing to support ELLs' oral language development in English?

5. How do you work with ESL teachers in your school or district to support ELLs in your classroom? For example, do you regularly meet with ESL teachers to discuss ways to support ELLs in your classroom?

REFERENCES
Au, K.H., Mason, J.M., & Scheu, J.A. (1995). *Literacy instruction for today*. New York: HarperCollins.
Cummins, J. (1979). Linguistic interdependence and the educational development of bilingual children. *Review of Educational Research, 49*(2), 222–251.
Duncan, S.E., & De Avila, E.A. (1998). *PreLAS2000 assessment kit*. Monterey, CA: CTB/McGraw Hill.
Dunn, L.M., & Dunn, L.M. (1997). *Peabody picture vocabulary test* (3rd ed.). Circle Pines, MN: American Guidance Service.

Fitzgerald, J., & Noblit, G.W. (1999). About hopes, aspirations, and uncertainty: First-grade English-language learners' emergent reading. *Journal of Literacy Research, 31*(2), 133–182.

Hudelson, S. (1986). ESL children's writing: What we've learned, what we're learning. In P. Rigg & D.S. Enright (Eds.), *Children and ESL: Integrating perspectives* (pp. 25–54). Washington, DC: TESOL.

Kim, Y., Lowenstein, K.L., Pearson, P.D., & McLellan, M. (2001). A framework for conceptualizing and evaluating the contributions of written language activity in oral language development for ESL students. In J.V. Hoffman, D.L. Schallert, C.M. Fairbanks, J. Worthy, & B. Maloch (Eds.), *50th yearbook of the National Reading Conference* (pp. 333–345). Chicago, IL: National Reading Conference.

Kim, Y., Roehler, L., & Pearson, P.D. (2009). Strength-based instruction for early elementary (K–3) students learning English as a Second Language (ESL). In H.R. Milner (Ed.), *Possibilities of diversity: A guide for practitioners* (pp. 103-115). Springfield, IL: Charles C. Thomas.

Kim, Y., & Turner, J.D. (2006). Creating literacy communities in multicultural and multilingual classrooms: Lesson learned from two European American elementary teachers. In R.T. Jiménez & V.O. Pang (Eds.), *Race, ethnicity and education: Language, literacy and schooling* (Vol. 2, pp. 219–236). Westport, CT: Praeger

Leslie, L., & Caldwell, J. (1995). *Qualitative reading inventory.* New York: HarperCollins.

Olson, D.R. (1996). *The world on paper: The conceptual and cognitive implications of writing and reading.* New York: Cambridge University Press.

Strizek, G.A., Pittsonberger, J.L., Riordan, D.M., Lyter, D.M., Orlofsky, G.F., & Gruber, K. (2006). *Characteristics of schools, districts, teachers, principals, and school libraries in the United States: 2003–04 schools and staffing survey.* Washington, DC: National Center for Education Statistics.

Tighe, P.L., & Ballard, W.S. (1991). IDEA Language Proficiency Test. Brea, CA: Author.

Valdés, G. (2001). *Learning and not learning English: Latino students in American schools.* New York: Teachers College Press.

Weber, R., & Longhi-Chirlin, T. (2001). Beginning in English: The growth of linguistic and literate abilities in Spanish-speaking first graders. *Reading Research and Instruction, 41*(1), 19–50.

Woodcock, R.W., & Muñoz-Sandoval, A.F. (1993). *Woodcock-Muñoz language survey.* Itasca, IL: Riverside.

CHAPTER 3

Children's Literature in Linguistically and Culturally Diverse Classrooms

Nancy Roser, Jennifer Battle, and Melody Patterson Zoch

Across time, theorists and researchers have implicated *story* as a place where identity, community, and learning take root (Bruner, 1992; Dyson & Genishi, 1994). Importantly, the stories shared in schools need not all be drawn from between book covers. Instead, they can be the stories of home and family, life and cultures. The indicators are strong that the compelling stories we tell, read, and write invite further thought and talk—and language learners must engage in both. The best of children's literature, like the finest of all writing, adds to the breadth and richness of children's own stories and invites them to consider (and perhaps to speak about) what links and distinguishes us as humans. This chapter looks closely at stories as invitations to language and literacy—with a close focus on teachers' well-planned mediations that surround books and children's stories in classrooms.

We begin with a brief summation of the research that cedes the critical importance of well-chosen literature for students' growing proficiency in their first and second languages. We next look into three classrooms with different populations of students learning language, supported by both good literature and informed teaching. Finally, we attempt to link the events in those classrooms with the implications from the evidentiary base.

Why Children's Literature in Linguistically and Culturally Diverse Classrooms?

We begin with a promise to examine closely the support for the seemingly obvious. That is, we want to examine some seemingly obvious precepts linking literature and language to determine if there are surprising and even counter-intuitive notions to consider. We present three well-accepted (or at least often-repeated) assumptions about learning language in the presence of children's literature, and then we inspect the evidence that supports each assumption. First, because the best of children's books are marked with some of the most exquisite uses of language—language that is poetic and metaphoric, as well as precise, detailed, and instructive—classroom literature collections marked by *variety, sufficiency, accessibility,* and *quality* can support growth in language proficiency. Second, language grows from use of language, so classroom conversations about books (as well as other language-centered response opportunities) can stretch and support language growth. Third, invitations to language are most readily responded to when they are encased within the familiar, so students who are offered texts relevant to their own experiences are more apt to develop proficiency with language. Following, we examine these "obvious" assumptions in ways that allow us to highlight the "not-so-obvious."

Classrooms filled with varied, sufficient, accessible, and quality books provide for growth in language proficiency. Hickman's (1981) careful observations in Ohio classrooms documented ways in which varied opportunities to read and to choose responsive activities were reflected in students' thoughtful book talk. From her targeted sample of students with rural and Appalachian backgrounds, Hickman raised an implication for linguistically diverse students as well: After classrooms are stocked with well-chosen children's literature, there must be time to read, enjoy, revisit, and talk over those books.

Others have contended that *interest or appeal* of the literature may be the obvious factor that deserves even more inspection. For example, after Elley and Mangubhai (1983) placed 250 high-interest English language books into 16 Fijian classrooms, they compared the students' reading and listening comprehension with matched controls to discover that high-interest story reading contributed to learning a second language. At the outset, the researchers noted "little empirical work has been done...to explore the proposition that L2 [second language] learning would be more effective when based on story reading and related activities" (p. 56). In a similar book flood within low-performing (on state tests) schools in south Texas, Roser and Hoffman and their colleagues (Roser, Hoffman, & Farest, 1990; Roser, Hoffman, Labbo, & Farest, 1992) placed children's books arrayed in study units into 78 kindergarten, first-, and second-grade classrooms (approximately 1,000 children's books in all). The 2,500 students were predominantly Mexican American, with Spanish as their home language.

Teachers were offered guidance for sharing books, initiating conversations, capturing students' observations and other comments on large "language charts" (in English or Spanish), and inviting students' drawing and writing. Although no direct measure of language growth was administered, teachers reported positive perceptions of their students' confidence with language and comfort with books. Further, scores for a cohort of second graders were compared with those of age-mates in comparison schools on the California Test of Basic Skills (CTB/McGraw Hill, 1992). Reading growth for these students who had met and talked over books in focus units was three times greater than that of comparison school students, as registered by shifts in percentile scores.

Worthy and Roser (2004) flooded a central Texas bilingual fifth-grade class with more than 300 books, based largely on the students' choices—providing a focused, "wish list book flood", such that the classroom collection contained books that students expressed preferences for, yet reported they could not always find in their schools and communities (see, for example, Neuman, 1999; Worthy, Moorman, & Turner, 1999). Literate in Spanish at the beginning of the school year (reading from second- to fifth-grade levels), these 18 fifth graders nominated titles, genres, and topics they hoped could be added to their classroom shelves. These included joke books, graphic novels, magazines, picture books, beginning chapter books, series books, mystery, horror, sports, information texts, and books with popular cultural currency, such as the Harry Potter series in English and Spanish. The descriptive data collected included student and teacher interviews, observational field notes, various written artifacts, book club transcripts, and comprehension checks. Yet, some important data were unanticipated. For example, a stack of books began to mark the corner of each student's desk (much like an avid reader's nightstand), and the students eagerly posted written recommendations for others. Ultimately, the end-of-year state reading assessment in English recorded that all the students (save one) passed at grade level.

Neuman (1999) found that a flood of books in 330 child care centers (at a ratio of five books per child) meant more time spent with books, more literacy-related activities, as well as increased interest in books. She pointed to the critical features accompanying books placed in young students' hands, including

> a caring adult who reads to children, exposing them to the rich vocabulary and linguistic forms of the language; who talks about the events in the stories; who focuses the children's attention on ways to better understand the text; and who shows them how they may participate.... (p. 301)

Yet, even with attention to good books, frequent reading, and invitations to talk, Neuman's measure of receptive vocabulary was unable to detect significant gains for the experimental group.

Nevertheless, across classrooms in which students are provided easy access to a menu of appropriate, appealing, high-quality, and varied books—and offered time to read—teachers observe students choosing to read. Krashen (2003) contends there is sufficient evidence to argue that "free voluntary reading may be the most powerful tool we have in language education...with a strong impact on reading comprehension, vocabulary, grammar, and writing" (p. 15). Even so, in an inspection of 14 empirical studies on voluntary reading, the authors of the National Reading Panel report (National Institute of Child Health and Human Development, 2000) contended that the 14 identified studies offered too little supporting evidence for the effects of independent reading opportunities to recommend the practice. The caveat, however, was that the studies typically involved students reading on their own without feedback. Further, the studies typically didn't describe the students' available book choices—such as their qualities, fit, and appeal.

The trouble may be, of course, that too few classrooms are well-stocked with books students can and like to read. Further, there may be too little opportunity to make choices and too little time to read good books. Further, although stories center our students' lives and offer connections and identity, it is informational text and the well-planned studies/units that sponsor their uses in classrooms, which encourage students' academic vocabulary and learning (Cummins, 1981; Morrow, Pressley, Smith, & Smith, 1997). Some studies indicate that students meet too few texts that offer them cognitive challenges (Duke, 2000; Hadaway, Vardell, & Young, 2002). Especially for linguistically and culturally diverse learners do the provision of books and choice seem critical. But once classrooms are filled with carefully selected books, relevant talk about those books becomes the second variable worth examining.

Conversations about books (as well as opportunities to respond in other language-centered ways) stretch and support language growth. Among teachers who subscribe to social-constructivist stances on learning (Vygotsky, 1978)—and who hold that learners are instrumental in their own knowledge making (Chang-Wells & Wells, 1992; Dewey, 1966)—time to talk may be as valuable as time to read.

When Sipe and Bauer (2001) brought picture storybooks into an urban kindergarten, they observed how students playfully entered the texts and exploited their potential for varied meanings. It could well be that the first invitations into story conversations happen not because students necessarily want to *talk* but, rather, because they want to extend the lived-through story experience and, as Hickman (1981) notes, to have their meaning making affirmed by others. Or, perhaps it is the natural gaps in stories, as Iser (1978) explains them, that invite students into conversations to fill the gaps with conjecture and inference.

For decades, researchers have argued that classroom conversations about books stretch thinking and contribute to deepening understandings. Certainly, a preponderance of descriptive evidence supports those contentions applied to monolingual speakers (e.g., Cochran-Smith, 1984; Eeds & Wells, 1989; Goldenberg, 1992/1993; Jewell & Pratt, 1999; Martinez & Roser, 1985; McGee, 1992). Yet, talk about good books is a subject of inquiry in diverse classrooms as well (see, for example, Morocco & Hindin, 2002). In a qualitative study of bilingual kindergartners' responses to story, Battle (1993) implicates the teacher's enthusiasm for the literature and her acceptance of the students' responses without correction as central to their willingness to converse.

Naturally, not all researchers use the same lens to inspect for the potential of classroom conversations about books. In some studies, children's literature seems to serve as the vehicle for addressing typical literacy objectives—yielding words for vocabulary instruction (Araujo, 2002; Collins, 2004; Hickman, Pollard-Durodola, & Vaughn, 2004; Silverman, 2007; Ulanoff & Pucci, 1999), providing text to be apprehended (Baumann, Hooten, & White, 1999; Hickman et al., 2004; Kucan & Beck, 1997), offering opportunities to inspect how written language works (Neuman, 1999), opening avenues to biliteracy and critical thinking (Martínez-Roldán & López-Robertson, 1999/2000), or offering invitations to build sensible interpretations together (Martínez-Roldán, 2005; Martínez-Roldán & López-Robertson, 1999/2000).

Within groups that gather around stories, there is, of course, remarkable potential for directly demonstrating useful skills and strategies to language users. But when the books are well chosen and the teacher is a skilled curator (Eeds & Peterson, 1991), there is also the potential for honoring the texts as well as the students—the potential for literary meaning making with picture books (Kiefer, 1994; Sipe, 2002), for basking in the choice of craft and elements (Eeds & Peterson, 1991), and for discovering the meanings in stories, books, and conversations (Rosenhouse, Feitelson, Kita, & Goldstein, 1997). Perhaps good book talk is most evident "when children grapple with core issues, observe closely, compare insightfully, question profoundly, and relate life experiences to story situations" (Roser & Martinez, 1995, p. 33). We may be placing too many language learners on a restricted talk diet.

There are other facets of discussion with diverse learners to learn more about. For example, although it is demonstrable that students make different and richer meanings when they bring diverse perspectives, it is less clear whether an optimal group size serves literature conversations. Again, it seems obvious that smaller groups mean the potential for more turns—more opportunities to speak (Martínez-Roldán, 2005; Taylor, Pearson, Clark, & Walpole, 2000)—while larger groups mean opportunities to have the stakes raised by the most proficient language user, the teacher (Morocco & Hindin, 2002; Roser, Martinez, Fuhrken, McDonnold, 2007; Whitmore, 1997). It is important to consider the trade-offs between the proficient modeling that occurs when teachers are present to demonstrate and negotiate meaning and the potential for growth when students themselves steer conversations, testing their ideas through language in ways comfortable and natural to them.

Finally, studies provide mixed results for the additional tasks and activities that follow book reading (Elley & Mangubhai, 1983). Like Turner (1995), who inspects the relative engagingness of tasks, others have begun to question the contributions of literature follow-up activities (Labbo, 1996), positing that the tasks themselves can make a difference in how students participate and learn. The evidence seems most promising for such meaning-making opportunities as open-ended writing (Araujo, 2002; Purves, 1993; Quiroa, 2004) and book-related dramatic play (Rowe, 1998; Seawell, 1985; Wolf, 1998).

In an inspection of linguistically and culturally diverse learners across studies, Meier (2003) contends that not all competent and purposeful language use indicates equivalent chances for school success. Rather, as Meier notes, it is the students' familiarity with books—their registers, content, cultural representations, and classroom treatment—that augurs well for school success. Literature becoming familiar introduces the third contention.

Students try out language more readily (at least initially) when they connect with the books being shared (i.e., when the book experiences are familiar). Bruner posits that stories "make the strange familiar and ourselves private and distinctive" (as cited in Crace, 2007, p. 2). Again it seems obvious that familiarity (and therefore connection) has at least three different bases. First, some research has demonstrated that familiarity with the story itself affects response. That is, when students meet the same story more than once, their thinking and talk about the text changes in powerful ways (Kaser & Short,

1997; Martinez & Roser, 1985; Yaden, 1988). Still another aspect of familiarity concerns students' comfort with the routines teachers establish to surround books in classrooms, as well as the teaching and modeling that allow students to learn how literary conversations sound (Eeds & Wells, 1989). The third base of familiarity belongs to the content of the literature—the conscious selection of books students embrace because they discover aspects of their own backgrounds and experiences within the pages (Meier, 2003; Sims-Bishop, 1992).

Blake (1998) suggests that cultural texts are those that "smell of context, of experience, of reality" (p. 239), arguing that these are the books students want to talk with, talk about, and perhaps, talk back to because these books speak to them. Sims-Bishop (1992) cautions that we must consciously attend to the books we share, noting that only some are culturally specific (as opposed to generic or neutral in their cultural content). When Quiroa (2004) inspected the responses of Mexican-origin students to culturally specific books, she argued that it is far too easy to assume monolithic cultural identity for all students within any classroom community, suggesting that the addition of "culturally relevant" texts to classroom libraries is much more complex than simply matching ethnicities, illustrations, authors/illustrators, and events.

Even so, it seems increasingly clear that students who identify with the texts they read are more thoughtfully engaged (Chinn, Anderson, & Waggoner, 2001). As Kaser and Short (1997) describe it, the goal is to allow students "to value their diversity in experiences, ways of learning, and outcomes" (p. 48). Roser and May and their colleagues (Roser et al., 2003) offered bilingual fourth graders approximately 50 culturally relevant books for talking over, as well as Readers Theatre scripts based on those books. The neighboring classroom served as a very loose control group in that the same books were provided without guidance as to how the books were to be incorporated. For students in the Readers Theatre classroom, the books were introduced, read aloud, discussed, and enacted. Using pre- and postcomparison scores on the Flynt–Cooter Reading Inventory (Flynt & Cooter, 1998), the researchers found that the average gain in reading (in Spanish) for the Readers Theatre class was 1.75 grades, compared with an average gain of 0.5 in the comparison class; the average gain for English reading was 1.34, while students in the comparison class gained 0.75 grade levels. Although it is clear that culture is not monolithic, these students seemed to link with the book characters and follow them into the story. As demonstrated in the following transcript excerpt (Roser et al., 2003), the students connected with the major character in *My Name Is Jorge on Both Sides of the River* by Jane

Medina, a set of poems in two languages revealing incidents in the life of a child who has emigrated from Mexico:

> Teacher: So, I think that some of us feel a little bit the same way as Jorge?
>
> C8: [in Spanish] Because he feels closer to where he was born...
>
> C4: I'm different. I don't feel like Jorge because I was born here.
>
> C5: No.
>
> C9: I was born in the middle [referring to the middle of the Rio Grande, the river that separates Texas from Mexico].
>
> C10: [in Spanish] When I'm here, I miss Mexico, and when I'm there, I miss here. (pp. 50–51)

There is more to learn about what it means for students to meet culturally relevant texts in their classrooms. For example, how can those who select books get more adept at choosing those that are accessible, relevant, appropriate, authentic, and without stereotype (Louie, 2006; Sims-Bishop, 1992; Yokota, 1993)? How is cultural identity strengthened when students find faces, ages, gender, class, religion, language, and life events like theirs in the classroom's texts? And can a given text be both culturally relevant and culturally irrelevant in the very same classroom? Researchers are hoping to find meeting points between embracing familiarity and countering resistance but have also begun to look at the value of placing texts in students' hands because they may evoke resistance, simply because the characters are different (Enciso, 1997; Galda & Beach, 2001). Just as students must find themselves in books so as to underscore their own identities, so must they meet texts that help them to understand others (Bieger, 1995/1996).

Finally, it is also widely held that students have the right, when feasible, to stories and literacy instruction in their home language (International Reading Association [IRA], 2001; National Council of Teachers of English, n.d.). And when instruction in the home language is not feasible, the students should be engaged in classroom dialogue—"especially the instructional conversation" (IRA, p. 3). Finding familiar literature and working to make the unfamiliar more familiar may make for the most challenging tasks of language teaching (Close, 1990; Samway & Whang, 1996).

The three classrooms we introduce in the next section were populated by students who became more able thinkers, learners, and speakers because of the power of books and story. The teachers' names have not been changed, but all of the students' names are pseudonyms.

Reading and Talking and Writing Together in a Bilingual Kindergarten

Cris Contreras's 18 Mexican American kindergarten students, 12 boys and 6 girls, demonstrate a wide range of language characteristics in their urban, central Texas classroom. Their language proficiencies range along a continuum from fluent (and monolingual) Spanish speakers to limited (and monolingual) English speakers. Cris is also Mexican American and fluently bilingual. It was Jennifer (second author of this chapter) who observed in Cris's classroom and who took the descriptive field notes that help to tell the story of students learning English surrounded by books and talk (Battle, 1994). Jennifer, too, has Mexican heritage and is bilingual.

Perhaps the first impression of Cris's instruction is that she deeply knows her students. She is a member of the same geographic and language community as they are, and she talks frequently with their parents and other family members. A second immediate impression is Cris's commitment to helping young students understand the forms and functions of text by making those forms visible and identifiable. Students' drawings, notes, records, messages, discoveries, stories, and news are pervasive: They can't be missed in the classroom. Teacher-modeled writing, too, is prominent.

But it is the classroom library center, cozy and comfortable, light and airy, organized and inviting, that announces how books play into this classroom's life. The library center seems always "open," providing ready access to shelves and cubbies, as well as an inviting rug for staying awhile to read. To supplement her classroom library collection, Cris regularly (each month) checks out 50 or more books in English and Spanish from the public library. She makes varied choices, but the titles support units of study—whether content or literature focused.

Central to her kindergarten program is daily storytime reading and time to talk over many pieces of children's literature in the thoughtful and intent style of kindergartners. The literary strand of Cris's curriculum is organized such that students meet related sets of books during storytime, with focus on genre, theme, author, or topic. Although language arts instruction is provided in Spanish for students who are Spanish dominant, Cris also reads aloud in English on a daily basis, providing for language acquisition and development. Some of Cris's interactive reading routines are identical to those in monolingual classrooms—such as introducing the book by identifying the title, author, and illustrator. But there are differences. For example, Cris supports her Spanish-dominant students when she reads in English by translating the title and then providing a short summary of the story in Spanish, using the book's illustrations as she highlights important language and invites them to share how they feel and what they like or don't like—much as a shared picture walk supports young students' reading. Cris uses her own Spanish storytelling markers, such as *Había en esos días...*[Back in those days there was...] or *Esta historia se trata de...* [This story is about...] to focus the students' attention. She sometimes pauses within the story to offer a direct translation of an important story event for the benefit of the Spanish-dominant students who might lose their way. And, even though there is talk throughout the story, Cris signals the appropriateness of continuing the talk at story's end by posing an open-ended invitation following the last word: "How does this story make you feel?" or "What do you think about this story?"

Each of these features of kindergarten storytime—systematic introductions to books, summaries in Spanish, and conversation at the story's close—contribute to lively talk among the students and their teacher—what Cazden (1988) has labeled cross talk. And as the students talk, so does Cris, weaving her own responses into those of the students—pointing out, translating, laughing, exclaiming over, fretting, protesting, appreciating, and anticipating—doing what an active reader does but doing it aloud. Cris's willingness to make her thinking transparent seems to stoke her students' talk. She has chosen the role of "participant" in storytime, showing her students how a literate person thinks and talks about books. But she does something further: Cris stops talking to make room for the students' talk, and through their talk, she monitors the meanings being constructed (Samway & Whang, 1996).

The following story talk example (Battle, 1994) from Cris's class centers on the interactive reading of *The Little Red Hen* by Paul Galdone (1979). (See Table 3.1 for a list of children's literature referenced throughout this chapter.) During the reading, the students lift an issue the story raises about the division of household chores:

Text: "So the Little Red Hen had to do all the housework. She cooked the meals and washed the dishes and made the beds. She swept the floor and washed the windows and mended the clothes..." (p. 9)

Pedro: That's what I have to do!

Cris: Does this sound like your mother?

Table 3.1. Children's Literature

Ada, A.F. (1997). *Gathering the sun.* New York: Scholastic.

Altman, L.J. (1993). *Amelia's road.* New York: Lee & Low.

Galdone, P. (1979). *The little red hen.* New York: Clarion.

Jiménez, F. (1998). *La mariposa.* New York: Houghton Mifflin.

Krull, K. (2003). *Harvesting hope.* New York: Scholastic.

Medina, J. (2004). *My name is Jorge on both sides of the river: Poems in English and Spanish.* Honesdale, PA: Boyds Mills Press.

Mora, P. (1997). *Tomás and the library lady.* New York: Alfred A. Knopf.

Ryan, P.M. (2000). *Esperanza rising.* New York: Scholastic.

Winthrop, E. (1985). *The castle in the attic.* New York: Holiday House.

Yvette: Yes.

Pedro: No! It sounds like me!

Cris: It sounds like you?

Carlos: I help my mom all the time.

Pedro: I do! I have to do all the chores. All she does is just sleep and watch T.V.!

Cris: Really?

Belia: I want to wash the dishes, but my mommy don't let me.

Cris: Maybe she is afraid that you will cut yourself.

Jo Jo: I cut myself one day.

Pedro's strong personal connection with the plight of the Little Red Hen sparked a conversation that revealed alternative perspectives on shared household chores. The ensuing discussion of the division of chores in the students' lives—such as age-appropriateness of, authority for, and safety of tasks—opened the story's themes to their perspectives.

Equally as important as uncovering students' identification with characters and events may be Cris's determination to accept each student's thoughts, ideas, and opinions in the language of choice. So, whether students' thinking comes in English or Spanish, in "standard," temporary, or "home usage," Cris doesn't use storytime to point out unconventional usage (Isenbarger & Willis, 2006). When a student offers, "I want to wash the dishes, but my mommy don't let me," Cris doesn't intervene to conduct a minilesson on subject–verb agreement. More like the parent who listens through the utterance to hear its intention, Cris believes that classroom literature sharing is a risk-free time and place for language learners. She leans forward to attend to meaning, and then, like a parent sharing a picture book with a child learning a first language, she extends the meaning: "Maybe she is afraid you will cut yourself." It is Cris's contention that only as students become more confident language users will they take more risks in their second language.

Further, Cris senses the value of including books that reflect multiple dimensions of the cultures of her classroom. The choices of books, she contends, directly affect students' eagerness to talk about the story. In the presence of stories with which they find connection, her students search for explanations, work to clarify their notions, pose logical reasons for events, connect with personal experiences, and express feelings evoked by stories. But Cris finds time to make the unfamiliar more familiar as well. For example, *The Little Red Hen* was new for her students, but they participated with delight in the story language, repeating refrains in English. Even Victor, a monolingual Spanish speaker developing some English language communicative competence readily joined in with others as Cris read: "'Not I,' said the cat, 'Not I,' said the dog, 'Not I,' said the mouse. 'Then I will,' said the little red hen. And she did" (Galdone, 1979, pp. 13–15).

Limits in language proficiency and inexperience with book talk did not preclude interpretive conversations in Cris's classroom. Jennifer's notes and analyses offer repeated evidence that the students are eager participants in story talk, can discuss a wide range of topics, and use language for many and varied purposes. Most of the discussion of stories is conducted in English by the students' own choice, possibly because the stories were read aloud in English. The extent of freewheeling talk argues that the students are not inhibited by fear of English language error correction. Rather, they repeatedly demonstrate their willingness to take risks in language use and to explore language issues. They provide rich demonstrations of what they know, what they can do together, and what they want to know.

And talk they do. Jennifer's field notes also record students' connections with other texts, their questions, and their forays into seeking confirmation, clarification, or information. The students turn their natural inclinations to understand their world (Donaldson, 1979) into making sense of the well-selected stories. Among the values of sharing literature with bilingual kindergartners in Cris Contreras's classroom are the opportunities literature creates to use language for communicative purposes and to become literate thinkers.

First Grade, First Chapter Book, First Language Not English

The elementary school in which Kathleen McDonald teaches first grade is set within a middle-class neighborhood in a Southwest U.S. city. The school of approximately 600 students serves a predominantly white and Asian prekindergarten through fifth-grade population. Many of the students have two-parent families, with a working father and mother. Kathleen's first graders, 22 in total, are nearly all English speakers. But it is the "nearly" that gives pause. Six have a first language other than English, and three speak little English at all. These students bring Korean, Japanese, Spanish, Portuguese, and Bengali languages to school, while Kathleen speaks English and some Spanish. No one else in the classroom speaks Korean, Japanese, Portuguese, or Bengali, so to communicate and to be understood, the students need English. It was Nancy (another of the chapter's authors) who observed in Kathleen's classroom, documenting how the students learn to become thoughtful comprehenders of challenging text through book talk and other response opportunities.

Kathleen's first grade is filled with language in many forms. There are demonstrations of oral and written language in play, in music, on charts, in class-made books, on labels, in puppetry, and in creative dramatics. Book sharing of both narrative and information texts has been part of the daily routine since the first day of school. During storytime, Kathleen often employs a read-aloud/read-along model—at first using Big Books and then offering each student an individual copy of the story being shared aloud. This up-close-and-personal experience with texts means penetrating observations from students who are invited to notice, label, and make meanings together. Although there is consistent attention to the language each student brings, English pervades.

When Kathleen agrees to be part of a classroom study with the purpose of investigating how teachers support students' reading when the books get longer (their first chapter book), she does not hesitate because of the English language learners (ELLs) in her classroom. The demands of a chapter book? "Hide and watch," she says. She is confident that students learning English can meet challenging text with the support she provides. Nancy doesn't hide, but she does watch—and videotape—so as to document ways in which all students are helped to make sense of a challenging book when there are no illustrations to help with meaning, and when the book itself offers a complex genre, plot, setting, and vocabulary.

The novel to be read aloud, talked over, playfully enacted, and written about is *The Castle in the Attic* by Elizabeth Winthrop. The chapter book is complex for a number of reasons. First, Winthrop's novel offers a flawed hero and puts that central character into genuine conflict with the people he loves most. Second, the settings include both a castle and an enchanted kingdom, meaning new concepts, technical words, and usages. Third, the passage of time is relative in this novel, contributing to plot complexity.

The videotapes of book conversation in Kathleen's room clearly show (as might be expected) that the most recent immigrants participate less in story-time talk. All the first graders require support for their first chapter book, but the students learning English register their difficulties in observable ways. For example, their attention (or at least their eyes) begin to wander, and they find places to itch, shoestrings to inspect, or corners to wriggle to while other kids make verbal observations and frame tentative meanings.

But some things happen that seem to make sense for the ELLs. First, Kathleen and Nancy make felt cut-outs of story characters and important features of the setting, so that the story can be retold as the characters and objects are moved about. Figure 3.1 shows how these students learning English meet in a small group to retell the chapter using the felt board and cut-outs.

Second, Kathleen shifts some of her strategies during reading time to support ELLs. For example, she increasingly incorporates dramatic interpretation into her reading, inflecting for dramatic emphasis, adding important gestures as she reads, and stopping to invite students into the enactment. She stabs a dragon and invites them to. She shudders in fear, and students talk about what it means to be brave. Each student in the discussion circle stands on an imaginary moat and then, stepping into the role of Sir Simon, invites young William into the castle. Each performs an Arabian roll in the story circle—the gymnastic feat that William used to conquer the evil wizard. As another example, Kathleen brings realia to concretely represent story in the discussion circle. For this story, the concrete objects include a fold-out castle that allows students to identify and inspect the turrets and drawbridge, the moat and portcullis, the galleries, and passages. But she also makes certain there are samples to experience—a piece

Figure 3.1. ELLs Using Felt Board and Cut-Outs to Retell a Chapter

of tapestry, the flute used to enchant a dragon, a tiny silver knight, as well as many, many information books to refer to. Further, she enlarges the setting map from the book's opening so that the students can track events physically.

Equally important, as each chapter concludes, the students write and draw their thoughts in a bound journal. Kathleen moves among students learning English to elicit a single idea for writing. When Hyun-Ki says, "William finds a knight," Kathleen helps the sentence get onto the page and then invites drawing to accompany the writing. On the following day, volunteers share their writing and drawing in preparation for the next chapter. Every student volunteers. "William finds a knight," Hyun-Ki reads, and there is great applause. Figure 3.2 shows examples of the students' work from their journals.

Across the 17 chapters of the chapter book, Kathleen's ELLs require less modeling of their own words and begin to try the sound system and meanings of English to record their ideas well before Kathleen stoops to hear what they

Figure 3.2. ELLs' Journal Entries

A.

B.

choose to write about. Eyes move toward print (as opposed to looking around, examining shoelaces, and so forth) during read aloud, and there are the beginnings of inference and meaning making: "The token is different!" Naruki shouts.

Each of Kathleen's invitational strategies—dramatic interpretations, enacting, rehearsing, retelling, making ideas concrete, and supporting meaning making with talk, drawing, and writing—treat language learners as language users. Although her ELLs do not speak as frequently as native speakers in her classroom, they speak and write with increasing frequency, confidence, and urgency. They want to.

When the Book Connects With Lives, Third-Grade Students Talk

Twenty-one third graders gather in a circle on the carpet located in the classroom library with its shelves stuffed with books in Spanish and English. They are careful to leave a space for their teacher next to the wicker basket from which David and Daniel pass copies of *Esperanza Rising* by Pam Muñoz Ryan. These bilingual Spanish and English speaking students are participating in the routines of daily literature study, something they anticipate each day. In Melody Patterson Zoch's (the bilingual teacher who is also author of this chapter) classroom, students spend time sharing and talking about books. They also depend upon response journals in which they record their thoughts for sharing; they use a language chart to make their thinking visible; and most important, they take time to make literature "mean" something to them.

Melody's urban Texas classroom is surrounded by mobile homes and community housing. Her students are either first-generation American or born in Mexico. Each is an ELL, with Spanish his or her first language. Although the dominant language in the classroom is Spanish, all of the classroom talk is translated into English for the purposes of this chapter. Melody is in her fourth year of teaching and has just begun working on her doctorate in literacy as the year begins. Through her university reading and study, she has become intrigued by the potential of book conversations focused around culturally relevant literature. Because Spanish is a second language for her, she feels the critical importance of helping her students understand the value both of being bilingual and of their heritage.

The novel study with *Esperanza Rising* fits into a larger study of family and community (Kaser & Short, 1997), initiated with oral stories, published memoirs, and finally a journey with Esperanza from a life of plenty in Mexico to a laborer's life in California as events change her life circumstances. Melody created an enlarged photo album as seen in Figure 3.3 for the students to share photos of their families. During the first week of the four-week unit, Melody reads aloud selected picture books that center on Mexican immigrants and farm workers. These include *Gathering the Sun* by Alma Flor Ada, *El Camino de Amelia [Amelia's Road]* by Linda Jacobs Altman, *La Mariposa [The Butterfly]* by Francisco Jiménez, *Cosechando Esperanza [Harvesting Hope]* by Kathleen Krull, and *Tomás y la Mujer de la Biblioteca [Tomás and the Library Lady]*) by Pat Mora. These books set the stage, open the talk, and stoke the inquiry.

In the second and following weeks, Melody gathers a class set of *Esperanza Rising* in Spanish so that each student has a copy. There will be read-aloud, partner reading, and even silent reading, as Esperanza's campesina story takes center stage in the classroom. The novel is a fictionalized memoir of author Pam Muñoz Ryan's grandmother, who migrated to California from Mexico during

Figure 3.3. Photo Album of Author Pam Muñoz Ryan's Ancestors and Photos of Bilingual Students' Families

the Great Depression. The story of Esperanza's wealthy family begins in Mexico, but after her father is murdered, she and her mother must flee to the United States to earn their livelihood through migrant labor. Esperanza must adjust to her new life of hardship while also growing in compassion. As each chapter is read, Melody keeps a teacher log of her students' thoughts and discussion about the novel, and it is from these notes that this description has been prepared.

Because each of the book's chapters bear the name of a fruit or vegetable significant to the story, Melody opens the day by sharing a taste of the fruit—whether papayas, figs, grapes, or avocados. As Melody reads aloud in Spanish, the students follow along in their own copies, many using the bookmarks she has made for them. Figure 3.4 shows the class reading along with Melody from *Esperanza Rising*. The bookmarks offer some of the book's Mexican proverbs—wisdom passed to Esperanza across generations. Melody plans for pauses in the reading to allow for comments, questions, conjectures, or clarification, but

Figure 3.4. Students Engaged in Daily Literature Study in Melody's Third-Grade Bilingual Classroom

as each chapter draws to a close, there is a time of quiet in which each student takes a few minutes for reflection and writing in a personal journal.

Melody maintains that journals should be special and fresh, so she has made one for each student in the same dimensions as the paperback book, and with a likeness of Esperanza on the cover. The response journal contains a page for each chapter, with the chapter title printed at the top of each page. But the journals are special in other ways as well: Photos of the real Esperanza Ortega appear on the first page of the response journal. The second page offers a space for students to record their unanswered questions about Esperanza: "Preguntas que tengo acerca de Esperanza," ["Questions I have about Esperanza"]. The last page of the journal provides space for students to write questions they have for the author—things they would ask if the author were a part of their discussion group. That page is labeled: "Preguntas que tengo para Pam Muñoz Ryan" ["Questions I have for Pam Muñoz Ryan"]. For the first two chapters, Melody demonstrates journal writing on chart paper, sharing her thoughts aloud to initiate her students into this form of discourse.

Once students have had time to reflect and write, the discussion begins. Melody notices that students talk freely, and she gently encourages response to one another's comments. With the exception of the first two days in which she does a lot of modeling, Melody is careful not to dominate the conversation.

There is great connection and identification with Esperanza among the students, perhaps because she, too, is of Mexican heritage. But the deep personal connection can also mean honest appraisal. Daniel judges Esperanza as selfish when she refuses to let a child touch her beautiful doll, the last gift from her father. Daniel shares: "I feel like Esperanza did a bad thing with that poor little girl. She was poor and now Esperanza is poor—what's the difference?"

Laura counters, "I don't think she should have to share it because her father gave it to her and it reminds her of her father. And her father is dead now." But Daniel is unconvinced and offers the example of generosity Esperanza's mother displayed when she made a yarn doll for the same child: "I think it's better to give it. There are a lot of people who don't have a lot. Maybe she wants to repay some of the people because they are poor." Carlos enters with, "I have a question: Why did Esperanza say that the doll her mom made was stupid? And why did her mom make it because it used a lot of string to do it?"

Melody's students so thoroughly climb into the story that their conjectures feel more like friendly neighbors talking around a table than a class discussing a book character. David wonders about the future prospects of a poor traveler who shared what she had when he asks, "How can she take care of her kids with just chicken eggs?" And Alexia is not at all sure Esperanza will be safe in America from her greedy uncles: "I think the uncles will follow them to the United States to look for them. They will put up posters to look for them." Jaime agrees with Alexia and adds, "I think the uncles will look for them and find the grandmother and then make her tell them where they [Esperanza and her mother] went."

As the talk comes to a close, Melody shifts the focus to the language chart— a serviceable graphic on large sheets of paper displayed on the wall to collect the thoughts that will be saved from the day's chapter. Melody organizes the chart to collect thinking about the theme-related picture books based on Chambers' (1985) ways of categorizing book talk (i.e., into the "three sharings" of observations, connections, and predictions). In addition, Melody adds a column to capture students' remaining questions.

The "Esperanza" language chart is structured with chapter names on the horizontal axis while the vertical axis provides for evidence gathering in three aspects of author craft: How Pam Muñoz Ryan shows us (1) Esperanza and how she changes, (2) time and setting, and (3) important themes. Figure 3.5 shows the original chart created by the class during their reading of *Esperanza Rising*. Table 3.2 shows excerpts from this chart translated into English.

Students' entries in their response journals seem similar to the issues they raise in discussion. That is, Melody's students use the response journals as a space to record their ideas, and as a way to recall their ideas during group discussion. Their written responses vary—possibly because there is time to write *before* end-of-chapter discussion: "I wonder if Miguel will help Esperanza be a good worker," "I imagined in my mind the part that said that Esperanza was 5 years old and hid from the robbers," "I feel sad for what happened to Esperanza's family," and "Maybe the dust storm was Esperanza's father." Overall, the language chart seems to serve as the reminder as students refer to the chart to reconstruct and interpret past chapters and events.

Even when trusted to steer the conversation for themselves, these students are able to find meaning and have discussions focused on the text. As Pam Muñoz Ryan (2006) stated in her address given at the Rising Star Writing Project conference, "It's my contention that we cannot simply look at another person's eyes, hair, and skin and understand him or her. We must look into other people's stories before we can accept differences or celebrate our similar humanity."

Figure 3.5. The Class "Esperanza" Language Chart

Pam Muñoz Ryan nos muestra...	Las Uvas	Las Papayas	Los Higos	Las Guayabas	Los Melones	Las Cebollas	Las Almendra
• Cómo es Esperanza y cómo cambia	• casi tiene 13 años • lleva un ligero vestido de seda • lleva un lazo en su largo cabello negro • es obstinada • ama mucho a sus padres	• Su padre está muerto • Está triste por su papa • no les gustan los higos • necesita Alfonso, Hortencia y Miguel • está furiosa con sus tíos	• Primero dice que está al Tío Luis pero luego le dice temas para el plan de ella y su mama • cambia su opinión de mudarse a Estados Unidos	• No quiere decir sus problemas a las compesinas • No quiere que la trate por mi hijo su indios porque es pobre y sucia • Eva enojada con su mayo porque trae la muerte de bajo para la rifla	• Trata en el consejo del valle • Defiende a su papá	• No sabe poner correas pañales a lavar la ropa • A ella no le gusta vivir en una habitación con otras personas	• No va a creer para pagar la alquiler y Hortencia un dólar • es fuerte • le gustó el jardín • que ya fue recoger la semilla • Esperanza espera para transmitir hasta la
• Cómo es importante el ambiente (cuándo y dónde)	• Aguascalientes, México, 1924 • El Rancho de las Rosas • viajan por caballo	• Hay bandidos • no es costumbre dejar la tierra a las mujeres	• el incendio puede influir la elección de mama • la carreta	• Viajan por Zacatecas • en el tren con otros que son pobres	• Viven sin agua caliente y electricidad • Viven en campamentos Separados las mexicana, los japoneses, los filipino y los "Okies"	• La cabaña es pequeña y el baño está cubierto con las personas y cortinas	• Llega están organizando una huelga
• temas importantes	• Aguantar bonita y la fruta cara en la mano, p.2 • "No hay rosas sin espinas", p.14 • Nueva temas empiezan de nuevo, p.13	• En tiempos difíciles, tenemos que apoyar a nosotros	• el cuento del fénix • la importancia de la abuelita (E. no quiere dormir) • No temas empezar de nuevo, p.50	• Carmen no le importa que es pobre y ella dice que es una pobre pero aun hijos • porque el pobre Carmen ayuda a los otros	• Deberas defender a las familias • Se puede ayudar en la elección de sus familia y la fruta Caros en la mano, p.93	• En cualquier situación en breve la elección de ser desgariarse a estar feliz	• Los que son pobres esta por nosotros pensar

What's Next? The "Take-Away" Understandings About Using Children's Lit With ELLs

Within this chapter, we have attempted to lift and examine the pervasive contentions that surround language and literature in diverse classrooms. We have argued that books provide both aesthetic and instructive opportunities for engaging with language in interesting and purposeful ways. Across three selected classroom examples, we reinforced that language learning is a social practice. We reiterated the "compellingness" of story, underscored the power of models, testified to the effects of instruction, and advocated trust in students to think and talk in powerful ways. But have we once again restated the obvious? Perhaps the distinction in our examples is this: What may seem obvious in precept is not always pervasive in practice.

Classrooms we visit from prekindergarten through high school are in need of hands-on collections of culturally relevant books. Even when school and community libraries are well stocked, books must be at hand to be inspected, read, referred to, compared, and talked over. Krashen (2003) contends that

Table 3.2. Excerpts of Bilingual Students' Reflections on *Esperanza Rising*

Pam Muñoz Ryan shows us...	Grapes	Figs	Guava	Onions	Almonds	Asparagus	Grapes
Esperanza and how she changes	• Is almost 13 • Wears a light silk dress • Wears a bow in her long, dark hair • Is stubborn • Loves her parents	• At first says she hates her uncle Tío but then is thankful for her and her mother's plan • Changes her mind about moving to the U.S.	• Doesn't want to tell her problems to the farm workers • Doesn't want the little girl to touch her doll because she is poor and dirty • Is mad at her mother for giving the yarn doll to the little girl	• Doesn't know how to sweep, change diapers, or wash clothes • Doesn't like to live with so many people	• She is going to pray for Miguel, her father, her grandmother, and a candy • Is strong • Likes the "jamaica"	• Gives beans and her piñata full of candy to a man who's family hasn't eaten in 2 days because they are on strike • Is more caring • Saves her money • Thinks she has the hands of a poor farm worker	• She feels content • Is 14 years old • Dreams of learning English, helping her family, and buying a small house some day • Can hear the valley's heartbeat
Setting and time	• Aguas-calientes, Mexico, 1924 • El Rancho de las Rosas • Travel by horse	• The fire can influence the mother's decision • The wagon	• Travel to Zacatecas on the train with other poor people	• The cabin is small and the ceiling is covered with newspapers and cartons	• Dust storm	• All children attend the same school because they are all poor • Men come from Oklahoma, Arkansas, Texas, and other places to look for work	
Important themes	• "Wait a little while and the fruit will fall into your hand." p. 2 • "There is no rose without thorns." p. 14 • "Do not be afraid to start over." p. 14	• The story of the Phoenix • The importance of the grandmother (Esperanza doesn't want to leave her) • "Do not be afraid to start over." p. 50	• Carmen doesn't mind that she is poor and says she is rich because of her children • Although she is poor, Carmen helps others	• In any situation you have the choice of being miserable or happy	• People are not so different—they all want to eat and feed their children	• "Wait a little and the fruit will fall into your hand." p. 227	• "Wait a little and the fruit will fall into your hand." p. 254 • "Do not be afraid to start over." p. 258

conversation about books in many classrooms tends to be less rich than the books that invite talk. If so, we who teach need to get better at planning and modeling thoughtful conjectures about books so as to raise the stakes on our students' literary and content conversations.

It may be, too, that in the face of increasingly high-stakes assessments, and in the press to cover material and demonstrate growth in reading levels, we have been willing to forego some of the time owed to reading and talking. Perhaps we have been willing to reduce the number of mediations between text and meaning (whether offers of drama, peer talk, writing, art, technology, or direct teacher support).

Between the lines, the chapter suggests that we may need to read research about literature and language more carefully. It is possible that large-scale studies with sweeping implications haven't observed closely enough what happens inside classrooms—particularly when it comes to the talk and writing that lean on literature. Similarly, smaller descriptive studies that enthusiastically proclaim outcomes must help the audience see *how* they make the claims.

Further, when literature and language are partners, there must be freedom to speak and act with one's literacy. Both Enciso (1997) and Sipe (2002) borrow the phrase "talking back" from bell hooks (1989), who refers to talking back as freedom to speak to authority with one's own arguments or opinions, including the freedom to disagree. In classrooms filled with books that help us to lift issues of critical importance, students, too, must feel free to raise issues and to dissent. As Enciso (1997) describes it, "all of us bring our own racial, ethnic, gender, class, political, intellectual, and linguistic differences to our reading," (p. 15) such that learning to talk back is learning to make a place for ourselves, our ideas, and our ways of expressing them. In a classroom in which differences are expected, honored, and attended to, students will speak to the class, race, gender, and power issues that touch their lives (Rogers & Soter, 1997). Choosing good literature with powerful themes also means making room for what students have to say about the implications of text to their own experiences.

To learn to think, to talk, to read and write, to participate in the lives of others, to find one's place, to stretch, and to understand more deeply—all these goals have obvious potential for inquiry into language and literature in classrooms.

REFLECTION QUESTIONS

1. In what ways can children's literature play a key role for teachers to consider the identities, backgrounds, and interests of ELLs?

2. In what ways do teachers and librarians in schools populated by ELLs make the critical selections of quality children's literature for their classrooms and libraries?

3. What is the nature of classroom environments that foster students' responsive talk among all students, including ELLs?

4. How can we develop informed instruction among ourselves as teachers that invites ELLs into the learning community that develops literate thinkers?

REFERENCES

Araujo, L. (2002). The literacy development of kindergarten English-language learners. *Journal of Research in Childhood Education, 16*(2), 232–250.

Battle, J. (1993). Mexican-American bilingual kindergarteners' collaborations in meaning making. In D. Leu & C.K. Kinzer (Eds.), *Examining central issues in literacy research, theory, and practice* (42nd yearbook of the National Reading Conference, pp. 163–170). Chicago: National Reading Conference.

Battle, J. (1994). *The collaborative nature of language learning and meaning making in Mexican-American bilingual kindergarteners storybook discussions.* Unpublished doctoral dissertation, The University of Texas at Austin.

Baumann, J.F., Hooten, H., & White, P. (1999). Teaching comprehension through literature: A teacher-research project to develop fifth graders' reading strategies. *The Reading Teacher, 53*(1), 38–51.

Bieger, E.M. (1995/1996). Promoting multicultural education through a literature-based approach. *The Reading Teacher, 49*(4), 308–312.

Blake, B.E. (1998). "Critical" reader response in an urban classroom: Creating cultural texts to engage diverse learners. *Theory Into Practice, 37*(3), 238–243.

Bruner, J.S. (1992). *Acts of meaning.* Cambridge, MA: Harvard University Press.

Cazden, C.B. (1988). *Classroom discourse: The language of teaching and learning.* Portsmouth, NH: Heinemann.

Chambers, A. (1985). *Booktalk: Occasional writing on literature and children.* London: Bodley.

Chang-Wells, C.G., & Wells, G.L. (1992). *Constructing knowledge together: Classrooms as centers of inquiry and literacy.* Portsmouth, NH: Heinemann.

Chinn, C.A., Anderson, R.C., & Waggoner, M.A. (2001). Patterns of discourse in two kinds of literature discussion. *Reading Research Quarterly, 36*(4), 378–411. doi:10.1598/RRQ.36.4.3

Close, E.E. (1990). Seventh graders sharing literature: How did we get here? *Language Arts, 67*(8), 817–823.

Cochran-Smith, M. (1984). *The making of a reader: Language and learning for human service professions monograph series.* Norwood, NJ: Ablex.

Collins, M.F. (2004). *ESL preschoolers' English vocabulary acquisition and storybook comprehension from storybook reading.* Unpublished doctoral dissertation, Boston University.

Crace, J. (2007, March 27). Jerome Bruner: The lesson of the story. *Education Guardian Weekly.* Retrieved May 30, 2007, from www.guardian.co.uk/education/2007/mar/27/academicexperts.highereducationprofile

CTB/McGraw Hill. (1992). *Comprehensive test of basic skills.* Monterey, CA: McGraw Hill.

Cummins, J. (1981). The role of primary language development in promoting educational success for language minority students. In C.F. Leyba (Ed.), *Schooling and language minority students: A theoretical framework* (pp. 3–49). Sacramento, CA: California Department of Education.

Dewey, J. (1966). *Democracy and education: An introduction to the philosophy of education.* New York: The Free Press.

Donaldson, M. (1979). *Children's minds.* New York: Norton.

Duke, N.K. (2000). 3.6 minutes per day: The scarcity of informational texts in first grade. *Reading Research Quarterly, 35*(2), 202–224. doi:10.1598/RRQ.35.2.1

Dyson, A.H., & Genishi, C. (Eds.). (1994). *The need for story: Cultural diversity in classroom and community.* Urbana, IL: National Council of Teachers of English.

Eeds, M., & Peterson, R. (1991). Teacher as curator: Learning to talk about literature. *The Reading Teacher, 45*(2), 118–126.

Eeds, M., & Wells, D. (1989). Grand conversations: An exploration of meaning construction in literature study groups. *Research in the Teaching of English, 23*(1), 4–29.

Elley, W.B., & Mangubhai, F. (1983). The impact of reading on second language learning. *Reading Research Quarterly, 19*(1), 53–67. doi:10.2307/747337

Enciso, P.E. (1997). Negotiating the meaning of difference: Talking back to multicultural literature. In T. Rogers & A.O. Soter (Eds.), *Reading across cultures: Teaching literature in a diverse society* (pp. 13–41). New York: Teachers College Press.

Flynt, E.S., & Cooter, R.B., Jr. (1998). *Flynt-Cooter reading inventory for the classroom.* Upper Saddle River, NJ: Merrill.

Galda, L., & Beach, R. (2001). Response to literature as a cultural activity. *Reading Research Quarterly, 36*(1), 64–73. doi:10.1598/RRQ.36.1.4

Galdone, P. (1979). *The little red hen.* New York: Clarion.

Goldenberg, C. (1992/1993). Instructional conversations: Promoting comprehension through discussion. *The Reading Teacher, 46*(4), 316–326.

Hadaway, N.L., Vardell, S.M., & Young, T.A. (2002). Highlighting nonfiction literature: Literacy development and English-language learners. *The New England Reading Association Journal, 38*(2), 16–22.

Hickman, J. (1981). A new perspective on response to literature: Research in an elementary school setting. *Research in the Teaching of English, 15*(4), 343–354.

Hickman, P., Pollard-Durodola, S., & Vaughn, S. (2004). Storybook reading: Improving vocabulary and comprehension for English-language learners. *The Reading Teacher, 57*(8), 720–731.

hooks, b. (1989). *Talking back: Thinking feminist, thinking black.* Boston: South End.

International Reading Association. (2001). *Second-language literacy instruction: A position statement of the International Reading Association.* Newark, DE: International Reading Association.

Isenbarger, L., & Willis, A.I. (2006). An intersection of theory and practice: Accepting the language a child brings into the classroom. *Language Arts, 84*(2), 125–135.

Iser, W. (1978). *The act of reading: A theory of aesthetic response.* Baltimore: Johns Hopkins University Press.

Jewell, T.A., & Pratt, D. (1999). Literature discussions in the primary grades: Children's thoughtful discourse about books and what teachers can do to make it happen. *The Reading Teacher, 52*(8), 842–850.

Kaser, S., & Short, K.G. (1997). Exploring cultural diversity through peer talk. In J.R. Paratore & R.L. McCormack (Eds.), *Peer talk in the classroom: Learning from research* (pp. 45–65). Newark, DE: International Reading Association.

Kiefer, B.Z. (1994). *The potential of picturebooks: From visual literacy to aesthetic understanding.* New York: Merrill.

Krashen, S.D. (2003). *Explorations in language acquisition and use: The Taipei lectures.* Portsmouth, NH: Heinemann.

Kucan, L., & Beck, I.L. (1997). Thinking aloud and reading comprehension research: Inquiry, instruction, and social interaction. *Review of Educational Research, 67*(3), 271–299.

Labbo, L. (1996). Beyond storytime: A sociopsychological perspective on young children's opportunities for literacy development during story extension time. *Journal of Literacy Research, 28*(3), 405–428.

Louie, B.Y. (2006). Guiding principles for teaching multicultural literature. *The Reading Teacher, 59*(5), 438–448. doi:10.1598/RT.59.5.3

Martinez, M., & Roser, N. (1985). Read it again: The value of repeated reading during storytime. *The Reading Teacher, 38*(8), 782–786.

Martínez-Roldán, C.M. (2005). The inquiry acts of bilingual children in literature discussions. *Language Arts, 83*(1), 22–32.

Martínez-Roldán, C.M., & López-Robertson, J.M. (1999/2000). Initiating literature circles in a first-grade bilingual classroom. *The Reading Teacher, 53*(4), 270–281.

McGee, L.M. (1992). An exploration of meaning construction in first graders' grand conversations. In C.K. Kinzer & D.J. Leu (Eds.), *Literacy research, theory, and practice: Views from many perspectives* (41st yearbook of the National Reading Conference, pp. 177–186). Chicago: National Reading Conference.

Meier, T. (2003). "Why can't she remember that?" The importance of storybook reading in multilingual, multicultural classrooms. *The Reading Teacher, 57*(3), 242–252.

Morocco, C.C., & Hindin, A. (2002). The role of conversation in a thematic understanding of literature. *Learning Disabilities Research & Practice, 17*(3), 144–159. doi:10.1111/1540-5826.00041

Morrow, L.M., Pressley, M., Smith, J., & Smith, M. (1997). The effect of a literature-based program integrated into literacy and science instruction with children from diverse backgrounds. *Reading Research Quarterly, 32*(1), 54–76. doi:10.1598/RRQ.32.1.4

National Council of Teachers of English. (n.d.). Research based policy statements on English language learners. Retrieved June 2, 2007, from http://www1.ncte.org/store/books/research/129130.htm

National Institute of Child Health and Human Development. (2000). *Report of the National Reading Panel. Teaching children to read: An evidence-based assessment of the scientific research literature on reading and its implications for reading instruction: Reports of the subgroups* (NIH Publication No. 00-4754). Washington, DC: U.S. Government Printing Office.

Neuman, S.B. (1999). Books make a difference: A study of access to literacy. *Reading Research Quarterly, 34*(3), 286–311. doi:10.1598/RRQ.34.3.3

Purves, A. (1993). The ideology of canons and cultural concerns in literature. In S. Miller & B. McCaskill (Eds.), *Multicultural literature and literacies: Making space for differences* (pp. 105–127). Albany, NY: State University of New York Press.

Quiroa, R.E. (2004). *Literature as mirror: Analyzing the oral, written, and artistic responses of young Mexican-origin children to Mexican American-themed picture storybooks*. Unpublished doctoral dissertation, University of Illinois at Urbana-Champaign.

Rogers, T., & Soter, A.O. (Eds.). (1997). *Reading across cultures: Teaching literature in a diverse society*. New York: Teachers College Press.

Rosenhouse, J., Feitelson, D., Kita, B., & Goldstein, Z. (1997). Interactive reading aloud to Israeli first graders: Its contribution to literacy development. *Reading Research Quarterly, 32*(2), 168–183. doi:10.1598/RRQ.32.2.3

Roser, N.L., Hoffman, J.V., & Farest, C. (1990). Language, literature, and at-risk children. *The Reading Teacher, 43*(8), 554–559.

Roser, N.L., Hoffman, J., Labbo, L., & Farest, C. (1992). Language charts: A record of story time talk. *Language Arts, 69*(1), 44–52.

Roser, N., & Martinez, M. (1995). The books make a difference in story talk. In N. Roser & M. Martinez (Eds.), *Book talk and beyond: Children and teachers respond to literature* (pp. 32–41). Newark, DE: International Reading Association.

Roser, N., Martinez, M., Fuhrken, C., & McDonnold, K. (2007). Characters as guides to meaning. *The Reading Teacher, 60*(6), 548–559. doi:10.1598/RT.60.6.5

Roser, N., May, L., Martinez, M., Keehn, S., Harmon, J., & O'Neal, S. (2003). Stepping into character(s): Using Readers Theatre with bilingual fourth graders. In R.L. McCormack & J.R. Paratore (Eds.), *After early intervention, then what? Teaching struggling readers in grades 3 and beyond* (pp. 40–69). Newark, DE: International Reading Association.

Rowe, D.W. (1998). The literate potentials of book-related dramatic play. *Reading Research Quarterly, 33*(1), 10–35. doi:10.1598/RRQ.33.1.2

Ryan, P.M. (2006, May). Address given at the Rising Star Writing Project conference, Texas State University, San Marcos.

Samway, K.D., & Whang, G. (1996). *Literature study circles in a multicultural classroom*. York, ME: Stenhouse.

Seawell, R.P. (1985). *A micro-ethnographic study of a Spanish/English bilingual kindergarten in which literature and puppet play were used as a method of enhancing language growth*. Unpublished doctoral dissertation, The University of Texas at Austin.

Silverman, R.D. (2007). Vocabulary development of English-language and English-only learners in kindergarten. *The Elementary School Journal, 107*(4), 365–384. doi:10.1086/516669

Sims-Bishop, R. (1992). Multicultural literature for children: Making informed choices. In V.J. Harris (Ed.), *Teaching multicultural literature in grades K–8* (pp. 37–54). Norwood, MA: Christopher-Gordon.

Sipe, L.R. (2002). Talking back and taking over: Young children's expressive engagement during storybook read-alouds. *The Reading Teacher, 55*(5), 476–483.

Sipe, L.R., & Bauer, J. (2001). Urban kindergartners' literary understanding of picture storybooks. *The New Advocate, 14*(4), 329–342.

Taylor, B.M., Pearson, P.D., Clark, K., & Walpole, S. (2000). Effective schools and accomplished teachers: Lessons about primary-grade reading instruction and low-income schools. *The Elementary School Journal, 101*(2), 121–165. doi:10.1086/499662

Turner, J.C. (1995). The influence of classroom contexts on young children's motivation for literacy. *Reading Research Quarterly, 30*(3), 410–441. doi:10.2307/747624

Ulanoff, S.H., & Pucci, S.L. (1999). Learning words from books: The effects of read-aloud on second language vocabulary acquisition. *Bilingual Research Journal, 23*(4), 409–422.

Vygotsky, L.S. (1978). *Mind in society: The development of higher psychological processes* (M. Cole, V. John-Steiner, S. Scribner, & E. Souberman, Eds. & Trans.). Cambridge, MA: Harvard University Press.

Whitmore, K.F. (1997). Inventing conversations in second-language classrooms: What students say and how they say it. In J.R. Paratore & R.L. McCormack (Eds.), *Peer talk in the classroom: Learning from research* (pp. 102–128). Newark, DE: International Reading Association.

Wolf, S. (1998). The flight of reading: Shifts in instruction, orchestration, and attitudes through classroom theatre. *Reading Research Quarterly, 33*(4), 382–415. doi:10.1598/RRQ.33.4.3

Worthy, J., Moorman, M., & Turner, M. (1999). What Johnny likes to read is hard to find in schools. *Reading Research Quarterly, 34*(1), 12–27. doi:10.1598/RRQ.34.1.2

Worthy, J., & Roser, N. (2004). Flood ensurance: When children have books they can and want to read. In D. Lapp, C. Block, E. Cooper, J. Flood, N. Roser, & J. Tinajero (Eds.), *Teaching all the children: Strategies for developing literacy in an urban setting* (pp. 179–192). New York: Guilford.

Yaden, D. (1988). Understand stories through repeated read-alouds: How many does it take? *The Reading Teacher, 41*(6), 556–561.

Yokota, J. (1993). Issues in selecting multicultural literature. *Language Arts, 70*(3), 156–167.

CHAPTER 4

Creating Opportunities for "Grand Conversations" Among ELLs With Literature Circles

Gisela Ernst-Slavit, Catherine Carrison,
and Jan Spiesman-Laughlin

Literature circles provide opportunities for oral language and literacy growth for all students, including English language learners (ELLs). Many teachers, however, are hesitant to use this instructional approach with students who are learning English. The purpose of this chapter, therefore, is twofold. First, we illustrate the benefits of literature circles for ELLs by showcasing Catherine's (the second author of this chapter) journey as she implemented literature circles in her culturally and linguistically diverse fourth-grade classroom. Throughout her journey, we will hear the voices of her students, many of whom had been silent, as they engage in rich, meaningful, student-directed dialogue about the books they read. This kind of "grand conversation" (Peterson & Eeds, 1990) affords students opportunities to critique, debate, and extend the discussion by building upon one another's ideas. Second, we present classroom teachers with a possible road map to follow as they implement literature circles with their students. Organization is the key for this kind of endeavor as it provides the invisible structure that supports optimum learning for participants.

This chapter is organized into three sections. The first section provides an overview of recent literature on successful teaching strategies for ELLs. We particularly focus on the intersection of two research areas: (1) effective practices that support literacy development for ELLs and (2) current research on the effectiveness of literature circles in K–12 classrooms. The second section presents Catherine's tribulations and joys as she implemented literature circles for the first time in her six years as a classroom teacher. Included in this section are the portraits of six ELLs in her classroom, examples of students' work, and

One Classroom, Many Learners: Best Literacy Practices for Today's Multilingual Classrooms edited by Julie Coppola and Elizabeth V. Primas. © 2009 by the International Reading Association.

Catherine's insights about the overall process. The last section contains a detailed outline of the components and steps necessary to successfully implement literature circles in K–12 classrooms because although the examples focus on elementary classrooms, the research and practices apply to grades K–12 and thus can be used with a wide range of age and proficiency levels. Descriptions of the most commonly used student roles and general procedures for implementing literature circles are provided, along with a list of resources for reference and further study.

Theoretical Background on Using Literature Circles to Develop ELLs' Oral Language and Literacy Skills

Literature circles are akin to monthly book club meetings, except that each student assumes a unique, rotating role. Every participant comes to the group prepared with notes and ready to perform his or her different role (Daniels, 1994). Several of these roles have become staples of literature circles, including Questioner, Literary Luminary, Character Captain, Illustrator, Summarizer, Researcher, Vocabulary Wizard, Passage Picker, and Scene Setter.

Literature circles work well because they are student centered. They extend students' opportunities to guide their own discussions and to focus on issues that are most meaningful to them. Most important, they encourage all students to interact with one another and with the text. As part of a balanced literacy program, literature circles afford students rich opportunities to use the many skills and strategies they learn in other areas of the literacy curriculum (Peterson & Eeds, 1990; Schlick Noe & Johnson, 1999; Short & Klassen, 1993) and to build confidence and enhance their language development (Carrison & Ernst-Slavit, 2005). Reading aloud, making personal connections, thinking critically, and using a variety of forms to demonstrate understanding are just some of the skills learners use as members of literature circles. Students also enjoy opportunities to develop oral language skills and to engage in independent and shared reading activities. For students involved in literature circles, literature becomes "lived through" as they actively engage with the text and with one another (Rosenblatt, 1995).

In their extensive literature review on elements critical to the fostering of literacy among ELLs, Meltzer and Hamman (2004) found three key elements in

Figure 4.1. Key Elements in Meeting ELLs' Literacy Needs

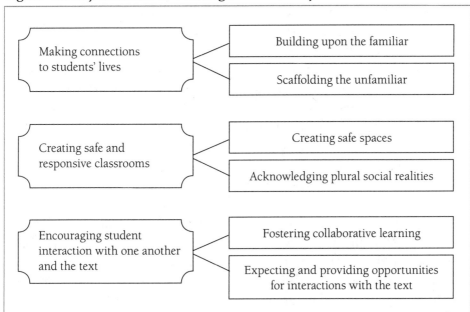

Note. Adapted from Meltzer and Hamman (2004)

the areas of motivation and engagement. Figure 4.1 depicts these key elements, which are making connections to students' lives, creating safe and responsive classrooms, and encouraging students to interact with one another and with the text.

We review each of these promising strategies in light of research supporting literature circles. Our purpose is to demonstrate how literature circles can be effective tools for developing the oral language and literacy skills of ELLs.

Making Connections to Students' Lives

Literacy development is enhanced when learners are meaningfully engaged with the text. According to Meltzer and Hamman (2004), two strategies have proven useful in motivating students to engage in literacy activities and, hence, in the learning process: (1) building upon the familiar and (2) scaffolding the unfamiliar by making text-to-text, text-to-self, and text-to-world connections. These two strategies provide a purpose for reading, sustain engagement with the text, and improve reading comprehension, all of which, in turn, promote students' academic literacy development across the content areas.

Literature circles provide students with ample opportunities to make connections to what they already know, what stimulates them, and what they need to know to achieve academic success. Choice is an important vehicle in establishing these connections. Depending on format and organization, students will most likely have a considerable amount of input in deciding what books to read, roles to play, and groups to join. They will also have a voice in making decisions about accountability methods, extension projects, and other responses to the text. Although the degree of student input will vary from classroom to classroom and from teacher to teacher, students will have opportunities to make choices and build upon their own strengths.

Fostering positive attitudes toward reading involves building on what students know. McKenna (1994) provides several suggestions for teachers to learn about their students' gifts and to create a positive environment where student input is valued. Among his ideas are (a) assessing students' beliefs about reading, (b) planning a varied program, (c) striving to show students the relevance of reading, (d) providing positive student models, and (e) recommending books on the basis of student opinions and preferences. These ideas are all natural components of literature circles.

Creating Safe and Responsive Classrooms

Culturally responsive pedagogy can be defined as teaching that uses the cultural knowledge, prior experiences, and performance styles of diverse students to make learning more appropriate and effective for them; it teaches *to* and *through* the strengths of these students (Ernst-Slavit & Wenger, 2006; Gay, 2000). Based upon their research, Meltzer and Hamman (2004) conclude that in responsive learning environments students feel safe and supported as they engage in literacy development and content area learning. More specifically, Meltzer and Hamman highlight creating safe spaces and acknowledging plural social realities as necessary for creating safe and responsive classrooms that are conducive to learning and achievement.

ELLs need to feel safe and accepted in all school contexts. This is of particular importance if we consider that many ELLs already feel marginalized in U.S. society. Literature circles, like book clubs, offer small, cozy settings where students can engage in literary discussions. These small groups provide a context for students to meet and discuss the books they have read; to reflect on and analyze themes, characters, and plot; and to share their opinions based on their personal experiences (Harvey & Goudvis, 2000) in an environment that is safe, nurturing, positive, and respectful. This kind of relaxed and welcoming atmosphere allows students to develop and discuss their own questions, to build knowledge based on the materials read, and to risk experimenting with more complex levels of thought and language.

Krashen's (1993) work indicates that "a great deal of learning occurs effortlessly, when learners consider themselves to be potential members of certain groups or 'clubs,' and expect to learn" (p. 71). This feeling of belonging coupled with a low-anxiety classroom environment allows students to lower their *affective filter* (that is, the mental block to learning that is based on emotional factors) and become more confident risk-takers and active participants in their own learning process. Plainly stated, the relationship between affect and second language learning is of major importance.

Similarly, there is a strong connection between affect and reading. Creating an environment in which students *want* to read will increase the chances that they *will* do so (Gee, 1999). Providing them with opportunities to work on specific tasks—such as reading within the literature circle context—combined with the awareness that they have some control over the activity will likely create some degree of intrinsic motivation to engage in the activity, thereby lowering the affective filter and thus increasing participation and learning.

When using culturally responsive pedagogy, students' life experiences and cultural and linguistic backgrounds are acknowledged and affirmed. All students, particularly ELLs, benefit from a learning environment where their home languages and cultures are acknowledged and valued (Ernst-Slavit & Slavit, 2007). Valenzuela's (1999) work indicates that many ELLs rarely encounter curricula and classroom practices that take into account their own backgrounds and experiences. Literature circles allow teachers to integrate students' languages and cultures in a variety of authentic ways, including (a) book choices, (b) first language use, (c) opportunities for multiple forms of participation, and (d) options for creative responses. When students find books that relate to their backgrounds and experiences, their opportunities to connect meaningfully with the text and to appear expert on the topic are magnified. Using the first language to scaffold students' writing and understanding of the material should be promoted at all times. Finally, encouraging a variety of response activities and extension projects permits all students—regardless of their level of English proficiency—to be active participants throughout the different phases of the literature circle.

Encouraging Student Interaction With One Another and the Text

Schlick Noe (2004) talks about the value of group work and interaction among students: "The power of working together to make meaning cannot be underestimated for challenged readers, whether their challenges are related to language, learning, or motivation" (¶ 25). Meltzer and Hamman (2004) found, in their thorough review of the literature, two important factors that promote interaction between students and the text: (1) fostering collaborative learning and (2) expecting and providing opportunities for interactions with the text.

Working in a group format offers ELLs an opportunity to reflect and relate elements from the reading back to their personal experiences. Students may also benefit from lively oral discussions, which allow for a deeper level of understanding about the topic. Well-designed collaborative activities foster meaningful discussions among participants.

This type of interaction is pivotal for ELLs, because oral language provides the foundation for literacy development (Snow, Burns, & Griffin, 1998). Unlike students who come to school already proficient in English, ELLs depend greatly upon school for interactions that support the development of authentic English skills, including both social and academic language (Gottlieb, Katz, & Ernst-Slavit, 2009; Teachers of English to Speakers of Other Languages, 2006). Although ELLs may learn social language from interactions with other students and adults in more informal settings (e.g., playground, lunchroom, park), they also require explicit instruction, interaction with peers, and modeling of the academic forms of language needed for success in the content areas (Wong Filmore & Snow, 2000).

Because of the nature of literature circles and their carefully scaffolded structure for participation, ELLs who are not yet confident speakers in a group are able to listen to their peers using academic language as they engage in grand conversations. This kind of exposure not only assists ELLs in learning how to ask questions and respond to inquiries but also models how peers interact with the text and with one another.

Daniels (1994) writes, "Small groups can be efficient, energizing, sometimes almost magical structures for learning" (p. 10). He further states that collaboration in small groups teaches efficient communication and brings the values of democracy, community, and shared responsibility to classrooms. Informal groups offer ample opportunities for students to "negotiate" the meaning of what they are reading and allow ELLs to become familiar with ways of discussing literature (Peregoy & Boyle, 2001). This kind of meaningful interaction with English-speaking peers enhances second language learners' opportunities to learn and practice both social and academic English.

Meaningful conversations about books can become grand conversations. Grand conversations are powerful and authentic literary experiences. The dynamic interaction, which expands the individual reader's conversation with the author to include other readers of the same text, demands active involvement. Within the context of the discussion, a reader can comment on personal connections, ask his or her own questions, and interpret the story through his or her unique experiences. The collaborative group format provides a context for individual members to take responsibility for sharing thoughts and opinions. Each member has a voice. Each voice adds stimulation and enriches the entire experience.

One Teacher's Experience: A Grand Experiment With Literature Circles

The Plan

Searching for an effective way to strengthen the literacy and communicative skills and the confidence of her ELLs, Catherine turned to literature circles as a possible approach. Her own experience in literature circles during a graduate school course first exposed her to the attributes of literary discussion, inspiring her to discover more about using the practice with her students to strengthen their literacy skills. With a belief that ELLs could benefit academically and socially from authentic conversations in a safe environment and armed with current research and a few good books on setting up and using literature circles (see Table 4.1), Catherine designed a research project to implement literature circles in her fourth-grade classroom. The project goal was to determine if, in fact, literature circles are an effective means of supporting literacy development as well as providing ELLs with authentic opportunities to gain communicative competence. Each of the two rounds planned by Catherine spanned about three weeks and involved reading one book and completing a reading reflection

Table 4.1. Professional Books, Articles, and Web Links on Literature Circles

Professional books and articles	Web links
Daniels, H. (2002). *Literature circles: Voice and choice in the student-centered classroom*. York, ME: Stenhouse.	Jim Burke www.englishcompanion.com Role sheets and other helpful items to organize your literature circles
Daniels, H., & Steineke, N. (2004). *Mini-lessons for literature circles*. Portsmouth, NH: Heinemann.	Brabham and Villaume Laura Candler www.lcandler.web.aplus.net (Click on "Literacy Lessons" then on "Literature Circles") Black line masters
Day, D. (2006). The ABC's of literature circles. *The Dragon Lode, 25*(1), 26–29.	EdSelect, The Canadian Encyclopedia edselect.com/literature_circles.htm
Peterson, R., & Eeds, M. (1990). *Grand conversations: Literature groups in action*. New York: Scholastic.	Literature Circles Resource Center School of Education, Seattle University www.litcircles.org
Samway, K.D., & Whang, G. (1996). *Literature study circles in a multicultural classroom*. York, ME: Stenhouse.	Literature Circles on Wikipedia en.wikipedia.org/wiki/Literature_Circles
Schlick Noe, K.L., & Johnson, N.J. (1999). *Getting started with literature circles*. Norwood, MA: Christopher-Gordon.	Pro Teacher Directory: Literature Circles www.proteacher.com/070172.shtml Contains information, resources, chats, and blogs

journal, extension projects, and a culminating group presentation (for additional information about this project, see Carrison and Ernst-Slavit, 2005).

The Classroom, the Students, and the Teacher

The research project was conducted in a K–5 elementary school in one of the fastest growing school districts in southwest Washington. At the time of the project, about 34% of the 720 students enrolled qualified for free or reduced lunch. About 6% of the students received learning support services and about 4% received English as a Second Language (ESL) pull-out services.

The study took place in Catherine's fourth-grade "English language learner cluster" classroom and involved a total of 24 students, 6 of whom were ELLs.

Table 4.2. Student Information

Name	Native language	Types of support received
Yulia	Ukrainian	ESL pull-out
Pavel	Ukrainian	(none)
Viktor	Russian	ESL pull-out
Ana	Spanish	(none)
David	Spanish	Learning support pull-out
Jason	English & Filipino/Tagalog	Learning support pull-out; speech therapy

At the time of the project, Catherine was in her sixth year of teaching, and although this was her first year having a designated cluster or group of ELLs, she did have previous experience working with ELLs in her mainstream classrooms. Over the years, as the numbers of ELLs in her classes increased so did her need for and interest in learning effective ways to provide more appropriate instructional support for these students.

Because the focus of the project was to examine the strengths of literature circles as a means of improving literacy and communication skills, particularly in relation to ELLs, a brief introduction to a few of these students (all student names are pseudonyms) will help set the stage and is provided in Table 4.2.

Putting the Circles Into Action

To establish baseline data, the project began with a survey of the students' previous experiences with literature discussion groups, their interests and preferences regarding reading, and a preassessment of the students' reading accuracy and comprehension levels. The reading interest and preference surveys and reading accuracy and comprehension assessments were readministered at the conclusion of the project to identify any notable changes of attitude or reading skill improvements.

Several books with themes addressing issues of diversity were selected. The texts were chosen with the goal of broadening students' understanding of these issues and inspiring discussion about these topics from a personal perspective. The books, many of which are listed in Table 4.3, varied in reading levels to ensure that all students had the opportunity to choose a book at their instructional level.

Table 4.3. Sample of Books Used for Literature Circles by Title

Book title	Author, date, publisher
Bearstone	Will Hobbs, l989, Avon
Esperanza Rising	Pam Muñoz Ryan, 2002, Scholastic
Hiroshima	Laurence Yep, 1995, Scholastic
Journey of the Sparrows	Fran Leeper Buss, 1991, Dell
Journey to America	Sonia Levitin, 1987, Aladdin
Local News	Gary Soto, 1993, Harcourt Brace Jovanovich
One Day in the Tropical Rain Forest	Jean Craighead George, 1990, HarperCollins
One Hundred Penny Box	Sharon Bell Mathis, 1986, Puffin
Sadako and the Thousand Paper Cranes	Eleanor Coerr, 1977, Scholastic
Sign of the Beaver	Elizabeth George Speare, 1983, Houghton Mifflin
Sing Down the Moon	Scott O'Dell, 1970, Houghton Mifflin
Stone Fox	John Reynolds Gardiner, 1983, HarperCollins
The Big Lie: A True Story	Isabella Leitner, 1994, Scholastic
The Crossing	Gary Paulsen, 1987, Orchard
The Jacket	Andrew Clements, 2002, Simon & Schuster
The Family Under the Bridge	Natalie Savage Carlson, 1958, HarperCollins
The Red Rose Box	Brenda Woods, 2002, Puffin
The Trouble with Tuck	Theodore Taylor, 1981, Dell Yearling
Yang the Youngest and His Terrible Ear	Lensey Namioka, 1992, Bantam Doubleday Dell

After a brief book talk about each of the literature books, students were invited to list their top three choices. Book groups of three to five students were formed, and students were given instructions via minilessons targeting (a) setting up reading schedules, (b) organizing reading journals, and (c) facilitating group discussions. Role sheets were distributed to the groups and completed by students after each discussion session. As the literature circles progressed, additional minilessons, such as those presented in Table 4.4, were presented on a variety of topics, such as author's craft and reading and writing response strategies.

In addition to students reading during their silent reading time and at home in the evenings, a 30–60 minute block (four days a week for about three weeks)

Table 4.4. Possible Minilesson Topics

Literature circle procedures	Literary—Elements of author's craft	Reading and writing response strategies
How to choose a book How to set up the reading schedule How to start a discussion How to be an active listener How to keep the conversation going How to disagree constructively What to do when you don't understand What to include in your response journal How to connect extension projects to the reading How to self assess What to do when your group finishes How to be a reading buddy	How the author grabs our interest Ways authors reveal the character of a person Characteristics of a good book title Ways to make dialogue in stories sound realistic Determining how much detail is too much Main components of a particular genre How an author sets the tone and mood of a story How an author uses "memorable" language Components of a story Ways to incorporate point of view and perspective	Self-correcting when reading doesn't make sense Making and checking predictions Incorporating ideas from sticky notes into a written response Supporting ideas with information from the book, your life, or other books Previewing Using flexible strategies to identify unknown words Building vocabulary through reading Creating pictures in your head or using sketches and illustrations to extend ideas Analyzing, interpreting, and inferring Writing a response on the character's point of view

Note. Adapted from Daniels (2002) and Schlick Noe & Johnson (1999)

was set aside for groups to read and reflect in their journals and to discuss what they had read. Once or twice a week Catherine joined each of the book groups to monitor the progress of the reading, the response journals, and the discussions. Throughout the reading of their books, students worked together to complete extension projects. Table 4.5 lists examples of extension projects based upon a variety of strategies for building comprehension and analytical skills. After completing the reading, groups planned and presented final projects designed to demonstrate their understanding of the book and to convince other students to read it.

Table 4.5. Examples of Extension Projects

Project	Brief description
ABC book	Create an alphabet book by focusing on key events, characters, and information from the book.
Accordion book	Use five to seven significant scenes from the book to make an illustrated accordion-shaped book representing the sequence of the story line.
Character bookmark	Create a bookmark by focusing on a favorite character or significant character in the story.
Collage	Using magazine photos, create a collage with images symbolizing events or themes important in the story.
Commemorative stamp	Focusing on an important theme from the story, choose a significant character or scene to depict on a stamp.
Jackdaw	Collect, label, and display artifacts, which are representative of the important elements in the book, such as characters, events, or ideas.
Literary weaving	On a strip of adding machine tape, use design, words, and colors to show the main themes or ideas in the book.
Map	Design a map to show a character's "journey" in the story. The journey might be physical, emotional or spiritual.
Open mind	Use illustrations or words to depict a character's possible dreams, fears, ideas, and so forth.
Setting pamphlet	In the form of a pamphlet or brochure, show four to five events or places that have an impact on a character in the story.
Story quilt	Design a quilt square that represents a favorite chapter or important scene from the book.

Note. Adapted from Schlick Noe & Johnson (1999)

Student Growth

Literature circles proved to be instrumental in the growth of students' reading skills and communicative confidence. In addition to improvement in students' reading accuracy and comprehension scores on postassessments, there were other notable improvements. As described in this chapter, ELLs found their voices not only during the grand conversations about the books but also during other classroom activities. The effects of their newfound confidence were seen throughout the remainder of the school year.

Although all students in the class reported being very motivated to participate in the literature circle activities, for the purposes of this chapter we highlight gains made by the six ELLs in specific areas: three of the students with the most significant gains followed by a discussion on selected accomplishments of three additional students.

Yulia. Prior to the literature circle project, Yulia, described by classmates as the "quietest girl in the class," rarely spoke out. Occasionally during math or social studies she would raise her hand to participate, but when called upon, she would shrink back and very quietly say, "Nevermind." In the instances when she was expected to read something in front of the class, Yulia would do so, but her whisperlike utterances went virtually unheard. During group projects, she would not assume any leadership roles, more often waiting to be given directions by other students before taking any action herself. In terms of her reading, Yulia had strong decoding accuracy, but her comprehension was fairly low.

Upon completing her first literature circle book, *The Trouble With Tuck* by Theodore Taylor, Yulia boldly took the lead role in organizing and presenting her group's final literature circle project. The group initially had trouble getting organized, so Yulia and another group member organized the drafts of their illustrations and wrote scripts for the accompanying narration. When the time came for their videotaped presentation in front of the class, Yulia, in the role of lead narrator, began the group's presentation by reading her lines aloud in front of the class. While her narration did not boom across the room, the students were finally able to hear Yulia's voice.

Yulia was the only girl in her second literature group. For their final presentation, the three students decided to perform a skit of two of their favorite scenes from the book *Sing Down the Moon* by Scott O'Dell. Once again, Yulia took on the responsibility of organizing the group and became the stabilizing force in writing the scripts for both the actor and narrator roles. When presentation time came, Yulia was the main narrator and memorized her lines for yet another part in the skit. The safety of taking on the persona of a character in the skit enabled Yulia to be animated and at ease in front of her classmates, when just being herself was too intimidating (Ernst-Slavit & Wenger, 1998). Although Yulia's extended character analysis projects and expository summary of the stories reflected some confusion with unfamiliar vocabulary, the story line, and the sequence of events, they were, however, more creative and detailed

Figure 4.2. Yulia's Open Mind Project

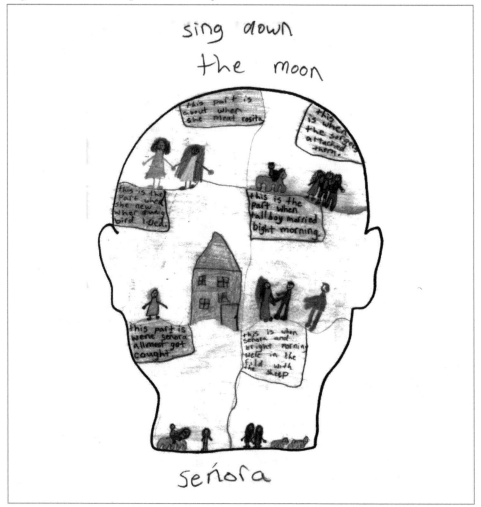

than many of her previous projects. A case in point is her Open Mind project as seen in Figure 4.2.

Pavel. With strong academic and literacy skills, Pavel's biggest challenge was participating in classroom activities. He was extremely shy, never volunteered to read aloud, and, up to the time of the literature circle project, rarely spoke out in class. Pavel was reluctant to assume any leadership role. However, during the final presentation of his first literature group project after reading *The Crossing* by Gary Paulsen, Pavel decided to assume the role of the narrator. He read to the class as the rest of his group performed a "theater in the round" rendition of several scenes from the book.

In the planning phase of the final project for his second literature book, *Yang the Youngest and His Terrible Ear* by Lensey Namioka, Pavel candidly shared in his discussion group how he related to the main character, Yang, feeling that his culture made him different. Later, he assumed the lead in designing the set—a large diorama, complete with background lighting. As he supervised the artwork and construction of the project, he explained his vision for the diorama and asked his group members to make adjustments in the assembly of their project. One student commented that she couldn't remember ever having heard Pavel "say so many words."

After completion of the project, Pavel continued to take a more active role in all classroom activities. He began volunteering to demonstrate math problems on the overhead projector and requesting to "go first" when making other presentations to the class. On a few occasions, Pavel even volunteered to read aloud in class.

Viktor. For most of the school year, Viktor displayed a great deal of apathy for school, especially when participating in learning activities or silent reading. His biggest struggles occurred while working in groups. Viktor refused to participate in any activity if he was partnered with a female student and had a very difficult time cooperating with other students.

Prior to the literature circle project, Viktor was very prompt in leaving each morning for his ESL pull-out class where things were "easy." As his classmates became more involved with the literature discussion, Viktor became less interested in leaving for ESL class on the days those activities overlapped. Catherine had chosen *Hiroshima* by Laurence Yep with Viktor in mind. The only topic that seemed to interest him academically was learning about wars, specifically World War II. Viktor was immediately drawn to the book and read it for his first literature circle book. On the second day of the project, Viktor, who rarely spoke to or even looked at the teacher, approached her before silent reading time to ask, "Can I read the literature circle book for the silent reading time?" The following day, as students were getting into their groups, Viktor asked, "Can I miss ESL today to be in the group?" The next week the teacher noticed that Viktor had checked out two books on Japan from the school library and was sharing them with the other students in his group during their discussion time.

For the final presentation of *Hiroshima*, Viktor's group decided to make large book posters and write haiku poetry about the story. Neither of these ideas appealed to Viktor, so he negotiated with the teacher to create a map of Japan with written facts about the bombing of Hiroshima. His map was a success with his group members, and they convinced Viktor to open their presentation with the map and his facts on the bombing.

During the second round of literature groups, Viktor's willingness to participate increased in spite of the fact that one of the other two members of the group was a female student. He was the star of the group's skit for *Sing Down the Moon*. Viktor's classmates so enjoyed his performance that they requested an encore, and he was clearly thrilled to oblige. Viktor's class participation level was at its highest all year during his involvement in literature circles. This participation, as well as an improved willingness to act as a positive member of the group, carried on through the rest of the school year.

Some Additional Successes. The three other ELLs in the classroom also seemed to blossom during the literature circle project. Ana, David, and Jason all struggled academically, partly due to their low literacy skills. They read their chosen books along with audiotaped, peer, parent volunteer, or teacher reading support. The oral participation of these students was notably stronger. The extension projects enabled Ana, David, and Jason to reflect upon and demonstrate comprehension visually rather than in writing (see, for example, Figure 4.3). This allowed them to use their visual representation as a springboard to verbalize their reflections and understanding to the rest of the group and thus to experience success.

In David's case, because of his significant learning challenges, he struggled to participate in many of the academic activities in class. As he began to read his first book, *Hiroshima*, he showed a renewed enthusiasm. He took his book with him to his learning support class and asked to read with the teacher during silent reading time. As evidenced by the following transcript, David, once quiet and withdrawn, began to find his voice and was a positive contributor to the grand conversation:

Catherine: Hiroshima is in about this area [indicating its location on a map of Japan]; actually, right where the little red dot is.

Figure 4.3. Ana's Coat of Arms

David: My mom has this big book about Hiroshima when they dropped the missile....

Catherine: The atom bomb?

David: Ya, the atom ball—and I think that, think that they showed a picture of what it looked like—what it looks like right now and I think, I think that's Hiroshima. And then they—instead of Hiroshima, they changed it into a park, uh....

Catherine: Yes, they did. You will read about what happened to it in the story. Okay, so Sam, what do you think? Get us going on our— on the story so far.

Sam:	[to the students in the group] Well, first of all, what was your favorite part so far?
David:	Well, the part I like about is when, um, when the mi...that was good luck when the—when the spaceship was gonna come and drop the atom bomb—there was some clouds right there, so they didn't know where to drop it and so they, they went to go attack 'em right there. See—that's the part I like because it was good luck.
Catherine:	Good luck that the clouds opened up or that the clouds were covering the city?
David:	Covering the city
Sam:	If you were Sachi—right before she passed out—what would you feel like?
Brianna:	I'd feel...
David:	[interrupting Brianna] I'd feel like I'm drowning—I don't know 'cause I've never passed out before, have you?
Brianna:	[louder] I'd pretty much feel scared because some people, when they pass out they die.
David:	[to Brianna] Ya! Ya, those are one of the reasons.

At one point, when Catherine complimented David on his increased participation, especially in the book discussions, he explained to her that he often felt "dumb" in school, but during the literature discussions he could share his ideas and feelings and ask questions about the book like the other students were doing. He felt "as smart as the other kids" while he was in a literature discussion circle.

Teacher Growth

The students were not the only learners in the literature circle project; the teacher learned a great deal as well. As a result, three main changes were made in her use of literature circles in the following school years. First, the procedures for the literature discussion circles were taught in subsequent years by clear modeling during a whole-class book study rather than having students participate in a variety of literature circles on their own. For instance, the year following this project, Catherine used *Shoe Shine Girl* by Clyde Robert Bulla to model the discussion roles and reading reflection journals.

Second, Catherine learned the importance of keeping minilessons "mini." Long, drawn-out directions for participating in literature circles were discarded and instead delivered in minilessons lasting a maximum of 10 to 20 minutes. Minilessons were immediately followed by opportunities for students to practice the skill or strategy taught. Finally, once students learned to participate in each of the discussion roles, the role accountability sheets were discarded and students rotated through the role responsibilities on their own.

In essence, the teacher learned to trust her students. Given solid preparation and the opportunity to assume the responsibility for participating, students rose to the occasion. Not only did their reading skills grow stronger but so did their willingness and enthusiasm to participate in other classroom activities. Additionally, the management skills students used during literature circles were evident in other group and classroom activities throughout the school year. In short, literature discussion circles fostered more than improvements in their literacy. Students learned to ask questions and to listen to and evaluate the opinions and perspectives of their peers about topics that were of interest to them—they learned to be active participants in grand conversations.

Procedures for Teaching Literature Circles: Creating the Scaffold

Teaching classroom procedures of any kind offers students emotional support, because students know what is expected. They do not have to question or wonder what they are supposed to be doing, which increases their feelings of safety and competence. As we have seen in Catherine's classroom, literature circles have the potential for providing a safe place to connect with others due to the collaborative small-group format. Participation in large- or whole-group dialogues is often less comfortable for ELLs; however, if one has only four or five other students with whom to interact, a student's comfort level is more likely to increase. In addition, the roles that are taught and assigned can at first act as a scaffold for students needing more conversational support.

The bonus with this student-centered method is that through the literature circle and the ensuing grand conversations, the community spirit that has already been established is further enhanced. The "snowball effect" of each student feeling safe to engage in dialogue in deeply personal ways strengthens the trusting relationships, and the supportive climate in the classroom continues to grow. This in turn can have an impact on the student's desire and ability to participate in other content area conversations.

The Roles

An examination of the responsibilities associated with each of the roles reveals that the skills needed to perform each role are varied and complex. The roles that most commonly are associated with literature circles include the following:

Discussion Director: Ensures that all group members are completing their tasks, prompts discussion of the text, selects the order of student response

Vocabulary Wizard: Locates and lists important words and phrases as well as the page numbers on which they appear; predicts the meaning of the words or phrases; uses a classroom resource, such as a dictionary, to locate the meaning of the words; shares this information with the other members of the group

Character Captain: Takes notes concerning the characters in the book, including characteristics, character development throughout the text, and personal reflections about the characters

Scene Setter: Documents various locations described (e.g., maps, illustrations, written descriptions), records details regarding the passage of time, and interprets how this information affects the characters in the text

Illustrator: Creates art work to illustrate the text and support the group's presentation to the class as a whole

Connector: Compares and contrasts the group's book (in terms of characters, settings, or actions) to other books, movies, or real life

Literary Luminary: Searches for one or more passages in the text that are very appealing or interesting and explains to the group why this is so

Researcher: Investigates a topic in the periphery of the story in order to contribute to the group's overall depth of understanding, researches the topic and reports back to the group (For example, in the book *Stone Fox* by John Reynolds Gardiner a student might investigate the science topics of Siberian Huskies or the climate or the social studies topics of Alaska or how dog sleds have been used.)

Summarizer: Prepares and presents a brief statement, poem, picture, or other item to summarize the reading completed by the group on any given day

Using role sheets, commonly found in literature circle books or on the Internet (see Table 4.1 on page 98 for sources), to teach students how to successfully participate in each role provides the scaffolding they need to engage in stimulating, literary conversation. Using role sheets is not a matter of simply handing roles to students and expecting them to perform. Each role is designed for the application of a comprehension strategy that may be new to students. Based on the kinds of responses the reading teacher is emphasizing and the roles being implemented, the success of the literature circle will be greatly increased as the teacher designs and teaches procedural lessons for each role.

After completing several literature circle experiences using the role sheets to prompt participation, more natural conversations do begin to occur. The use of the role sheets should be considered temporary. The ultimate goal is to rely less and less on the support provided by the assigned roles. In this way the performance of literature circle roles can have the power to scaffold readers toward grand conversations.

Instructional Methods

There are several ways to approach teaching literature circle roles, as shown in Table 4.6. Lessons for each role can be taught to the whole group first by teaching all students the responsibilities for a particular role, next by having them read a short piece of text such as a poem or a picture book, and then having all students learn the role at the same time. This whole-group instruction approach concludes with a short debriefing of the activity, which provides students with opportunities for asking questions and discussing how to improve role performance. If this procedure is repeated over the course of a school week with several different roles, enough roles would be learned to form actual literature circle groups consisting of the various roles. Then, with a new piece of text, students could be assigned to a collaborative group to perform one of the roles and a trial literature circle could occur. After debriefing this dress rehearsal, students should be prepared for literature circle discussions to begin. In this way students who have been taught all the roles and procedures have a clear vision of how literature circles work.

Another approach to teaching the roles is to utilize the "fishbowl" strategy, which offers a detailed road map for implementing literature circles. This approach consists of selecting a group of students and teaching them how to perform the various roles. Essentially this group becomes a training model.

Table 4.6. Implementing Literature Circles

Components	Method for implementing	Materials	Teacher	Student
Teaching roles: Whole class	**Week 1** Monday: Teach Discussion Director Tuesday: Teach Illustrator Wednesday: Teach Connector Thursday: Teach Literary Luminator Friday: Teach Summarizer **Week 2** Monday–Friday: Practice using all roles	Short chapter book or several poems	• Choose text or a chapter book that can be read in a short amount of time. Each selection is used to teach a literature circle role. • Assign reading. • Teach responsibilities of one role each day for a week. • Conduct debriefing for clarification. • During the second week, form literature circles utilizing all roles. • Practice and debrief for clarification.	• Read the text. • Perform the role. • Ask clarifying questions.
Fishbowl	Day 1: Teach a group of students to participate in a literature circle. This group will be used as a model for others to observe. Day 2: Model students teach their role to small group of peers. Day 3: Whole class forms literature circles composed of one of each of the roles. Read, practice, debrief.	Chapter from a book or poem	• Select a group of students who will be taught to perform various literature circle roles. • Assign the reading. • Teach the roles. • Practice until students feel confident as models. • Facilitate "fishbowl" literature circle for other members of class. • Debrief.	Day 1: Observe the "fishbowl." Ask questions. Day 2: Learn a role. Practice. Debrief. Day 3: Form literature circles. Practice. Debrief.

Components	Method for implementing	Materials	Teacher	Student
Book selection	Book talk/teacher choice Bulletin board posting/student choice	Books of a variety of levels and interests Connections to student lives	• Prepare short book talk to introduce the story.	• Have first and second choice of books that teacher has read. • Student choice: Post the title of a book or the book jacket he or she would like to read on the bulletin board. Other students can choose to be in the group by writing their name on an attached sign-up sheet.
Scheduling the reading	Whole-class minilesson	Calendar for time period, usually 3–4 weeks	• Provide each student with calendar. • Discuss possible schedules for the completion of the book. • Require reading at school or at home. • Discuss accountability issues. • Model or show examples of completed schedule.	• Collaborate with others to schedule the reading. • Make decisions regarding accountability for the reading.
Reading	Buddy or paired reading Books on tape Learning assistant	Books chosen by teacher or students	• Assess class to determine which students might need support with the reading. Pair up more capable readers with students needing assistance, or provide students with other reading support such as the book on tape or the support of a knowledgeable adult.	• Capable students provide support to students needing assistance.

(continued)

Table 4.6. Implementing Literature Circles (continued)

Components	Method for implementing	Materials	Teacher	Student
Minilessons	Brief explanations of areas that will facilitate improvement of literature circle experience. These lessons could be on content, process, or management.	Materials as needed	• Observe or participate in literature circles and assess needed skills or strategies. • Prepare and present short lessons to address student needs.	• Participate in lesson.
Response activities	Formal: Journal or log demonstrating what students have learned or how they connect with the reading. Informal: Notes, sticky notes, questions	Materials as needed	• Present options for individual or group response. • Present possible prompts for writing as needed.	• Write response to share connections, reflections, or other learning.
Extension projects	Writing, drama, art, music, dance	Materials as needed	• Present menu of ideas for extending the learning. • Give options for individual or group extension.	• Choose from the menu. • Create and present extension projects.
Assessment	Group notebook binder: Each literature circle is provided with a binder containing forms such as calendar, log response sheets, role sheets, etc. Student portfolio, journal, or log: Individual students maintain a record of the calendar, learning, responses, and reflections associated with the reading. This can be used for individual self-assessment purposes upon completion of the book.	Three-ring binder	• Prepare a binder for each literature circle group. • Teach minilesson on record keeping and accountability. • Assess work in notebook as part of assessment process.	• Keep individual and group records pertaining to the work of the literature circle group. • Use portfolios for self-assessment.

After learning and practicing each of the roles, these readers perform a literature circle for other classmates to observe. By grouping "expert" students together and having their peers stand on the perimeter of the group, the fishbowl effect provides the untrained students with a demonstration of the roles as well as the kind of conversations that can occur. Debriefing the fishbowl session gives students opportunities to further explain their roles and others to ask clarifying questions.

Using either the fishbowl approach or teaching every student each of the roles gives students the skills and knowledge they need for participation in literature circles. The psychological comfort of knowing what to do and how to do it benefits both the student and the teacher. Teaching the procedures helps to ensure that time and energy will be spent on literary conversations and less on classroom management.

The Reading Schedule

Literature circle participants can also be empowered when they are given the responsibility for creating their own reading calendar or schedule. With the support and encouragement of the teacher, readers can be taught how to divide up the chapters of the book and organize their reading time so that the selection being read is completed in the amount of time allotted for literature circles. (See Table 4.6 for suggestions for scheduling the reading.)

Next, the group can formulate its own code of accountability so that, prior to beginning the book study, students have mutually agreed on the consequences for not completing the reading needed for each discussion session. Having an agreed-upon accountability system in place makes for less disagreement if students do not fulfill their responsibilities for the reading.

Once trusting relationships are established and the organizational procedures have been taught and practiced, students can proceed almost independently. The intentional teacher has put in place the scaffolds that support effective literature circle discussions that can grow into grand conversations.

What Can Literature Circles Bring to Your Classroom?

The primary goal of this chapter has been to encourage all teachers, especially those working with ELLs, to explore the use of literature circles to benefit students by (a) increasing participation in reading and speaking, (b) strengthening literacy and oracy skills, and (c) enhancing motivation to read. Through a discussion of some of the theoretical arguments supporting the use of literature circles and in sharing some of the discoveries of one teacher's exploration of the practice, we have attempted to demonstrate how literature circles can be an effective avenue for developing ELLs' literacy and oracy skills.

Literature circles provide students with ample opportunities to make connections with what they already know, what stimulates them, and what they need to learn to succeed in educational settings. Additional opportunities exist to scaffold learning when students encounter the unfamiliar, take risks, and engage in grand conversations. We recommend that the various aspects of literature circles be practiced or modeled when students are first introduced to this approach. Teachers who design, organize, and implement literature circles to address the needs of their students provide much-needed support as they demonstrate a procedure, guide students through a task, break complex tasks into smaller steps, and supply information (Gilmore & Day, 2006). As students gain knowledge and expertise about how to collaborate in literature circles, teachers gradually decrease their support, encouraging students to become confident, self-directed participants in grand conversations.

REFLECTION QUESTIONS

1. What are some specific benefits of literature circles for ELLs?
2. Select 5–6 minilessons from Table 4.4 and outline how you will present those to your students to support literature circles.
3. Before starting literature circles, it is important to inquire about students' interests. For that purpose, prepare a brief survey to gauge students' previous experiences with literature and their current interests and preferences.
4. What specific actions can you take to include parents and family in literature circles?

REFERENCES
Carrison, C., & Ernst-Slavit, G. (2005). From silence to whisper to active participation: Using literature circles with ELL students. *Reading Horizons, 46*(2), 93–113.
Daniels, H. (1994). *Literature circles: Voice and choice in the student-centered classroom.* York, ME: Stenhouse.

Daniels, H. (2002). *Literature circles: Voice and choice in book clubs and reading groups*. York, ME: Stenhouse.

Ernst-Slavit, G., & Slavit, D. (2007). Educational reform, mathematics, and diverse learners: Meeting the needs of all students. *Multicultural Education, 14*(4), 20–27.

Ernst-Slavit, G., & Wenger, K.J. (1998). Face-to-face encounters: Using creative drama in the elementary ESL classroom. *TESOL Journal, 7*(4), 30–33.

Ernst-Slavit, G., & Wenger, K.J. (2006). Teaching in the margins: The multifaceted work and struggles of bilingual paraeducators. *Anthropology & Education Quarterly, 37*(1), 62–81. doi:10.1525/aeq.2006.37.1.62

Gay, G. (2000). *Culturally responsive teaching: Theory, research, and practice*. New York: Teachers College Press.

Gee, R.W. (1999). Encouraging ESL students to read. *TESOL Journal, 8*(1), 3–7.

Gilmore, D.P., & Day, D. (2006). Let's read, write, and talk about it: Literature circles for English learners. In T.A. Young & N.L. Hadaway (Eds.), *Supporting the literacy development of English learners: Increasing success in all classrooms* (pp. 194–209). Newark, DE: International Reading Association.

Gottlieb, M., Katz, A., & Ernst-Slavit, G. (2009). *Paper to practice: Using the TESOL English language proficiency standards in prek-12 classrooms*. Alexandria, VA: Teachers of English to Speakers of Other Languages.

Harvey, S., & Goudvis, A. (2000). *Strategies that work: Teaching comprehension to enhance understanding*. York, ME: Stenhouse.

Krashen, S.D. (1993). *The power of reading: Insights from the research*. Englewood, CO: Libraries Unlimited.

McKenna, M.C. (1994). Toward a model of reading attitude acquisition. In E.H. Cramer & M. Castle (Eds.), *Fostering the life-long love of reading: The affective domain in reading education* (pp. 18–40). Newark, DE: International Reading Association.

Meltzer, J., & Hamman, E.T. (2004). *Meeting the literacy development needs of adolescent English language learners through content area learning, part one: Focus on engagement and motivation*. Providence, RI: Brown University, Education Alliance. Retrieved April 8, 2007, from www.alliance.brown.edu/pubs/adlit/adell_litdv1.pdf

Peregoy, S.F., & Boyle, O.F. (2001). *Reading, writing, and learning in ESL: A resource book for K–12 teachers* (3rd ed.). New York: Longman.

Peterson, R., & Eeds, M. (1990). *Grand conversations: Literature groups in action*. New York: Scholastic.

Rosenblatt, L.M. (1995). *Literature as exploration* (5th ed.). New York: Modern Language Association of America.

Schlick Noe, K.L. (2004). Literature circles build excitement for books. *Education World*. Retrieved May 20, 2007, from www.education-world.com/ a_curr/curr259.shtml

Schlick Noe, K.L., & Johnson, N.J. (1999). *Getting started with literature circles*. Norwood, MA: Christopher-Gordon.

Short, K.G., & Klassen, C. (1993). Literature circles: Hearing children's voices. In B.E. Cullinan (Ed.), *Children's voices: Talk in the classroom* (pp. 66–85). Newark, DE: International Reading Association.

Snow, C.E., Burns, S., & Griffin, P. (1998). *Preventing reading difficulties in young children*. Washington, DC: National Academy Press.

Teachers of English to Speakers of Other Languages. (2006). *PreK–12 English language proficiency standards*. Alexandria, VA: Author.

Valenzuela, A. (1999). *Subtractive schooling: U.S.-Mexican youth and the politics of caring*. Albany, NY: State University of New York Press.

Wong Filmore, L., & Snow, C. (2000). *What teachers need to know about language*. Washington, DC: U.S. Department of Education.

Language, Literacy, and Learning in Middle and Secondary School Classrooms

CHAPTER 5

Implementing Scaffolded Reading Experiences in Diverse Classrooms

Michael F. Graves and Jill Fitzgerald

The Scaffolded Reading Experience (SRE) was developed some 30 years ago (Graves, Palmer, & Furniss, 1976) as an instructional framework for planning prereading, during-reading, and postreading activities that assist all students—including students with the varied linguistic and cultural backgrounds found in today's classrooms—in successfully comprehending and learning from the many different types of narrative and expository texts they read in school. As we write this chapter, the two of us together have had over 40 years of experience observing teachers as they use SREs in their classrooms and talking to them and their students about doing so, teaching scores of college classes and inservice sessions in which we used SREs, considering reviewers' feedback on the books and articles we have written on SREs, and conducting studies of the effectiveness of SREs. As a result, we have learned a tremendous amount about successfully incorporating SREs in many types of classrooms and with diverse groups of students.

Research on SREs has involved children and adolescents of various ages, reading abilities, and social groups and has investigated a number of outcomes. Watts and Rothenberg (1997) demonstrates the effectiveness of SREs in improving the comprehension of high school, special education students reading the literature of William Shakespeare. Fournier and Graves (2002) demonstrates the effectiveness of SREs in improving average and below-average ability middle school students' comprehension of short stories. Cooke (2001) shows that SREs could be used with stronger and weaker middle-grade readers to improve their understanding of multicultural stories and increase their involvement and enthusiasm toward reading multicultural stories. Graves and Liang

(2003), working with high school students in a suburban school and an inner-city school, shows the effectiveness of SREs in improving students' higher order thinking. Liang (2004), working with urban sixth graders, demonstrates that SREs could be effectively designed to emphasize either reader response goals or more cognitive goals. And Liang, Peterson, and Graves (2005), working with culturally and linguistically diverse third graders, shows that students receiving SREs score higher than students receiving a more response-oriented approach but that both approaches include worthwhile activities.

Clearly, SREs can be effective with students of various ages, reading abilities, and social groups; with various types of texts; and for various purposes, as seen in Table 5.1. However, constructing and using SREs are creative efforts that require teachers to plan carefully and make a number of decisions. In the next section of this chapter, we discuss some of the principal decisions and challenges teachers face as they plan and implement SREs in their classrooms. In the third section, we consider using SREs for the special purpose of fostering higher order thinking, a proficiency much needed in the 21st century and something emphasized by teachers who have helped students in diverse classrooms "beat

Table 5.1. Possible Components of a Scaffolded Reading Experience

Prereading activities	During-reading activities	Postreading activities
Motivating	Silent reading	Questioning
Activating or building background knowledge	Reading to students	Discussion
Providing text-specific knowledge	Supported reading	Building connections
Relating the reading to students' lives	Oral reading by students	Writing
Preteaching vocabulary	Modifying the text	Drama
Preteaching concepts	Using students' native language	Artistic, graphic, and non-verbal activities
Prequestioning, predicting, and direction setting	Engaging students and community people as resources	Application and outreach activities
Using students' native language		Using students' native language
Engaging students and community people as resources		Engaging students and community people as resources
Suggesting strategies		

the odds" and succeed beyond expectations (Taylor, Pearson, Clark, & Walpole, 2002; Taylor, Pressley, & Pearson, 2002). In the fourth section, we consider assessing the effects of SREs, a clear necessity in all classrooms.

Decisions and Challenges in Implementing SREs

Some of the decisions and challenges teachers face when implementing SREs include the frequency of SREs, how much scaffolding to provide, how often to differentiate activities for different students, the importance of providing a balance between challenging and easier reading material, adjusting and differentiating postreading tasks to ensure student success, and involving students in constructing SREs.

The Frequency of SREs

Clearly, SREs are only one part of a comprehensive reading program and certainly not something that should be used with everything students read. But just how frequently should they be used? Of course, the answer to this question varies for different students, different teachers, different goals, and different grade levels—to name just a few myriad factors affecting what takes place in any classroom. Nevertheless, we can suggest some considerations and guidelines.

To begin, we believe that SREs provide some of the best opportunities for extending students' zones of proximal development (the range of tasks they can complete) by supporting their efforts, helping them succeed in their reading, and giving them some common experiences to talk about, write about, and know that they share. In this sense, SREs have an intrinsic value that would lead us to use them quite frequently for their own sake—for the stretching, success, and shared experiences they can provide. To take advantage of these benefits, we would generally include at least one SRE as a part of reading instruction during most school weeks.

From another perspective, SREs are useful for the extrinsic reason that they facilitate students' reading and learning in various content areas. Because students need to do a good deal of reading in social studies, science, health, and the like—and because some of this reading is challenging—SREs are often called for in content area reading. Although SREs used in content areas will sometimes be brief, most school weeks will call for several of them.

Finally, the question of how the frequency of SREs should differ at various grade levels and for students with varying levels of proficiency requires careful consideration. Two somewhat opposing lines of reasoning come into play here. On the one hand, students obviously need to become increasingly independent and self-sufficient as they move toward becoming proficient and independent adult readers. This of course argues for SREs becoming less frequent over time. On the other hand, one very important purpose of SREs is to stretch students, enabling them to read material that would be too challenging without the assistance of an SRE. Certainly, we do not want to stretch older and more proficient students any less than younger and less proficient ones.

The situation, then, appears to be this: Over time, students get increasingly competent. Over that same time, however, the materials students read and the tasks they complete with those materials become increasingly challenging. Thus, there continues to be a place for SREs throughout high school. In fact, in our judgment, giving reading assignments without any scaffolding—the proverbial "Read Chapters 4 and 5 and come to class on Tuesday prepared to discuss them"—is generally inappropriate even in graduate school. Consequently, although SREs will certainly be different for students of various ages and abilities, they continue to be an important component of a complete and balanced program, even in the upper grades and for very competent readers.

How Much Scaffolding to Provide

The main thing to recognize when considering how much scaffolding to provide is that it is neither a case of the more the merrier nor one of the less the merrier. The general rule is to provide enough scaffolding for students to be confident and successful in their reading but not so much that they are not sufficiently challenged, feel that they are being spoon fed, or become bored. In general, then, the suggestion is to provide enough scaffolding but not too much. Further reinforcing the notion of not providing more scaffolding than is needed is the fact that constructing scaffolds takes valuable teacher time, time that is always at a premium. At the same time, there is no getting away from the fact that in today's classrooms many students need and deserve a significant amount of scaffolding if they are to succeed.

How Often to Differentiate Activities

Today's diverse classrooms very often contain students representing a huge array of background knowledge and reading proficiency. Thus, differentiating SREs is at times necessary. Two sorts of differentiation are worth considering. On the one hand, a teacher will sometimes want to differentiate SREs based on students' interests. For example, students can read different books while pursuing a common topic or theme. Thus, in exploring the themes of death and grieving, some upper elementary students might read Marion Dane Bauer's *On My Honor,* others Katherine Paterson's *Bridge to Terabithia,* and still others Candy Dawson Boyd's *Breadsticks and Blessing Places.* Similarly, some students may choose to respond to a reading selection in writing, others with some sort of artwork, others with an oral presentation, and others by using the Internet to pursue the topic further. The constraints on differentiation of this type are the teacher's time, ingenuity, and ability to orchestrate diverse activities. Additionally, a teacher needs to keep in mind that the more different activities students are involved in the less time there is available to assist students with each activity. At the extreme, if 30 students are each involved in a different activity, a teacher can give each student less than two minutes of individual attention each hour. Thus, there are a number of practical limits on differentiating on the basis of student interest. However, if these limits are kept in mind, differentiation based on interest is frequently desirable.

The other sort of differentiation to consider is differentiation based on students' reading and language proficiency. Here, the same limits that influence differentiation based on interest apply. That is, constraints include a teacher's time, ingenuity, ability to orchestrate diverse activities, and ability to assist students when many activities are going on at once. Beyond these considerations, however, is that of the effect of being repeatedly placed in a group that receives more assistance. Being a member of the group that repeatedly receives more assistance certainly has the potential to weaken students' self-image and motivation to learn. Singling out students for special, essentially remedial, assistance is not something we want to do any more frequently than necessary.

However, these are not the only facts to consider. There is also the fact that success begets success and failure begets failure. Thus, the suggestion that differentiation based on reading and language proficiency should be infrequent because of the psychological effect it might have must be tempered by the realization that differentiation can make the difference between success and failure. With less proficient readers, it is often important to differentiate instruction to ensure success, even though that differentiation should be no more frequent than is necessary.

Providing a Balance of Challenging and Easy Reading

Consideration of differentiating SREs leads directly to the matter of providing a balance of challenging and easy reading. All students need and deserve opportunities to read easy material that they can understand and enjoy without effort and challenging material that they need to grapple with (Graves, Juel, & Graves, 2007). Reading easy material fosters automaticity, builds confidence, creates interest in reading, and provides students with practice in a task they will face frequently in their everyday lives. Reading challenging material builds students' knowledge bases, their vocabularies, and their critical thinking skills. Reading challenging material also provides students with practice in a task they will face frequently in school and college, in their work outside of school, and in becoming knowledgeable and responsible members of a democratic society. Moreover, reading challenging materials builds students' confidence in their ability to deal with difficult reading selections. Teachers must, however, ensure that students are successful with the challenging material.

The point that needs to be stressed here is that each student—more proficient and more knowledgeable students as well as less proficient and less knowledgeable students—needs both challenging and easy reading. This condition cannot be met by providing only material that is of average difficulty for the average student. Assuming classrooms made up of students with varying skills and knowledge—and this description fits most classrooms—routinely providing only reading selections of average difficulty ensures that some students will repeatedly receive material that is difficult for them, others will repeatedly receive material that is of average difficulty for them, and still others will repeatedly receive material that is easy for them. Such a situation is inappropriate for all students. Because the reading tasks we face in the world outside of school vary and because the benefits of reading vary with the difficulty of the reading tasks, all students need frequent opportunities to read materials that vary in the challenges and opportunities they present. Thus, in a 10th-grade English class, some students might be reading a simple and brief novel such as An Na's *A Step From Heaven*, others a more complex and longer novel such as Khaled Hosseini's *The Kite Runner*, and others a still more complex book like James McBride's *The Color of Water*.

Tailoring Postreading Tasks to Ensure Success

In constructing and using SREs ourselves and talking to other teachers who have done so, we have found that sometimes—even after considering the students, the text, and the learning task and arranging a sturdy set of prereading, during-reading, and postreading activities—some students are still not likely to have a successful reading experience unless something more is done. In such cases, we recommend two approaches: (1) simplifying postreading tasks and (2) offering alternative postreading tasks. Five general approaches to simplifying postreading tasks include the following:

1. Asking students to do less rather than more
2. Requiring recognition rather than recall
3. Requiring assembly rather than creation
4. Cueing students to the place where answers can be found
5. Preceding production tasks with explicit instruction

Almost certainly the most straightforward approach to simplifying postreading tasks is to ask students to do less rather than more. We realize this sounds a bit flippant, but we are quite serious. Everything else being equal, tasks in which students answer fewer questions, construct less involved models, or write shorter pieces are distinctly easier. For example, after they read *The Island of the Blue Dolphins* by Scott O'Dell, students may be asked to identify *two* instances of courage and explain why these were courageous rather than having them deal with *four* instances.

Requiring recognition rather than recall is another straightforward approach to simplifying postreading tasks. Any time a teacher allows students to return to the text to find answers or presents them with alternatives from which to choose rather than requiring them to construct answers, the students' task is simplified. In the case of *The Island of the Blue Dolphins* described above, for example, letting students return to the text to find instances of courage is likely to make the task markedly easier.

Requiring assembly rather than creation is quite similar to requiring recognition rather than recall. For example, some students might find it difficult to construct a timeline of major events after reading a chapter on the U.S. Civil Rights movement. However, these students would be greatly aided if you gave them a list of those events and a list of dates out of order and asked them to reorder the events and dates to construct a timeline.

Cueing students to the places where answers can be found is an easily implemented approach and a particularly powerful one to use when students are dealing with lengthy and challenging selections. This approach was first suggested by Herber (1970). Depending on the difficulty students face, a teacher can cue them to the chapter, page, or even paragraph in which the information needed to answer a question is found.

Our final suggestion here is to precede challenging production tasks with explicit instruction (Graves et al., 2007). If students will be expected to summarize information, synthesize information, make inferences, and complete other activities that require them to construct new information, teachers may need to explicitly teach students how to do these tasks before asking them to complete them. Of course, some students will already have been taught the needed procedures. However, even when students have been taught a procedure, it will often be a good idea to review it. For example, if the students' task is to compare and contrast two boys growing up during the U.S. Revolutionary War—perhaps Johnny in *Johnny Tremain* by Esther Forbes with Tim in *My Brother Sam Is Dead* by James Lincoln Collier and Christopher Collier—a teacher might review the notion of a comparison and contrast essay, suggest some of the characteristics on which students might compare and contrast these two particular characters, and suggest some order for their essay, perhaps that of first listing the ways in which the two were the same and then listing the ways in which the two differed.

At this point, it may seem as if we have suggested a great deal of simplification and that what we are recommending amounts to spoon feeding and thus robs students of the opportunity to grapple with difficult tasks. We want to stress that this is not our message. We are not recommending that postreading tasks always be simplified, and we are certainly not recommending that some students routinely be given simplified postreading tasks. On the contrary, the simplifications suggested here are fix-up strategies to be used *sparingly* and only in cases in which students might otherwise fail. The essence of the SRE approach is to choose reading selections wisely and involve students in prereading and during-reading activities that will enable them to succeed with the postreading activities in which they engage. Occasionally, however, even with everything a teacher has done to accomplish this, there will be some students who will struggle to complete postreading activities. This is the point at which simplifying postreading tasks becomes both appropriate and advisable.

The other suggestion we have for tailoring postreading tasks to ensure success is to offer students alternative postreading options. The work of Gardner (1983, 2003) on multiple intelligences is particularly insightful in this regard. Gardner believes that there is more than one sort of thinking and that schools largely neglect many of these. Gardner has now described eight of these intelligences:

1. Linguistic
2. Logical–mathematical
3. Spatial
4. Bodily kinesthetic
5. Musical
6. Interpersonal
7. Intrapersonal
8. Environmental

Traditionally, only two of these—linguistic intelligence and logical–mathematical intelligence—have received much attention in school. Unfortunately, although a good deal has been written about Gardner and his theories and we frequently hear his conception of intelligence praised, we see little attention to the other six intelligences in school. We view this as most unfortunate. In today's diverse classrooms, all of these ways of thinking and demonstrating understanding have a real place and ought to be considered as valid options. Thus, after reading a text, students of all ages and proficiency levels should sometimes be given the opportunity to respond through such activities as dance, music, and drawing.

Involving Students in Constructing SREs

One of the central themes of current thinking about learning and instruction is that to really learn something students need to be actively involved in their learning. One approach to getting students actively involved in their learning is cross-age tutoring, involving older students in the instruction of younger students. Our experience as teachers, a substantial body of research and writing produced over a number of years (for example, Cohen, Kulik, & Kulik, 1982; Juel, 1996; Utah State Office of Education, 2006), and common sense suggest that cross-age tutoring is extremely effective. We very much agree with the sentiments expressed by McKeachie (McKeachie, Svinicki, & Hofer, 2006), a scholar who has spent more than 50 years studying instruction, when he says this:

> The best answer to the question, "What is the most efficient method of teaching?" is that it depends on the goal, the student, the content, and the teacher. But the next best answer is, "Students teaching other students." There is a wealth of evidence that peer teaching is extremely effective for a wide range of goals, content, and students of different levels and personalities. (p. 81)

One way in which older or more proficient students can assist in teaching younger or less proficient students—and in doing so become actively involved in their learning—is by preparing SRE materials for younger or less proficient students. Consider what the student who is going to prepare a preview, a set of discussion questions, or a summary of chapter needs to do to construct first-rate materials. He or she needs to read the chapter, understand it, pick out what is important, decide what sort of language to use in addressing the younger or less proficient student, and then prepare materials that will be interesting, informative, attractive, and engaging. In other words, he or she needs to understand and appreciate the chapter fully, use his or her creative and problem-solving skills to create material, and use his or her linguistic skills to communicate with a genuine audience.

It is hard to imagine a task that presents more opportunities for learning, for doing something useful, and for feeling a sense of accomplishment. Moreover, the possibilities are certainly not limited to previewing, summarizing, or writing discussion questions. Many prereading, during-reading, and postreading activities require some sorts of materials; with a teacher's help, older students are quite capable of constructing those materials. Selecting and teaching vocabulary and concepts, identifying the organization of a selection, recording parts of a selection on tape, developing a writing assignment, and many other SRE activities are within older students' range. Finally, not only will students learn more from creating SRE activities, but having students participate in constructing SRE materials will free up some of the teacher's time to work with students who really need individual help. We almost always agree with the adage that if something seems too good to be true it probably is. However, we feel compelled to believe that students assisting teachers in constructing SRE activities is the proverbial exception that proves the rule.

Using SREs to Foster Higher Order Thinking and Deep Understanding

As we have noted, SREs are intended to foster a variety of sorts of reading, not giving special consideration to any one sort. Thus, for example, they can and should be used in situations in which teachers want students to gain only a rudimentary knowledge of a text as well as in situations in which teachers want students to gain rich and deep understanding. Here, however, we want to discuss the use of SREs to promote higher order thinking, which as we have noted is both much needed in the 21st century and something emphasized by teachers who have helped students in diverse classrooms "beat the odds" (Taylor, Pearson et al., 2002; Taylor, Pressley et al., 2002).

Fortunately, using SREs to foster higher order thinking is a straightforward process. Doing so simply requires objectives that require higher order thinking and understanding and SRE activities that scaffold students' efforts to achieve those objectives. Here, we discuss three sources that we have found particularly useful in planning and implementing higher order thinking activities: Resnick's *Education and Learning to Think* (1987); Anderson and Krathwohl's *A Taxonomy for Learning, Teaching, and Assessing* (2001); and Sternberg and Spear-Swerling's *Teaching for Thinking* (1996).

After noting that higher order skills resist precise definition, Resnick (1987) lists some features of higher order thinking. Although lengthier than a typical definition, Resnick's list does an excellent job of providing a real feel for the concept.

- Higher order thinking is *nonalgorithmic*. That is, the path of action is not fully specified in advance.
- Higher order thinking tends to be *complex*. The total path is not "visible" (mentally speaking) from any single vantage point.
- Higher order thinking often yields *multiple solutions*, each with costs and benefits, rather than unique solutions.
- Higher order thinking involves *nuanced judgments* and interpretation.
- Higher order thinking involves the application of *multiple criteria*, which sometimes conflict with one another.
- Higher order thinking often *involves uncertainty*. Not everything that bears on the task at hand is known.

- Higher order thinking involves *self-regulation* of the thinking process. We do not recognize higher order thinking in an individual when someone else calls the plays at every step.

- Higher order thinking involves *imposing meaning*, finding structure in apparent disorder.

- Higher order thinking is *effortful*. There is considerable mental work involved in the kinds of elaborations and judgments required. (p. 3)

Making use of Resnick's (1987) features when planning SREs simply requires deliberate decision to include some activities that engage students in the features she describes. For example, suppose when working with middle-grade students and planning a SRE for Laurie Halse Anderson's *Fever 1793*, a historical novel about the yellow fever epidemic in Philadelphia, Pennsylvania, during the U.S. Revolutionary period, students are asked to consider the factors that make a similar epidemic today likely or unlikely. This task requires higher order thinking in that it is complex, may have multiple answers, and involves uncertainty. Or, suppose when working with high school students and planning an SRE for Walter Dean Myers's *Monster*, a gripping novel about a 16-year-old on trial for murder, students must attempt to determine the truthfulness of the various participants in the trial—defendants, witnesses, and lawyers—and establish criteria for their determinations. This activity clearly involves students in higher order thinking because it requires the application of multiple criteria, involves uncertainty, and is effortful.

Anderson and Krathwohl (2001) take a different tact in considering types of thinking. With the assistance of a group of colleagues, Anderson and Krathwohl extensively revised Bloom's (1956) well-known and widely used *Taxonomy of Educational Objectives*. Their revision encompasses an entire book, which we recommend highly. We will not, however, attempt to summarize the book here. Instead, what we describe here are seven of the types of thinking described in the revised taxonomy that we find particularly useful in working with SREs. The definitions of the first six types are taken nearly verbatim from Anderson and Krathwohl (2001, p. 31). The last definition reflects a mixture of their thinking and our own.

1. Remembering—Retrieving relevant knowledge from long-term memory

2. Understanding—Constructing meaning from instructional messages, including oral, written, and graphic communications

3. Applying—Carrying out or using a procedure in a given situation

4. Analyzing—Breaking material into its constituent parts and determining how the parts relate to one another and to an overall structure or purpose

5. Evaluating—Making judgments based on criteria and standards

6. Creating—Putting elements together to form a coherent or functional whole, reorganizing elements into a new pattern or structure

7. Being metacognitive—Being aware of one's own comprehension and being able and willing to repair comprehension breakdowns when they occur

Any of these except the first one—remembering—and perhaps the second one—understanding—has the potential to engender higher order thinking. In planning SREs, it is a simple matter to include activities requiring some or even all of them. Oftentimes, these activities come as questions for students to respond to, as in this set of questions on "Mom, Did You Vote?" a chapter from Joy Hakim's middle-grade textbook *War, Peace, and All That Jazz*.

1. Remembering—About when did Alice Paul begin her campaign for women's suffrage?

2. Understanding—Why were women denied the vote when the United States was first formed?

3. Applying—Identify some sort of social injustice that exists today, and consider ways in which tactics used by the suffragists might be used to improve the situation or draw attention to the problem.

4. Analyzing—Which of the suffragists' approaches do you think was the most effective? Why do you believe that?

5. Evaluating—Do you think the suffragists did the right thing in mounting their protests? Why or why not?

6. Creating—Suggest some tactics the suffragists did not use that might have been effective.

7. Being metacognitive—Think about your own attitude toward women having the vote, and consider how your attitude might affect your reading and understanding of the chapter.

Of course, not all these types of questions need to be asked with every selection, but over time students should get opportunities to work with all of them.

Additionally, we want to note that exactly how questions are classified is not the issue here. Many questions might be placed in several different categories of the taxonomy, and that is fine. What is important is that teachers ask many sorts of questions and that a significant number of these be higher order questions.

Sternberg (Sternberg & Spear-Swerling, 1996) takes a similar but simpler tack to categorizing types of thinking. The central thesis of Sternberg's theory is that there are three basic kinds of thinking: analytic, creative, and practical. Sternberg defines these three sorts of thinking thusly:

1. Analytic thinking involves analyzing, judging, evaluating, comparing and contrasting, and examining.
2. Creative thinking involves creating, discovering, producing, imagining, and supposing.
3. Practical thinking involves practicing, using, applying, and implementing. (p. ix)

As Sternberg (Sternberg & Spear-Swerling, 1996) notes, schools typically focus on analytic thinking and largely neglect the other two sorts. This, he argues, is very unfortunate because all three sorts of thinking are important, both in the classroom and beyond it. We very strongly concur, and we have found it extremely useful to deliberately offer students opportunities for all three sorts thinking as postreading tasks. As with Anderson and Krathwohl's (2001) system, the most straightforward way to use Sternberg's plan is to ask questions. To show how widely applicable the system is, here we present questions illustrating Sternberg's three types of question with a preschool story, "The Three Little Pigs" by Steven Kellogg and the chapter "Mom, Did You Vote?" from Joy Hakim's (2002) middle-grade textbook *A History of U.S.: War, Peace, and All That Jazz*.

"The Three Little Pigs"

1. Analytic thinking—Why isn't straw a very good building material?
2. Creative—What are some things the first little pig might have done to make his house safer from the wolf?
3. Practical thinking—Suppose you had to build a house. What material would you build it with?

"Mom, Did You Vote?"

1. Analytic thinking—Which of the suffragists' approaches do you think was the most effective? Why do you believe this?

2. Creative thinking—Suggest some tactics the suffragists did not use that might have been effective.

3. Practical thinking—Identify some sort of social injustice that exists today, and consider way in which tactics used by the suffragists might be used to improve the situation or draw attention to the problem.

As you will see if you compare the questions illustrating Sternberg's system to those illustrating Anderson and Krathwohl's system, the two systems overlap. However, we believe it is useful to consider Sternberg's scheme as well as Anderson and Krathwohl's to avoid putting too much emphasis on analytic thinking, which happens too frequently in many classrooms.

Assessing the Effects of SREs

In assessing the effects of SREs on students' understanding and learning, we have found a particular approach to generating questions a very valuable tool— the "story map" as described by Beck and McKeown (1981). This is not, we should point out, the graphic that goes by this title. As described by Beck and McKeown, a story map is a listing of the major events and ideas in a selection in the order in which they occur. To create a story map, a teacher must first identify the major elements, both explicit and implicit, of a selection. Then, a teacher must generate a question for each major element for the students to answer. These questions elicit information that is central to understanding the selection, and the answers to the questions constitute the essence of the meaning of the selection. Figure 5.1 shows a set of story map questions for Flannery O'Connor's "A Good Man Is Hard To Find," a challenging and violent story that critics had described as both disturbing and humorous and that would be read by high school students.

The answers to the story map questions are one important part of what we would expect students to know after reading a selection. Story map questions are not, however, the only questions to ask on a reading selections. Once students understand the essence of the selection, then interpretive, analytical, and creative questions are appropriate and important to pursue. For example, with "A Good Man Is Hard To Find," extension questions such as the following might be included:

Figure 5.1. Story Map Questions for "A Good Man Is Hard to Find"

1. In the beginning of the story, the grandmother clearly does not want to go to Florida. How does she try to dissuade Bailey from taking his family there?

2. Is the grandmother concerned about being a "lady?" How do we know this?

3. How does the children's perception of the South differ from the grandmother's perception of it?

4. At the restaurant, the grandmother and Sammy discuss "better times." What are some specific things they discuss?

5. Why does Bailey give into the kids' desire to visit the old plantation?

6. Immediately before the accident, the grandmother has a "horrible thought" that she decides not to share with anyone. What is this horrible thought?

7. To whom does the grandmother tell, "I know you're a good man at heart"? Under what circumstances does she tell him this?

8. Name some things that The Misfit does that are ironic?

9. The grandmother and The Misfit discuss the life of Jesus. What does The Misfit believe about Jesus?

10. Why does The Misfit "spring back as if a snake had bitten him"?

11. Do you think that the grandmother actually believes that The Misfit is one of her own children? Why do you think that she tells him that he is?

- There are several references in this story to better times when children respected their elders. Find some examples in the story of descriptions of both the past and the present society. Do you agree with these descriptions? Do you think the story gives an accurate description of present-day United States?

- This story shares many features found in Shirley Jackson's story "The Lottery." Both contain a considerable amount of foreshadowing, and the idea of "tradition" is an important concept. Discuss how these stories are both similar and different in their use of foreshadowing or in how they deal with the idea of "tradition."

There are several ways to use the story map and extension questions to assess students' comprehension and learning following an SRE. One is to have students study and answer the story map and extension questions individually and then have them or some of them discuss their responses individually with the teacher. Another is to have students write out the answers to the questions and turn them in. And still a third is to have students discuss their responses in small groups as the teacher sits in and considers the contributions of individual students. The goal is to find out if students understood and learned from reading the selection and participating in the teacher-created SRE activities and if they can make valid inferences and generalizations based on the selection. If they can, that's terrific. This is evidence that SREs are assisting students in effectively dealing with texts. If they cannot, a teacher will need to make modifications—creating stronger SREs, using different texts, giving students more time with the selections, or whatever it takes to lead students to successfully reading and learning from what they read.

Concluding Remarks

We began this chapter by describing the SRE framework and research demonstrating that SREs can be effective with students of various ages, reading abilities, and social groups; with various types of texts; and for various purposes. We next cautioned that while SREs have been shown to be effective, constructing and using them requires teachers to plan carefully and make a number of decisions. Among the decisions to be made are how frequently to use SREs, how much scaffolding to provide, how often to differentiate activities for different students, how to provide an appropriate balance between challenging and easier reading material, how to adjust postreading tasks to ensure student success, and how to involve students in constructing SREs. The majority of the chapter provided guidelines for making these decisions. We also took up the special case of using SREs to foster higher order thinking, a type of thinking particularly important in today's complex world and a type of thinking that has been shown to help students in diverse classroom succeed. Finally, we discussed the use of story maps to assess students' performance when working with SREs. We hope we have both convinced readers of the potential of SREs and assisted them with the always challenging task of fitting a particular instructional strategy to a particular classroom. That is never an easy task, but with hard work it can be a very rewarding one for teachers and students alike.

REFLECTION QUESTIONS

1. Scaffolded Reading Experiences (SREs) can be created to provide virtually any level of support your students need. A sturdy and fairly lengthy SRE can assist students in understanding a text they simply could not comprehend independently, while a much briefer and less robust SRE can be designed simply to garner students' interest in reading a particular text. Given the range of SREs you might create, how often do you think you would use SREs in your class or classes? Why you think you would use SREs this often or this seldom?

2. Differentiating SREs is quite a bit of work because you have to create more than one set of reading activities. Nevertheless, doing so can certainly be worthwhile. In what ways would this be worthwhile in your classroom?

3. One suggestion in the chapter is to simplify postreading tasks if necessary in order to ensure that all students succeed. Think about a text you might use in a class and a fairly challenging postreading task that students might do after reading that text. Then describe a postreading task that is considerably simpler and therefore more doable by students who may struggle with reading.

4. Another suggestion in the chapter is to involve students in creating SREs. Consider the age and ability levels of your students and describe some parts of SREs that they could create or at least help you create. Also consider and discuss the pros and cons of have older students create SREs for younger students.

5. Identify a text you use in your classroom and construct some questions that promote analytic thinking, some that promote creative thinking, and some that create practical thinking.

REFERENCES

Anderson, L.W., & Krathwohl, D.R. (2001). *A taxonomy for learning, teaching, and assessing. A revision of Bloom's Taxonomy of Educational Objectives*. New York: Longman.

Beck, I.L., & McKeown, M.G. (1981). Developing questions that promote comprehension: The story map. *Language Arts, 58*(8), 913–918.

Bloom, B.S. (1956). *The taxonomy of educational objectives: Handbook I: Cognitive domain*. New York: David McKay.

Cohen, P.A., Kulik, J.A., & Kulik, C.C. (1982). Educational outcomes of tutoring: A meta-analysis of findings. *American Educational Research Journal, 19*(2), 237–248.

Cooke, C.L. (2001). *The effects of scaffolded multicultural short stories on students' comprehension, response, and attitudes.* Unpublished doctoral dissertation, University of Minnesota.

Fournier, D.N.E., & Graves, M.F. (2002). Scaffolding adolescents' comprehension of short stories. *Journal of Adolescent & Adult Literacy, 46*(1), 30–39.

Gardner, H. (1983). *Frames of mind: The theory of multiple intelligences.* New York: Basic.

Gardner, H. (2003, April). *Multiple intelligences after 20 years.* Invited address presented at the annual meeting of the American Educational Research Association, Chicago.

Graves, M.F., Juel, C., & Graves, B.B. (2007). *Teaching reading in the 21st century* (4th ed.). Boston: Allyn & Bacon.

Graves, M.F., & Liang, L.A. (2003). Online resources for fostering understanding and higher-level thinking in senior high school students. In D. Schallert, C. Fairbanks, J. Worthy, B. Maloch, & J. Hoffman (Eds.), *51st yearbook of the National Reading Conference* (pp. 204–215). Oak Creek, WI: National Reading Conference.

Graves, M.F., Palmer, R.J., & Furniss, D.W. (1976). *Structuring reading activities for English classes.* Urbana, IL: National Council of Teachers of English.

Herber, H.L. (1970). *Teaching reading in content areas.* Englewood Cliffs, NJ: Prentice-Hall.

Juel, C. (1996). What makes literacy tutoring effective? *Reading Research Quarterly, 31*(3), 268–289. doi:10.1598/RRQ.31.3.3

Liang, L.A. (2004). *Using scaffolding to foster middle school students' comprehension of and response to short stories.* Unpublished doctoral dissertation, University of Minnesota.

Liang, L.A., Peterson, C., & Graves, M.F. (2005). Investigating two approaches to fostering children's comprehension of literature. *Reading Psychology, 26*(4/5), 387–400. doi:10.1080/027027 10500285748

McKeachie, W.J., Svinicki, M.D., & Hofer, B.K. (2006). *McKeachie's teaching tips: Strategies, research, and theory for college and university teachers* (12th ed.). Boston: Houghton Mifflin.

Resnick, L.G. (1987). *Education and learning to think.* Washington, DC: National Academy Press. Retrieved March 24, 2009, from books.nap.edu/catalog/1032.html

Sternberg, R.J., & Spear-Swerling, L. (1996). *Teaching for thinking.* Washington, DC: American Psychological Association.

Taylor, B.M., Pearson, P.D., Clark, K., & Walpole, S. (2002). Effective schools and accomplished teachers: Lessons about primary grade reading instruction in low-income schools. *The Elementary School Journal, 101*(2), 121–165. doi:10.1086/499662

Taylor, B.M., Pressley, M., & Pearson, P.D. (2002). Research-supported characteristics of teachers and schools that promote reading achievement. In B.M. Taylor & P.D. Pearson (Eds.), *Teaching reading: Effective schools, accomplished teachers* (pp. 361–373). Mahwah, NJ: Erlbaum.

Utah State Office of Education. (2006). *Cross-age tutoring.* Salt Lake City, UT. Author.

Watts, S.M., & Rothenberg, S.S. (1997). Students with learning difficulties meet Shakespeare: Using a scaffolded reading experience. *Journal of Adolescent & Adult Literacy, 40*(7), 532–539.

CHAPTER 6

Developing Language and Literacy in Science: Differentiated and Integrated Instruction for ELLs

Fay Shin, Robert Rueda, Christyn Simpkins, and Hyo Jin Lim

English language learners (ELLs) present a specific set of challenges to educators because of difficulties in the acquisition of academic language proficiency and content area knowledge (Francis, Rivera, Lesaux, Kieffer, & Rivera, 2006). Like other populations of learners with academic challenges, underachieving ELLs require specialized instruction and interventions to prevent further difficulties. Therefore, educators must become knowledgeable about and also continue to develop effective instructional practices and interventions to augment and support academic attainment for these students.

The primary goal of this chapter is to present an approach to effective instruction in science education for ELLs. Our approach attempts to describe instruction in science education for ELLs that is differentiated (from a language acquisition perspective) and integrated (language and content instruction) with the goal of promoting growth in English language development (ELD) *and* scientific knowledge and skills. Thus, this framework shares Huntley's notion of "synergistic integration" in effective language instruction, which emphasizes the interaction and mutual supports for two different disciplines (Stoddart, Pinal, Latzke, & Canaday, 2002). This view of integration also focuses on the reciprocal processes in science and language learning; effective language instruction enhances the learning of science concepts, and effective science instruction fosters language and literacy development and promotes the development of higher order thinking skills (Casteel & Isom, 1994). In addition to describing our approach, we also demonstrate how Christyn, a chapter author and sixth-grade teacher, planned and implemented differentiated and integrated instruction in her sixth-grade language arts classroom that enrolled ELLs with a wide range of English language and literacy skills.

Special Considerations in Teaching Language and Content to ELLs

Achievement Gaps

In all grades and content areas, results from national assessments show that ELLs fall behind their native English-speaking peers. In 2007, only 7.5% of fourth-grade ELLs achieved at or above the proficient level in National Assessment of Educational Progress (NAEP) reading test, compared with 35.5% of native English speakers (Lee, Grigg, & Donahue, 2007). The situation is similar in mathematics achievement; only 12.9% of fourth-grade ELLs scored at or above proficient level, while 42.2% of native English speakers scored at or above the same level (Lee, Grigg, & Dion, 2007).

In science, 2005 NAEP test results show that only 4% of fourth-grade ELLs scored at or above the proficient level, compared with 31% of native English-speaking students. Also, 28% of fourth-grade students identified as ELLs performed at or above basic level, while 71% of English-speaking peers achieved at that level (Grigg, Lauko, & Brockway, 2006). Although ELLs' test performance is confounded by the fact that their lack of English proficiency interferes with their ability to demonstrate content knowledge, it is important to note that these statistics on performance suggest that two thirds of fourth-grade ELLs do not demonstrate the knowledge and reasoning required for understanding the earth, physical, and life sciences at grade-appropriate levels. That is, they are not able to carry out basic investigations and read uncomplicated graphs and diagrams and do not demonstrate understanding of classification, simple relationships, and energy.

Taken together, these assessment data show that ELLs face many difficulties on the road to academic success. Of major concern are the numbers of students who struggle with literacy in general—and vocabulary in particular, one of the key components in academic language and reading comprehension.

Within-Group Diversity

Although ELLs are often considered a unitary group, there are many within-group differences. These differences include culture, language and language proficiency, socioeconomic status (SES), immigration history and status, amount of schooling in the native language, and family constellation (e.g., single versus dual parent families, nuclear versus extended families, and so forth) to name a few. These differences or factors play a role in an ELL's opportunity to learn because they influence other factors such as background knowledge and life experiences, print environment, access to adults with extended school literacy experience, development of academic language, and perspectives on education. Each factor may have an independent effect on language, literacy, and learning, but these factors often interact in complex ways as well.

Science Instruction and ELLs

In science, perhaps more than in other domains, language is critical. In some cases, there are words used primarily in academic/scientific contexts (e.g., *diameter, condense*) but not commonly used in everyday settings. In other cases, there are words with equivalent meanings that are used mainly in one or the other context (e.g., *gather* in everyday settings and *collate* in academic settings; Bailey, 2007; Maatta, Dobb, & Ostlund, 2006). Researchers and practitioners concerned with ELLs have come to recognize the importance of academic language, or Academic English as it is sometimes called, as a unique dimension of general language acquisition, especially as it relates to science achievement. In spite of some controversy (MacSwan, 2000) over the "privileging" of Academic English over other, especially everyday forms of discourse or language, most educators and parents believe that students need to become proficient in Academic English. Because of its importance to the ELL population, we begin this section with a brief overview of this area.

Academic Language and Literacy

Critical language and literacy skills that are essential to acquiring scientific content knowledge are problematic for ELLs. Some of these key skills include demonstrating facility with technical vocabulary and concepts, writing and following procedures, reviewing information, summarizing data, constructing logical arguments, responding to critical analysis of peers or teachers, and communicating results for a variety of different audiences with a specific focus on the expository genres associated with science. Often, little attention is paid to teaching these necessary skills to ELLs, even in inquiry-based science programs. The acquisition of Academic English, therefore, is a significant issue for ELLs, particularly those who are not exposed to highly literate peers, adults, and environments with school-based experience and knowledge (August & Hakuta, 1997; Bailey, 2007; Scarcella, 2003). Promoting competence in academic language is complex for these learners because it involves teaching academic subjects such as science while teaching literacy and language skills at the same time.

Academic literacy is fundamental to school success, including science, and to succeed in everyday life beyond school, increasingly sophisticated levels of literacy knowledge and skills are required (Moore, Bean, Birdyshaw, & Rycik, 1999). These forms of "high literacy" include the following:

> the ability to use language, content, and reasoning in ways that are appropriate for particular situations and disciplines. Students learn to "read" the social meanings, the rules and structures, and the linguistic and cognitive routines to make things work in the real world of English language use, and that knowledge becomes available as options when students confront new situations. This notion of high literacy refers to understanding how reading, writing, language, content, and social appropriateness work together and using this knowledge in effective ways. It is reflected in students' ability to engage in thoughtful reading, writing, and discussion about content in the classroom, to put their knowledge and skills to use in new situations and to perform well on reading and writing assessments including high stakes testing. (Langer, 2001, p. 838)

Some educational researchers have taken an empirical approach to operationalize the components of academic literacy demonstrating that it is characterized by unique and recognizable features. Butler, Lord, Stevens, Borrego, and Bailey (2004), for example, focus on organizational features, language functions, structural features, and lexical features in the contexts of science, math, and English as a second language (ESL) standards, textbooks in science and math, and analysis of videotapes of classroom instruction. Common language functions across all three contexts included classification, comparison and contrast, definition, description, evaluation, explanation, inference, and labeling. Butler and colleagues' (2004) analysis suggests that there is an identifiable science register that uses academic language features that include formulating hypotheses, proposing alternative solutions, describing, classifying, using time and spatial relations, inferring, interpreting data, predicting, generalizing, and communicating findings (National Research Council, 1996; National Science Teachers Association, 1991).

We take the view that *both* scientific content knowledge and language acquisition are necessary for meaningful academic success for all students—but especially ELLs. Our position is that integrating science and language acquisition enhances rather than hinders either domain. The subject matter content provides a meaningful context for the learning of academic language structure and functions, and the language provides the medium for analysis and communication of subject matter knowledge (Stoddart et al., 2002). This integrated approach builds on studies that have successfully attempted to integrate science instruction with academic literacy (Casteel & Isom, 1994; Gasking et al., 1994; Keys, 1994; Palincsar & Magnussen, 2000; Rivard, 1994).

Current Approaches for Science Education in ELLs

Although many teachers do not feel competent to teach science due to inadequate course work or training, especially to ELLs (Gándara, Maxwell-Jolly, & Driscoll, 2005), there is a growing body of work that provides some guidance, and important progress is being made in work that targets ELLs specifically. In much of this work, researchers and practitioners have emphasized effective instruction and interventions for ELLs that are quite similar to those found in research on science instruction conducted with monolingual English speakers but include attention to building English language knowledge and skills.

A dominant perspective in elementary science teaching and learning, including that with ELLs, is based on theoretical approaches with strong roots in cognitive psychology and constructivism (Cobern, 1993; Crowther, Vilá, & Fathman, 2006; Gibbons, 2003). Much of this work focuses on students' engagement in science learning activities, in particular "active learning" or "inquiry learning" (Bybee, 2002; National Research Council, 2000) that includes participation in a variety of meaningful activities including problem solving and critical thinking with real-world application. The goal for the active learning is to develop and construct knowledge through physical and mental activities including hands-on experience in experimentation and investigation through observing, collecting and analyzing data to replicate research, and exploring new questions. From this perspective, effective teachers need to structure learning environments to foster experiences that enhance students' knowledge application in the real world. The guiding principles of constructivism in science teaching suggest teachers utilize problems relevant to students and structure learning around primary concepts and students' suppositions (Brooks & Brooks, 1993).

Lee (2005) conducted a review of research on science education and ELLs. She categorized work into the following areas: science learning (including cultural beliefs and practices, scientific reasoning and argumentation, and linguistic influences on science learning), science curriculum, science instruction (including culturally congruent instruction, cognitively based instruction, and instruction focused on linguistic processes), science assessment, and science teacher education. Lee identified some general important patterns in the research that are worth noting in the context of the present discussion. Some of the major conclusions were as follows:

- There is a surprising number of studies with ELLs overall (over 40 studies total between 1982 and 2004, but most after the mid-1990s)—but research in specific subareas is limited.

- The research tends to use different research traditions and approaches and is sometimes contradictory. For example, Kearsey and Turner (1999) find positive effects of home language for science learning, where other research focuses on limitations (Lynch, 1996a, 1996b). Experimental or quasi-experimental studies were rare.

- Cultural and linguistic factors seem to be important in science learning for ELLs but are rarely considered in general education science classrooms.

- Research conducted outside of the United States was more likely to focus on the role that the home language plays in science learning than research conducted in the United States.

- Efforts to assess science learning reflect different views on ELLs (i.e., either to eliminate home language and culture or to understand and incorporate home language and culture to guide assessment efforts).

- Most teachers assume that ELLs must acquire English before learning content area subject matter such as science, even though it often leads to achievement gaps with English-speaking peers.

- There were *no* studies found on preservice teacher education for science instruction for ELLs; there are only a small number of studies that address professional development, and these suggest that both teacher beliefs and attitudes as well as student science outcomes can be affected and approved.

- There were only a few examples of programmatic research, for example the Science for All Project (Lee, 2002) and the Chèche Konnen Project (Roseberry, Warren, & Conant, 1992).

In summary, there is a growing body of work on various aspects of science education for ELLs and students from diverse cultural backgrounds. As Lee's (2005) review indicates, however, there are many areas that have not been systematically covered, and significant work needs to be done to have a stronger research base to guide practice.

Despite these gaps in the research, increased attention to teaching science to ELLs has resulted in an expanding literature (Carrasquillo & Rodriguez, 2005; Dobb, 2004; Fathman & Crowther, 2006; Fradd, Lee, Sutman, & Saxton, 2001; Gibbons, 2003; Hampton & Rodriguez, 2001; Lee, 2005) that suggests several guidelines for teachers as they plan and implement science instruction for ELLs:

- Students' language and experience should be seen as instructional resources rather than obstacles to learning and achievement.

- Instructional activities should be differentiated by learners' language proficiency levels.

- Materials and activities should build on language that is meaningful and comprehensible as a foundation and entrée into science.

- Learning should be promoted as an active process in which students are given opportunities and support to engage the content.

- Instructional planning should attend to affective (motivational) factors such as connections to students' existing interests and experience.

- Materials and activities should provide scaffolding designed to promote self-regulation (i.e., increased student independence and control over their own learning).

- Teaching and activities should be responsive, that is, beginning where the learner is and shifting the type and amount of assistance as needed. All students should be held to the same challenging content so that what varies is the level of assistance rather than the content.

- All activities should emphasize the close connections among reading, writing, listening, and speaking.

We turn our attention to differentiated and integrated language and content instruction in classroom practice. We begin with a discussion of the role of an ESL program and classroom grouping practices in this instructional approach, and we provide some examples of how teachers might integrate language and content instruction.

Grouping Students for Instruction

A major factor in effective differentiated and integrated language and content instruction for ELLs is that students receive instruction appropriate to their level of English proficiency and that the instruction addresses their language and literacy learning needs. Ideally, if it is practical and realistic, one teacher should teach one class of students at the same proficiency level during this time. In fact, some schools with large populations of ELLs do currently follow a model where students from one grade level are grouped according to their proficiency levels for one period of the day or alternatively during a designated ESL time within the grade-level language arts period. Some models even forgo traditional grade-level groupings and group students according to English proficiency level. For example in some classrooms, sixth- and seventh-grade ELLs at the beginning level may learn together. This configuration makes it possible for the teacher to provide instruction at one English proficiency level. In California, for example, the ELD standards group grade levels K–2, 3–5, 6–8 and 9–12 together according to English proficiency levels (Ong, 2002). It is important to note, however, that caution must be taken not to exceed these recommended grade-level grouping arrangements to ensure that all students receive age- and grade-appropriate instruction.

Although having an ESL class where all students are at the same proficiency level is ideal, we recognize that for the majority of classrooms this is not possible. More often, the typical classroom enrolls ELLs with differing English proficiency levels. Furthermore, these classrooms may also include students who are fluent or native English speakers. Therefore, teachers must consider their teaching schedules and student populations as they plan and implement integrated language and content instruction. In classrooms of students with different levels of English proficiency, successful language and content integration occurs when teachers provide (a) whole-group instruction that is comprehensible to all students and (b) small-group instruction that is differentiated according to language needs. We address grouping practices in the following sections, and then we turn out attention to language arts activities that may be used to support content learning.

Whole-Group Instruction

During this time, both fluent English speakers and ELLs are taught together in order to provide an introduction to the lesson, build background knowledge, and address motivational considerations. This part of the lesson is crucial for gaining students' interest and finding out how much they know about the particular topic. During whole-group instruction, teachers set a foundation for guided inquiry that allows students to become engaged and use information to reason through a scientific issue, master concepts, and complete oral and written projects. Most important, during this time instruction must be *comprehensible* to all students, regardless of English proficiency. Some ways that teachers make content comprehensible are by (a) showing students realia (fruits, plants, animals, rocks) and encouraging students to touch and share what they know about each object; (b) showing students pictures or models related to the science content; or (c) providing an activity where students can observe, predict, classify, and analyze objects. These activities can take the form of an experiment, a nature walk to study the environment, an outdoor weather-related investigation, or seed planting to study the life cycle of a plant. During whole-class instruction, new vocabulary is clearly displayed, and graphic organizers (tables, charts, graphs, Venn diagrams) are used to capture student responses about what they know and learn about the topic under investigation. All of these teaching activities help to ensure that all students have access to the science content and language they need for success.

Differentiated Instruction

Differentiated instruction is the time when teachers group students according to English proficiency levels and provide small-group instruction that addresses students' needs. The most common proficiency level groupings are Level 1—Beginning, Level 2—Intermediate, Level 3—Advanced, and Fluent English speakers. The teacher works with each group for 10–15 minutes, providing instruction appropriate to the language proficiency level ensuring that all students have access to the same science content. While the teacher is working with one small group, the other groups are working in learning centers, on independent reading activities, or on supplemental activities that support the science theme. Some suggested learning center activities, which may also be differentiated according to proficiency level, include a short reading assignment, a group oral or written project, or vocabulary activities such as word–picture match cards, memory game cards, or word definition cards (Shin, 2005/2006).

In addition to providing whole-group instruction that is comprehensible to all students and small-group instruction that targets students' needs, teachers also must pay attention to the integration of language and content instruction. Incorporating poetry and using carefully designed graphic organizers are two examples of how language arts can be integrated with science instruction.

Integrating Language and Content Instruction

Poetry

Integrating poetry with science is an excellent way to allow students to creatively express their understanding of science concepts as they build word knowledge and sentence-level skills. Poetry brings a sense of meaning and experiences together in words and sentences. In addition, when students create poems, teachers can assess students' comprehension and personal interpretation of what they learned. We provide examples of two types of poetry that allow students to write and share their reflections through word play.

Diamante Poem. This is a seven-line poem written in the shape of a diamond. This form helps students apply their knowledge of the subject, opposites, and parts of speech. This takes a lot of thought and is not as easy as it looks.

Line 1: one noun as the subject

Line 2: two adjectives describing the subject

Line 3: three verbs or participles (ending in –ing)

Line 4: four nouns (two related to the subject and two related to the opposite)

Line 5: three verbs telling about the opposite

Line 6: two adjectives describing the opposite

Line 7: one noun that is the opposite

Following is an example of this type of poem:

Elephants

big, gray

exciting, standing, eating

animal, zoo, fish, bird

boring, jumping, flying

small, colorful

mouse

Children often like to make their own choices and interpretations of words or concepts with diamante poems. When children know the topic and the parts of speech, teachers can combine both grammar and content by using patterns that create a verse for a poem (for example, the word "elephant" is a noun that can be described in several ways).

Biopoem. Another type of poem that supports language and content learning is the biopoem. Although the biopoem may be used to explore a scientist or a well-known figure in the science word, it may also be used to personify a scientific term or concept.

I am _____.

I feel _____.

I think _____.

I like _____.

I don't like _____.

I have _____.

I _____.

Following is an example of this type of poem:

I am the sun.

I feel hot.

I think people like me.

I like to make the earth warm.

I am made of hydrogen and helium.

I have light.

I provide heat.

This version of the biopoem allows students to deepen their content knowledge as they express their thoughts and feelings as if they were an object. Students integrate the facts they have learned about the topic and use their imagination to create a poem. Sentence prompts or "starters" are used to scaffold the writing of the poem.

Graphic Organizers

Well-constructed graphic organizers can be used to support students during a science investigation that integrates reading and writing. For example, one of the science standards used by teachers in California is that students know how to observe and describe similarities and differences in appearance and behavior of plants and animals. As students compare and sort plants or animals by one physical attribute (color, shape, texture, size, weight), a variety of graphic organizers including tables, Venn diagrams, flowcharts, and double-entry journals can be used to record and organize data from observations and scaffold attempts to compose written responses such as a paragraph about similarities and differences between two plants or animals. Graphic organizers such as semantic maps, clusters, webs, charts, and Venn diagrams are effective for helping ELLs see how words are related to one another. Students can also brainstorm words related to the science topic and classify the words as they record them on a cluster or semantic map.

In the following section, we share Christyn's successes and challenges as she planned and implemented differentiated and integrated language and content instruction with her sixth-grade ELLs. We begin with some background information about Christyn, her school, and her language arts classroom.

Implementing Differentiated and Integrated Language and Content Instruction With Sixth-Grade ELLs: Christyn's Story

Background

Christyn is a sixth-grade general education teacher with 13 years of teaching experience. Christyn teaches all subject areas including ESL, a school requirement. Like most teachers in California, Christyn possesses a Cross Cultural Language Development credential that allows her to teach ELLs.

Christyn's urban school district has a student population of approximately 34,000, and most students are minorities: 45% Hispanic, 21% Southeast Asian, 13% African American, and 16% Caucasian. Over half of the students (67%) receive free or reduced-cost lunch. In addition, 35% of the students are ELLs. Students in Christyn's school are grouped heterogeneously for content area classes such as mathematics and social studies; however, students are grouped according to English proficiency level for language arts instruction. At the time of the classroom implementation described in this chapter, Christyn's language arts class was composed entirely of students classified as ELLs. Therefore, Christyn also taught ESL during this class period.

As in many other urban classrooms, there was great diversity in terms of language proficiency among the 30 ELLs in Christyn's classroom. For example, there was one new student with very few English language skills and who was considered a beginner, four or five students at the intermediate level, and the rest of the students were at the advanced level. Most of the advanced-level students had been at that same level for several years. Many of these students appeared to be orally proficient, and they had adequate reading comprehension skills. They performed far below grade level in writing, however. These poor writing skills and the students' poor performance on the California English Language Development Test prevented the students from being reclassified as Fluent English proficient. And as in other urban areas, high student mobility rates was also a challenge that Christyn faced. Christyn's class enrollment was 30 students, yet typically only 15 of those students attended the class for the entire school year.

ESL Instruction and Instructional Materials

Christyn taught ESL 45 minutes daily as part of her daily 90-minute language arts class. On Mondays and Fridays, Christyn taught ESL using the district-adopted core ESL/language arts curriculum and accompanying reading and grammar materials. Christyn used the ESL time at the beginning of the week to prepare students for the weekly reading selection. For example, students engaged in previewing and predicting activities, and Christyn taught vocabulary and grammar necessary for success with the reading selection. On Fridays, ESL time was devoted to reviewing the reading selection.

Christyn was dissatisfied with her students' progress using this approach. Aside from the vocabulary and previewing and predicting activities, she found that much of the ESL time was consumed by reteaching grammar skills as students completed workbook pages. This approach, according to Christyn, did little to increase test performance or writing skills. For example, although students could locate and correct errors on Daily Oral Language worksheets, they were unable to edit their own writing. Christyn believed that her students needed opportunities to write for authentic purposes and learn strategies for comprehending informational text and vocabulary that would be useful across the curriculum. Therefore, on Tuesdays, Wednesdays, and Thursdays, Christyn devoted the 45 minutes of ESL time to teaching language embedded within content-based science lessons. To do so, Christyn used a variety of language-teaching strategies and techniques to provide comprehensible input to her students. For example, during a whole-group lesson on the environment, students viewed pictures of different environments and took a walk outside the school to observe living and nonliving things in their immediate environment. Back in the classroom, students worked in heterogeneous groups to create mobiles using pictures to demonstrate their understanding of living and nonliving objects in their environment. Christyn then provided differentiated instruction as she grouped students according to their proficiency levels to teach language- and literacy-related skills. During this time, Christyn's beginning-level student labeled orally and in writing key parts of his mobile. Christyn's intermediate-level students worked on composing a short paragraph in which they described their mobiles, and the advanced-level students read and responded orally and in writing to a text about the environment using content-related vocabulary (Shin, 2005/2006).

Integrated Instruction

As Christyn planned and implemented integrated language and content instruction, she noted several successes. These included (a) opportunities to provide her students with comprehensible input necessary for language learning, (b) opportunities to build oral language skills, (c) attention to vocabulary building, and (d) use of effective strategies beyond the language arts classroom.

Providing Comprehensible Input. Christyn found that the integrated language and science lessons provided daily opportunities to provide her students with the comprehensible input they needed to learn in and about their second language. For example, Christyn found that many concepts and terms could be demonstrated and thus understood more fully during the ESL/science lesson than when students were exposed to a written text only as was the case in the traditional ESL curriculum. For example, during a weather unit, students acted out the spinning motion of air currents ensuring all grasped the concept in a very short time. Christyn routinely used realia to help her students learn science concepts and vocabulary. When Christyn wanted her students to learn about cells as "building blocks," she and her students used math manipulatives to put together "blocks" of cells to make a stem, a leaf, a heart, and an eye. Christyn also used pictures and diagrams to help her students learn. Using pictures was particularly helpful for the students with lowest levels of proficiency as these students participated in the lessons first by pointing to pictures before they began using the oral and written language associated with each science theme. Students learned how to use a variety of graphic organizers such as Venn diagrams to record what they were learning such as differences between plant and animal cells. Christyn found that after students participated in these activities designed to make content comprehensible, language and literacy tasks such as sharing findings orally with group members, identifying terms, or reading and responding to the science text were far less formidable.

Oral Language Development. Embedding language instruction within a content area provided meaningful opportunities for students to develop oral language skills. Christyn found that for her students "it was far more real to doing science than learning English." Group work as students completed vocabulary activities and oral and written final products connected to each science theme promoted purposeful talk among the students. As students worked in small groups, they freely used a home language, English, or a combination of a home language and English. Students routinely presented results of their group projects orally, and they embraced the need to use English at this time because it was the one language shared by all class members. For many students, the group presentation was the safest place to talk, and even limited English speakers participated using gestures as more proficient group members provided the information orally.

Building Vocabulary. Christyn found that she provided more opportunities for her students to learn and use new vocabulary during the integrated language and content lessons. For example, when introducing a new concept or theme, Christyn and the students mapped out keywords as a whole class and arrived at working definitions. Christyn also provided differentiated vocabulary instruction according to proficiency levels. Working in small groups, students created posters that included the assigned vocabulary, definitions written in their own words, a sentence using each new word, and a visual representation of each word to help students remember word meanings. Students then presented their word work orally to the class to provide pronunciation practice. Although students worked on words appropriate to their language proficiency levels, the presentations ensured that each student was exposed to all of the new vocabulary associated with the science theme. Christyn then displayed the posters to provide support for students as they read. Christyn also provided many opportunities to students to use their newly learned words such as in the following acrostic poem from a unit on extreme weather.

Warm

Extreme weather

Air pressure

Thunder storm

Heat wave

Evaporate

Rain storms

Beyond the Language Arts Classroom. Christyn found that many of the strategies and activities that she used with her students during the integrated language and content lessons were useful as she taught in other content areas. She first began to apply the teaching strategies in her science class and later in her social studies and math classes. For example, vocabulary activities first introduced in the ESL/language arts classroom were equally helpful to the students as they read their social studies text or tackled word problems. In addition, in social studies class students began to dramatize some of the historical events they were studying. They found that similar to the science demonstrations in their language arts/ESL class, these dramatizations helped them more fully understand the social studies content. And although much of the science vocabulary learned during the ESL/science lesson was subject specific, students encountered many of their newly learned words in other content areas and made connections to their earlier learning. According to Christyn, "It was always a wonderful moment to be reading in social studies or math and have one of the students say, 'Hey wait a minute. That's the thing we read about in ESL yesterday!'"

Although Christyn and her students experienced many successes using an integrated and differentiated approach to language and literacy learning, she also noted some challenges that she will continue to address.

Ongoing Challenges

It was an ongoing challenge to ensure that all students had the necessary vocabulary knowledge to successfully complete language and literacy tasks. For example, Christyn's students routinely made and confirmed predictions as they read. Yet when asked to do so as they read a passage about the ocean during one ESL/science lesson, many students struggled. Christyn quickly discovered that she had mistakenly assumed that her students knew the meaning of the word *coastal*, and therefore, she did not anticipate that she needed to preteach this word prior to assigning the reading passage. Christyn found that even with the increased attention to teaching vocabulary in the integrated lessons she frequently had to stop a lesson to address these gaps in vocabulary. Christyn also believed that she was successfully differentiating instruction according to a student's proficiency level, yet she identified meeting the needs of students with such a wide range of proficiency levels as an ongoing challenge that had to be faced daily. Finally, Christyn found that even though students were writing more during the integrated language and content lessons she was not satisfied with the overall quality of the written products. According to Christyn, "Oftentimes this was because of time pressures. Over and over again we ran out of time before I felt [the students] had gotten what they needed to get out of the writing pieces. This is the area I find that I would like to work to improve the most. I need to find and put into place more scaffolds to help students write thoughtful, detailed, descriptive sentences and thorough paragraphs."

Despite these challenges, Christyn found that overall her students experienced more success with content-based lessons than with her former approach to ESL instruction. She plans to continue to differentiate and integrate language and science instruction to meet the diverse needs of her ELLs.

What Else Can Be Done to Raise Science Achievement?

Although there are guidelines for best practice and the availability of good models of instruction, there is some evidence that many teachers lack a sense of self-efficacy in teaching science content. For example, the results of a recent large-scale study of teachers in California demonstrated that teachers indicated a strong need for help in the areas of ELD and content teaching such as science

(Gándara et al., 2005). This suggests a strong need for professional development in this area so that all students can benefit.

In addition to consideration of investing in teacher development, there may be other avenues to help improve science achievement. For example, in a Hierarchical Linear Model analysis of NAEP science data, Von Secker (2004) found that protective factors may mitigate what are often called "risk factors" for low science achievement (low SES, ethnic minority status, and gender). The protective factors included parental education, home environment, attitudes and beliefs about science, and quality of instructional opportunities. Intervening in these domains may be an important way of influencing student outcomes. These results suggest that low achievement in science is not inevitable for students who do not as a group do well and that there are points for strategic intervention both in and out of the classroom.

An additional factor to consider in improving science instruction is re-examining how we as a nation approach the task. Large-scale, cross-national comparisons of how science is taught suggests some important differences between the United States and four other countries that outperform U.S. students on science achievement (National Center for Education Statistics, 2006). Although there were commonalities as well as differences among the high-achieving countries (Czech Republic, Australia, Japan, and the Netherlands), one commonality was holding students to some type of high content standards. In the United States, there was more variety in terms of organizational structures, content, and activities, and typically these features did not make the science content coherent and challenging. Thus, there remains work to be done not only for ELLs but also for all students.

REFLECTION QUESTIONS

1. What strategies do you use currently in your classroom to meet the language, literacy, and content area learning needs of ELLs who are at different levels of English proficiency?

2. Based on Christyn's experiences, what additional strategies might you try?

3. What are some ways that you might differentiate and integrate language and literacy instruction in your science lessons? What are some ways you might differentiate and integrate language and literacy instruction in other content areas such as social studies?

REFERENCES

August, D., & Hakuta, K. (Eds.). (1997). *Improving schooling for language minority children: A research agenda*. Washington, DC: National Academy Press.

Bailey, A.L. (2007). *The language demands of school: Putting academic English to the test*. New Haven: Yale University Press.

Brooks, J., & Brooks, M. (1993). *In search of understanding: The case for a constructivist classroom*. Alexandra, VA: Association for Supervision and Curriculum Development.

Butler, F.A., Lord, C., Stevens, R., Borrego, M., & Bailey, A.L. (2004). *An approach to operationalizing academic language for language test development purposes: Evidence from fifth-grade science and math*. Los Angeles, CA: Center for the Study of Evaluation, National Center for Research on Evaluation, Standards, and Student Testing.

Bybee, R.W. (2002). *Learning science and the science of learning*. Arlington, VA: National Science Teachers Association.

Carrasquillo, A., & Rodriguez, V. (2005). Integrating language and science learning. In P.A. Richard-Amato & M.A. Snow (Eds.), *Academic success for English language learners* (pp. 436–454). White Plains, NY: Longman.

Casteel, C.P., & Isom, B.A. (1994). Reciprocal processes in science and literacy learning. *The Reading Teacher, 47*(7), 538–545.

Cobern, W.W. (1993). Contextual constructivism: The impact of culture on the learning and teaching of science. In K. Tobin (Ed.), *The practice of constructivism in science education* (pp. 51–69). Hillsdale, NJ: Erlbaum.

Crowther, D.T., Vilá, J.S., & Fathman, A.K. (2006). Learners, programs, and teaching practices. In A.K. Fathman & D.T. Crowther (Eds.), *Science for English language learners: K–12 classroom strategies* (pp. 9–21). Arlington, VA: National Science Teachers Association.

Dobb, F. (2004). *Essential elements of effective science instruction for English learners* (2nd ed.). Los Angeles, CA: California Science Project.

Fathman, A.K., & Crowther, D.T. (2006). *Science for English language learners: K–12 classroom strategies*. Arlington, VA: National Science Teachers Association.

Fradd, S.H., Lee, O., Sutman, F.X., & Saxton, M.K. (2001). Materials development promoting science inquiry with English language learners: A case study. *Bilingual Research Journal, 25*(4), 479–501.

Francis, D.J., Rivera, M., Lesaux, N., Kieffer, M., & Rivera, H. (2006). *Practical guidelines for the education of English language learners: Research-based recommendations for instruction and academic interventions*. Portsmouth, NH: RMC Research Corporation, Center on Instruction.

Gándara, P.C., Maxwell-Jolly, J., & Driscoll, A. (2005). *A survey of California teachers' challenges, experiences, and professional development needs*. Santa Cruz, CA: Center for the Future of Teaching and Learning.

Gasking, I.W., Guthrie, J.T., Satlow, E., Ostertag, J., Six, L., Byrne, J., et al. (1994). Integrating instruction of science, reading, and writing: Goals, teacher development, and assessment. *Journal of Research in Science Teaching, 31*(9), 1039–1056.

Gibbons, B.A. (2003). Supporting elementary science education for English learners: A constructivist evaluation instrument. *The Journal of Educational Research, 96*(6), 371–379.

Grigg, W., Lauko, M., & Brockway, D. (2006). *The nation's report card: Science 2005* (NCES 2006-466). Washington, DC: U.S. Government Printing Office.

Hampton, E., & Rodriguez, R. (2001). Inquiry science in bilingual classrooms. *Bilingual Research Journal, 25*(4), 461–478.

Kearsey, J., & Turner, S. (1999). The value of bilingualism in pupils' understanding of scientific language. *International Journal of Science Education, 21*(10), 1037–1050. doi:10.1080/095006999290174

Keys, C.W. (1994). The development of scientific reasoning skills in conjunction with collaborative writing assignments: An interpretive study of six ninth-grade students. *Journal of Research in Science Teaching, 31*(9), 1003–1022.

Langer, J.A. (2001). Beating the odds: Teaching middle and high school students to read and write well. *American Educational Research Journal, 38*(4), 837–880. doi:10.3102/00028312038004837

Lee, O. (2002). Science inquiry for elementary students from diverse backgrounds. In W.G. Secada (Ed.), *Review of research in education* (Vol. 26, pp. 23–69). Washington, DC: American Educational Research Association.

Lee, O. (2005). Science education with English language learners: Synthesis and research agenda. *Review of Educational Research, 75*(4), 491–530. doi:10.3102/00346543075004491

Lee, J., Grigg, W.S., & Dion, G.S. (2007). *The nation's report card: Mathematics 2007* (NCES 2007-494). Washington, DC: U.S. Department of Education.

Lee, J., Grigg, W.S., & Donahue, P.L. (2007). *The nation's report card: Reading 2007* (NCES 2007-496). Washington, DC: U.S. Department of Education.

Lynch, M. (1996a). Students' alternative frameworks: Linguistic and cultural interpretations based on a study of a western-tribal continuum. *International Journal of Science Education, 18*(3), 321–332. doi:10.1080/0950069960180305

Lynch, M. (1996b). Students' alternative frameworks for the nature of matter: A cross-cultural study of linguistic and cultural interpretations. *International Journal of Science Education, 18*(6), 743–752. doi:10.1080/0950069960180607

Maatta, D., Dobb, F., & Ostlund, K. (2006). Strategies for teaching science to English learners. In A.K. Fathman & D.T. Crowther (Eds.), *Science for English language learners: K–12 classroom strategies* (pp. 37–59). Arlington, VA: National Science Teachers Association.

MacSwan, J. (2000). The Threshold Hypothesis, semilingualism, and other contributions to a deficit view of linguistic minorities. *Hispanic Journal of Behavioral Sciences, 22*(1), 3–45. doi:10.1177/0739986300221001

Moore, D.W., Bean, T.W., Birdyshaw, D., & Rycik, J.A. (1999). *Adolescent literacy: A position statement for the Commission on Adolescent Literacy of the International Reading Association.* Newark, DE: International Reading Association.

National Center for Education Statistics. (2006). *Highlights from the TIMSS 1999 video study of eighth-grade science teaching.* Retrieved May 22, 2007, from nces.ed.gov/pubs2001/2001027.pdf

National Research Council. (1996). *The national science education standards.* Washington, DC: National Academy Press.

National Research Council. (2000). *Inquiry and the national science education standards: A guide for teaching and learning.* Washington, DC: National Academy Press.

National Science Teachers Association. (1991). *Scope, sequence, and coordination of secondary school science: A project of the National Science Teachers Association.* Washington, DC: Author.

Ong, F. (2002). *English-language development standards for California public schools: Kindergarten through grade twelve.* Sacramento, CA: California Department of Education.

Palincsar, A.S., & Magnussen, S.J. (2000). *The interplay of firsthand and text-based investigations in science class.* Ann Arbor, MI: Center for the Improvement of Early Reading Achievement.

Rivard, L. (1994). A review of writing to learn in science: Implications for practice and research. *Journal of Research in Science Teaching, 31*(9), 969–983. doi:10.1002/tea.3660310910

Roseberry, A.S., Warren, B., & Conant, F.R. (1992). Appropriating scientific discourse: Findings from language minority classrooms. *Journal of Learning Sciences, 2*(1), 61–94.

Scarcella, R. (2003). *Accelerating academic English: A focus on the English learner.* Oakland, CA: Regents of the University of California.

Shin, F. (2005/2006). *Journeys-ESL in the content area: Science*. New York: Rosen Publishing.

Stoddart, T., Pinal, A., Latzke, M., & Canaday, D. (2002). Integrating inquiry science and language development for English language learners. *Journal of Research in Science Teaching, 39*(8), 664–687. doi:10.1002/tea.10040

Von Secker, C. (2004). Science achievement in social contexts: Analysis from National Assessment of Educational Progress. *Journal of Educational Research, 98*(2), 67–78. doi:10.3200/JOER.98.2.67-78

Organizing Classroom Instruction That Supports ELLs: Promoting Student Engagement and Oral Language Development

Julie Nora and Julie E. Wollman

Schools throughout the United States are currently experiencing a growth in the number of older English language learners (ELLs) who represent increasingly diverse countries of origin, educational experiences, and native languages. The challenge to simultaneously learn academic content and a new language experienced by all ELLs is pronounced especially in middle and secondary schools for several reasons.

Immigrants who arrive to the United States as adolescents have less time to master academic content at a time when graduation requirements are becoming more rigorous (Darling-Hammond, Rustique-Forrester, & Pechione, 2005). These students often must achieve in subject areas that require high levels of Academic English with limited access to native language support (Center for Applied Linguistics, 2008). In addition, the curriculum is frequently Eurocentric, and thus provides students with few opportunities to build on prior knowledge and experiences (Short, 1993). Another factor that contributes to the challenge experienced by older ELLs is the departmentalization that characterizes middle and secondary level education and limits the amount of time teachers have available to learn about and build upon their students' prior knowledge and experiences (Gándara, Maxwell-Jolly, & Driscoll, 2005). Taken together, limited time, little to no access to first language support, minimal incorporation of students' prior knowledge and experiences, and the structure of middle and secondary schools can lead to lower levels of student engagement.

The U.S. educational system is currently not meeting the needs of the growing population of ELLs (Gándara et al., 2005; Genesee, Lindholm-Leary, Saunders, & Christian, 2006). One cause is a shortage of qualified personnel. Suárez-Orozco and Suárez-Orozco (2002) estimate that 290,000 qualified teachers for bilingual or English as a second language (ESL) classes are needed; however, there are only 50,000 (Zhao, 2002). Urban, poor communities more frequently have less access to qualified teachers. According to a report issued by Fideler, Foster, and Schwartz (2000), urban schools face an immediate need for special education teachers (97%), mathematics and science teachers (80%), and ESL and bilingual teachers (57–67%). Some argue that we need to provide incentives for qualified teachers to accept employment in low-income communities (Futrell, Gomez, & Bedden, 2003). Efforts to address staffing issues in schools that enroll ELLs are necessary but not sufficient alone to improve student achievement. Schools need to be structured specifically to meet the needs of this student population.

Although some school restructuring efforts have attended to the needs of ELLs (Olsen, 1997), most schools are not appropriately organized for these students. There are few programs for those with limited prior schooling and low literacy skills, a growing population of ELLs (Ruiz-de-Velasco, Fix, & Clewell, 2000). A common reaction to less-than-fluent English is for teachers to expect lower level cognitive performance (Chamot & O'Malley, 1989) and, as a result, the few programs that do exist rarely provide students with access to academic concepts and skills. Both quantitative (Arreaga-Mayer & Perdomo-Rivera, 1996) and qualitative studies (Ruiz, 1995) have shown that the result of such pedagogy is low-level student engagement, which ultimately leads to "educational deadends" (Valdés, 2001, p. 3).

The goal of this chapter is to provide teachers with the information they need to organize classroom instruction to support engagement and oral language development among ELLs at the middle and secondary levels. To do so, we begin by examining student and teacher interactions in one Sheltered Instruction (SI), middle school social studies classroom. We share the results of our study, which employed ethnographic methodologies—classroom observations, interviews with the teacher and students, and field notes—to identify patterns of student involvement in activity settings. Analysis was thematic and recursive and initial research questions evolved based on what was discovered in the context. Data collection took place from January to June of a school year. A glimpse into this middle school social studies, ESL classroom revealed how one teacher—who had good intentions, appropriate certification, and was viewed widely as a "good teacher"—at times organized learning in his classroom in ways that engaged students and at other times unintentionally limited student engagement and prevented students from accessing academic material and developing oral proficiency. We conclude with recommendations for organizing instruction that promote student engagement and lead to opportunities to learn and develop oral language in middle schools that serve ELLs. While any teacher observed for months may have better and worse moments and it is easy to critique from the observer's perspective, this chapter focuses instead on what we can learn from current practices about what works for middle school ELLs.

Engaging ELLs

To be successful in school, all students need to be engaged in productive ways. School engagement has been defined primarily in three ways in the research literature: behavioral engagement, emotional engagement, and cognitive engagement (Fredricks, Blumenfeld, & Paris, 2004). Behavioral engagement refers to student participation in academic or social activities. Emotional engagement involves reaction (positive or negative) to teachers, classmates, and school. Cognitive engagement refers to student investment or willingness to put in the effort to understand ideas and master new skills. Students who are engaged will demonstrate sustained involvement in learning activities. Low levels of student engagement in any one of these domains can lead to low levels of success in school (Marks, 2000; Roderick & Engle, 2001; Willingham, Pollack, & Lewis, 2002).

Engagement in typical middle and secondary school classroom learning requires academic and oral language proficiency. Academic language is the language used to talk about complex concepts, participate in class discussions, comprehend lectures, and read and write about events that are not immediately present (Cummins, 2000). Oral language knowledge and skills provide access to the academic content ELLs need to experience success in school (Snow, Cancino, Gonzalez, & Shriberg, 1987). The results of two major reviews of research on educating ELLs shows that ELLs need opportunities to develop English oral language in structured ways that allow them to use and expand oral language and academic skills (August & Shanahan, 2006; Genesee et al., 2006). For example, students need to acquire the facility in English oral language to benefit from being taught specific strategies, such as those for reading comprehension or decoding and vocabulary development (August & Shanahan, 2006). However, the development of English oral proficiency alone will not lead to greater academic skills. While increased use of language promotes greater language development, structured academic language use at school plays a more significant role than language use at home or other interpersonal communication in developing greater levels of language and literacy (Genesee et al., 2006). Classroom language use and task-oriented peer language use are significant predictors of second language reading comprehension (Genesee et al., 2006). To provide these necessary academic language learning opportunities, teachers need to rethink the ways that classrooms are organized for student learning. In particular, they need to address their use of the most common language exchange in middle and secondary school classrooms—Initiation-Response-Evaluation (IRE) sequence.

Looking Closely at Initiation-Response-Evaluation

Nearly 30 years ago, Mehan (1979) identified three phases in typical classroom interactions. In the first phase, Initiation, the teacher begins an exchange by asking a question. These inquiries are called quiz questions, or requests for known answers, because the teacher wants to know whether the students know information the teacher already knows. In the second phase, Response, all students are expected to bid for nomination to respond. If no student bids, the teacher has the right to nominate a student. The student who is nominated by the teacher has the obligation to respond to the teacher at the appropriate moment in the appropriate way. Students who do not respond may be seen as uncooperative, lacking knowledge, or sometimes disruptive. During the third phase, Evaluation, the teacher evaluates the students' responses. By placing the student responses between teacher's turns, the teacher retains conversational initiative and can direct the discourse (Holmes, 1978). While the most common sequence in both general education and ESL classrooms (Arreaga-Mayer & Perdomo-Rivera, 1996; Cazden, 2001), the IRE structure minimizes students' interactions and does not allow them to engage in complex interactions and meaning exchanges. Nor does it allow students opportunities to learn by talking to explore a concept. Student interaction is essential to having ELLs test their language hypothesis through output and to use their own knowledge and experiences to create meaning through the interaction (Echevarria, Vogt, & Short, 2008; Long, 2006). Because it limits such opportunities, the IRE pattern is less motivating and less meaningful for students (Duff, 2001) and is considered problematic for ELLs (Long, 2006).

We now take a closer look at the school, the teacher, and students to reveal a setting that is fairly typical, in that using the IRE structure is common, and to provide the context of this discourse setting.

The School

East Middle School (names of places and people are pseudonyms) is a public school in a Northeast, urban district. Typical of an urban school, 92% of the students in the school qualify for free or reduced lunch. Thirty-six percent of the students are Hispanic, 36% are African American, 18% are Caucasian, 8% are Asian, and 2% are Native American. Twenty percent of the students receive ESL services. Built in 1929, East Middle School is a brick building in disrepair and deemed a "school in crisis" by the state department of education.

The Program

The program model used to educate ELLs is SI, an approach intended to prepare students for mainstream, content area classes by promoting the development of a second language while simultaneously facilitating mastery of academic content taught through that second language (Echevarria et al., 2008; Freeman & Freeman, 1988). In this approach, teachers identify language and content goals for each lesson and "shelter" instruction to make it comprehensible by using such strategies as extralinguistic contextual clues, modifications of language, and frequent monitoring of comprehension. However, in the district, there was no social studies curriculum and there were no local language objectives. There was also little coordination between the content teachers and the ESL teachers. The teacher reported to being "on his own" to develop curriculum and design teaching and learning.

The Teacher

The teacher, Mr. Gil, is a monolingual, English-speaking, middle class male. He attended a local university to obtain his bachelor's degree in teaching history. He also had earned ESL and middle school endorsements and at the time of this study was pursuing a master's degree in reading. In his fourth year of teaching, he is a member of the lead team who travels to another state to participate in professional development in standards-based education from a national organization with whom the district had partnered. Although he was relatively new, he had fulfilled all certification requirements, sought to continue to develop professionally, and was well respected by his colleagues, principal, and district leaders.

The Students

The students in Mr. Gil's class came from various countries: Liberia, China, Haiti, Dominican Republic, Guatemala, and Puerto Rico and had been in the United States for varying periods of time—from one who was born in the United States to one who had just arrived—and the amount of time students had spent in an ESL program in the United States spanned from 1 month to 10 years. All were classified by the district's central intake office as intermediate- or advanced-level ESL students; as is increasingly the case in ESL classes, there was significant diversity in the level of English language proficiency. Like many of his colleagues and teachers nationwide (Gándara et al., 2005), Mr. Gil struggled to meet the needs of his diverse students. According to Mr. Gil, "I struggle with what to do with students who really haven't been to school a day in their lives. What do you do with that kind of kid? I struggle with that. I struggle with that every day. A kid can't read or write. What do you do? How do you teach that kid about exploration?" Despite having the required credentials for his position, similar to many of his colleagues, Mr. Gil struggled to meet the diverse needs of his students.

Mr. Gil's Instructional Approaches

Mr. Gil's positive reputation came from a series of activities that promoted students' access to content and provided opportunities for oral language development. He designed activities in which the students creatively depicted historical concepts. These creative representations were often displayed in the school hallways. For example, in the Three Branches of Government poster project students were asked to use cooperative learning (Chips, 1993) to make posters representing the three branches of government as seen in Figure 7.1. Mr. Gil facilitated student success by providing a criteria chart, in which he described the goals and requirements, and by giving students several graphic organizers to record their research in preparation for making their posters. All students were

Figure 7.1. Students' Three Branches of Government Poster Project

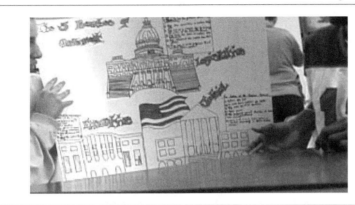

engaged during class time when they were working on these projects. Students overwhelmingly reported enjoying working on these projects.

Mr. Gil also introduced the Preamble Collage, in which students made a collage and wrote their own version of the Preamble to the U.S. Constitution as shown in Figure 7.2. Providing hands-on interaction with academic content is frequently cited as a "best practice" for engaging ELLs and promoting language development. These projects represent examples of using pictorial, hands-on, or performance-based assessments to determine student comprehension of the subject matter and language growth (Echevarria et al., 2008) often found in an SI approach. In an SI approach, students are given multiple opportunities to show their understanding of content through informal class discussions, oral reports, written assignments, and portfolios. Although the teacher initiated the tasks, students primarily directed the activity within these structures, another recommended practice when teaching ELLs (Genesee et al., 2006). Students in Mr. Gil's class were afforded supportive environments for using oral language in these small-group settings.

While these hands-on activities engaged students, other activities—which consumed a good percentage of time—limited student engagement. Mr. Gil regularly led an activity he called Rapid Review characterized by the IRE sequence for approximately 10–15 minutes during many of his 50-minute class sessions. For example, during a unit on the presidency, he began the class by asking, "What does it mean to be the head of the armed forces?" the day following a

Figure 7.2. Students' Preamble Collage

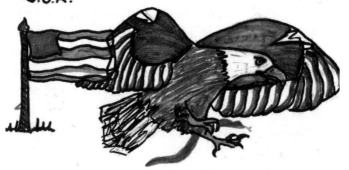

PREABLE

We the people of U.S.A., USA

To make sure that our country to be together no matter what happens, to make sure we have courts system, to make sure we have peace at home, to make sure that we have Protection by building army and navy, to make sure that people have everything that they need to survive in there homes, to make sure that we have freedom and our childrens that comes after us, we make these laws in the U.S.A.

class discussion of presidential duty. As Mehan (1979) documented, Mr. Gil expected all students to raise their hands, wait to be called on, and then respond. Following a response that Mr. Gil deemed correct, the student was awarded a "check plus." At the end of the class, the "check pluses" were tallied in the teacher's grade book, and they could be cashed in at the close of the quarter for small rewards.

Rapid Review appears to be best practice for ELLs with the goal of providing a daily review of material to activate schema (Echevarria et al., 2008). However, as the following exchange suggests, Mr. Gil focused on having students follow the norms of participation rather than engaging students cognitively. In the following Rapid Review exchange, Mr. Gil called on Juan, who had not volunteered.

Mr. Gil: What is separation of powers? What is separation of powers? Juan.

Juan: The state.

Mr. Gil: Separation of powers. What is separation of powers?

Juan: Separation.

Mr. Gil: Okay. Separation. Okay. What does that mean? Do you have a notebook?

Juan: [shakes his head no]

Mr. Gil: Where's your notebook?

Juan: Lost it.

Mr. Gil: What are you going to study from? Get one of those books up there, right now. Look it up. What is separation of powers? [pause] Get one of the blue books. This is important stuff, you need to know. As soon as you find it raise your hand, okay? Separation of powers.

Mr. Gil called on Juan despite Juan not having raised his hand, likely because he knew he could not or did not feel comfortable responding without being nominated. Juan's response "separation" was evaluated negatively by Mr. Gil, who asked, "What does that mean?" Before allowing Juan to respond, Mr. Gil realized that Juan did not have his notebook, an expected norm in this class. Mr. Gil immediately directed Juan to get a textbook to look up the answer. It is significant what Mr. Gil did *not* do. He did not continue questioning Juan to see if he knew what Separation of Powers was. Instead, he instructed Juan to get a blue book to replace his lost notebook and look up the concept. While Rapid Review could have been a whole-class oral activity in which the teacher models academic oral language (Genesee et al., 2006), for Juan this quickly became a silent, independent activity using a text because he had not followed classroom norms. Juan was also humiliated in the exchange, affecting his willingness to take advantage of an invaluable opportunity to converse with the teacher, the only native U.S. English speaker (Genesee et al., 2006). This example is representative of other exchanges that were commonly observed.

Moments in History, an activity students did for approximately 15 minutes nearly each day at the beginning of their class, also limited student learning. As in most middle schools, these seventh and eighth graders moved daily from classroom to classroom for each subject for five 50-minute periods. Every day, before the students entered his classroom, Mr. Gil wrote two moments in history—sentences describing events that occurred on that day in history—on the chalkboard. Each sentence had grammatical errors, such as "Prohibition *gos* into effect." These moments included topics as diverse as May 14, 1653—when Louis XIV became king at age 5—to March 27, 1912—when the first Japanese cherry tree was planted in Washington, DC. For the first part of this activity, students entered the room, sat down, took out their notebooks, copied the moments in their incorrect form, and attempted to correct the sentences individually in their notebooks. Mr. Gil then circulated and evaluated the student responses, saying "good" for each appropriate correction, and "gotcha!" for each missed or inappropriate correction, which he tallied in his grade book. Moments in History was Mr. Gil's self-described way of transitioning the students from the hallway to his classroom by silencing students as they entered his room. This approach effectively prohibited the students from participating in an interactive learning environment that fosters the development of language skills that are connected to literacy and academic domains (Genesee et al., 2006).

Mr. Gil stated, "Moments in History is my way of focusing the students. Like I make them line up outside of the room, they come in here and they know that the first thing they need to do is they have their little notebooks and they open their notebooks and they copy moments in history quietly." By having students work independently and silently, he cut off any social interaction or talk that could be "disruptive" but also which could be productive for sharing ideas and promoting cognitive engagement with the material (Genesee et al., 2006).

Because the skills and abilities required for the initial, written part of this activity—copying down moments in history and making grammatical corrections in their notebook—were the ability to read and copy the sentences and to understand the grammar sufficiently to recognize and correct the errors, the primary goal of the this part of this activity appeared to be to help students learn English grammar. This is a laudable goal because research suggests that to develop oral proficiency ELLs need to gain control over English grammar, and carefully planned direct instruction of target language skills is an effective instructional approach with ELLs (Genesee et al., 2006). However, there was little to no explicit teaching or discussion of grammar, and the errors were generated by the teacher and did not arise from an analysis of common student errors. Students were expected to correct the mistakes independently, without teacher or peer assistance.

A secondary goal could have been to teach history by focusing on the content of each of the statements. However, the choice of what to include in the moments was based on the calendar: Mr. Gil chose events that occurred that day in history. And, as the example of Louis XIV becoming king at age 5 reveals, the moments were not always related to the focus of this class—U.S. history. For the moments that were related to U.S. history, the content was rarely related to the topic that was being studied at that time. Nor were the moments connected to one another. By using the calendar to choose moments each day that ranged over a wide span of years and encompassed a wide range of unconnected topics, the teacher was not helping students understand "how things progressed, how things build on each other, how things are related, how things are connected," his stated goal for teaching history. The presentation of such unrelated facts did not represent what research suggests works best for ELLs: having high expectations for students and providing access to academic domains through meaningful curriculum that is carefully aligned with standards (Genesee et al., 2006).

Best practice for educating ELLs connects teaching and learning to students' prior knowledge or experiences, which often differ from those of students from mainstream backgrounds (Echevarria et al., 2008). In the following example, Mr. Gil lost an opportunity to build on the student's prior knowledge.

Mr. Gil: The American League baseball team was formed in the early days of baseball in 1900. Over a hundred years ago, this all started years ago. And of course, baseball is America's favorite pastime. Still play it today.

León: What? It's America's favorite *what*?

Mr. Gil: America's favorite *pastime*, baseball.

León: It's still the best, one of the best Spanish sports ever.

Mr. Gil: *American* sport.

León: No it's not. It's a Spanish sport.

Mr. Gil: Why is it a Spanish....León, why do you say it's a Spanish sport?

León: [inaudible]

Mr. Gil: You think so, is it popular in the D.R. (Dominican Republic)?

León: Don't you see all the people coming over here?

Mr. Gil: I do.

León: Cause they all [inaudible]

Mr. Gil: [interrupting] Do you know where it originated? Like what baseball was based on? Do you know anything about the history of baseball?

León: [no response]

Mr. Gil: What's that?

León: I don't know.

Mr. Gil: You don't *know*. It's an English game that's very similar to baseball called cricket. So it's actually an *English* game. And the U.S. originated as colonies of *what* country?

León: England.

Mr. Gil: [continues on to the next moment in history] 1919, on this date Prohibition goes into effect.

When Mr. Gil began discussing the moment in history, he used a word that León did not understand—*pastime*. León asked for clarification. Mr. Gil responded by emphasizing the word *pastime*. León was enthusiastic about baseball and began to engage in a discussion with Mr. Gil about baseball, how it was the best "Spanish sport ever." The teacher responded by emphasizing that baseball was an American sport, to which León, a native of the Dominican Republic, responded that it was a "Spanish sport." Mr. Gil's response was, "Why do you think it's a Spanish sport?" León said that there were many Spanish players in the United States. The teacher agreed that there were many Spanish players in the United States and then immediately cited history to defend his argument that baseball was an *American* sport. By asking León if he "knew anything about the *history* of baseball," he stripped León's authority, which was based on knowledge of contemporary baseball. As a teacher of U.S. *history*, the teacher had authority in this content domain. Mr. Gil interrupted León, silencing him. By connecting his argument directly to the content of the class that they had been studying, Mr. Gil repositioned himself as an authority. León accepted this discourse and retreated from his initial statement that baseball was a Spanish sport.

What We Learned From Practice in the Classroom

The beginning of nearly each class was consumed by an activity that was designed—per the teacher's admission—merely to silence students as they transitioned from the hallways to his classroom, not to teach social studies content, develop oral language proficiency, or systematically teach students English. A significant percentage of class time was spent in the traditional IRE format, where the teacher controlled conversational norms and student interpretation of content in ways that restricted learning and did not build on students' prior experiences or knowledge. The way the teacher organized learning during these times did not provide students with opportunities for exchanges that would allow for academic growth. Most ELLs do not have prior knowledge about U.S. history, or, when they do, they have a different perspective than their mainstream teachers. Tapping into students' experiential knowledge can facilitate their understanding of the concepts being presented. In Mr. Gil's classroom, students lost opportunities to develop oral language with the teacher or with peers.

The findings from Mr. Gil's classroom reflect the research findings discussed earlier. When students were working on group projects, there were good opportunities for emotional, behavioral, and cognitive engagement (Fredricks et al., 2004) and access to content through informal student-directed discussion (Genesee et al., 2006) and creative depiction of new concepts. On the other hand, the pattern of interaction between students and the teacher during the more predominant, whole-class discourse events was IRE (Mehan, 1979). This pattern made it impossible for students to use their developing oral language skills to further develop their English and their content understanding (August & Shanahan, 2006; Genesee et al., 2006; Long, 2006).

Moreover, students were discouraged from tapping their own prior knowledge and experiences in favor of getting through the lesson and getting to the right answer. They were unable, as Echevarria and colleagues (2008) suggest, to activate and use existing schema and build upon what they knew to make sense of new information. Also during these whole-class activities, the teacher spent less time modeling academic oral language and using authentic questioning and interactive exchanges with students (Genesee et al., 2006) than he did focusing on student compliance to avoid what he saw as disruptive behavior. Ironically, defying widespread research implications when faced with a very wide range of student skill and ability, the teacher organized the classroom to eliminate discussion in English rather than encourage the talk that we know, from previous research, would be most beneficial to students.

Alternative Practices to Engage ELLs

Although we need to continue to research educational practices for ELLs, we do have consistent findings in the research literature that we need to apply in educational settings. Many of these findings could be applied to Mr. Gil's classroom to address what we saw as missed opportunities—both at the classroom level and in the larger context of the school and district.

At the classroom level, Mr. Gil could have organized teaching and learning in ways that demonstrated higher expectations for students, provided greater access to academic content, built on students' prior knowledge, and increased opportunities for oral language (Genesee et al., 2006). We witnessed how Mr. Gil accomplished this with the Three Branches of Government poster project and the student version of the Preamble Collage. We also witnessed how students' prior knowledge was not honored, in the case of "Spanish baseball." Mr. Gil could have made connections to the native culture and interpretation of content to build bridges to an understanding he was trying to achieve, as opposed to dismissing it altogether. Mr. Gil could have increased opportunities for task-oriented peer language use. He also could have done more interactive reciprocal teaching, which research suggests is more beneficial than the transmission model. When teachers facilitate as opposed to control learning, students are more successful (Skinner & Belmont, 1993). Interactive reciprocal teaching has students engaged in higher order cognitive skills, not just factual recall. In one of the passages, we showed how students' lack of familiarity with vocabulary (*pastime*) impeded understanding. Direct teaching of the vocabulary would have facilitated learning (Genesee et al., 2006).

In the frequently observed IRE format, the teacher mediated each student utterance. Mr. Gil could have engaged students in meaningful learning by promoting cross discussion or a dialogue between students in which the teacher does not serve as the intermediary (Lemke, 1985). To facilitate cross discussion, he could have arranged the chairs in a circle so that students look at one another when they are speaking. He could have not regained the floor after every student's turn but could have allowed students to follow one another without nomination. Moving away from teacher nomination eliminates the need for students to raise their hands and allows students to address one another directly, as illustrated in the exchange that follows:

Teacher: Let's pick up where we left off yesterday. Separation of powers is a key concept in the U.S. government. Do you think separation of powers creates a more balanced government?

Student 1: It separates...I don't know how to say it.

Student 2: Yeah, like what Mr. G. said, it separates the courts, the laws, and the president so nobody have more power. So, yeah, I think it's more balanced.

Student 3: But sometimes one branch does have more power.

Teacher: Okay, can anyone think of an example when one branch of government had more power than the others?

This exchange represents a different kind of discourse, in which students can explore their own understanding of the concepts being discussed (Cazden, 2001). Unlike the IRE sequence, interaction among students allows for the exploration of a concept, as opposed to limited responses.

Teachers who build upon students' ideas, experiences, and funds of knowledge give students access to academic content. Teachers who value students' contributions and demonstrate through evaluation of student responses that they believe students have knowledge that would be relevant engage students in learning. Students become engaged because their contributions are valued. Such exchanges can follow the IRE sequence, giving students access to this commonly found classroom format. However, the interactions must be inclusive. Teachers' evaluation of students must value their contributions and prior knowledge. Instead of evaluating the students' responses as correct or incorrect, a teacher's slight modification to the evaluation phase allows students to elaborate and generates more discussion. For example, instead of evaluating the student's response, in the previous exchange the teacher encourages greater elaboration by asking "Can anyone think of an example?" Research has shown that such elaboration stimulates more complex interactions (Long, 2006). In addition, the teacher used a visual to scaffold students' learning, which is essential in an SI approach.

Beyond the Classroom

The recommendations listed in the previous section demonstrate some ways a classroom teacher can organize classroom instruction to support ELLs. A teacher does not, however, work in isolation. There are also changes that can be made in the context of school. Mr. Gil felt the need to spend the first 10–15 minutes transitioning students with moments in history because of the limited 50-minute block he had. Longer blocks could eliminate the need to respond to such transitions. The school, as is the case with most secondary schools, did not use the native language systematically as a foundation. Implementing more bilingual programs would allow for native language to be used as a resource to build upon. The examination of this classroom occurred in the context of No Child Left Behind, and as a result, much of the professional development occurring at the district level was focused only on improving student performance on standardized tests. While some of the professional development was appropriate for mainstream, native English-speaking students, none of the professional development considered how to meet the specific needs of ELLs. It is important that programs for ELLs stress higher order thinking, are academically challenging, and are aligned with standards and achievement and that successful teachers of ELLs have knowledge of bilingual theory and second language development. Districts need to carefully consider programs and provide systematic and sustained professional development for all teachers to reflect on and improve their practice with ELLs. Research suggests that schools with high-quality programs where staff share a cohesive schoolwide vision, have shared goals and clearly defined expectations, have a clear instructional focus on and commitment to achievement, and have high expectations for students are successful in helping ELLs achieve academic success (Genesee et al., 2006).

By looking at one teacher's classroom, we were able to unearth ways that the organization of teaching and learning was effective for ELLs, as well as areas for improvement in engaging ELLs in one middle school classroom. Teachers such as Mr. Gil need opportunities for reflection to determine whether the perception of their teaching and actual practice match. Researchers and practitioners need to continue to document the concrete details of practice that can help us understand the points of view of the participants (Erickson, 1986) so that we can improve teaching and learning and programmatic response to the students most in need.

REFLECTION QUESTIONS

1. Consider some of your daily instructional routines. In what ways do these routines foster or potentially inhibit ELLs' opportunities to engage in meaningful language and literacy interactions?

2. What are some modifications that you can make in your teaching practice to increase student engagement and promote language development?

3. How can you provide more opportunities for ELLs to build upon and share the background knowledge and experiences in your classroom?

4. What steps can you take to build time into your teaching practice for serious reflection on what you do in the classroom each day? What steps can you take to collaborate with peers to create networks of "critical friends" who visit each other's classrooms and provide constructive feedback?

REFERENCES

Arreaga-Mayer, C., & Perdomo-Rivera, P.D. (1996). Ecobehavioral analysis of instruction for at-risk language-minority students. *The Elementary School Journal, 96*(3), 245–258. doi:10.1086/461826

August, D., & Shanahan, T. (Eds.). (2006). *Developing literacy in second-language learners: Report of the National Literacy Panel on Language-Minority Children and Youth.* Mahwah, NJ: Erlbaum.

Cazden, C. (2001). *Classroom discourse: The language of teaching and learning* (2nd ed.). Portsmouth, NH: Heinemann.

Center for Applied Linguistics. (2008). *Directory of two-way immersion programs in the United States.* Retrieved August 12, 2007, from www.cal.org/twi/directory/index.html

Chamot, A.U., & O'Malley, J.M. (1989). The cognitive academic language learning approach. In P. Rigg & V. Allen (Eds.), *When they don't all speak English: Integrating the ESL student into the regular classroom* (pp. 108–125). Urbana, IL: National Council of Teachers of English.

Chips, B. (1993). Using cooperative learning at the secondary level. In D. Holt (Ed.), *Cooperative learning. A response to cultural and linguistic diversity* (pp.81–97). McHenry, IL: Center for Applied Linguistics and Delta Systems.

Cummins, J. (2000). *Language, power and pedagogy: Bilingual children in the crossfire.* Buffalo, NY: Multilingual Matters.

Darling-Hammond, L., Rustique-Forrester, E., & Pechione, R. (2005). *Multiple measures approaches to high school graduation.* Stanford, CA: School Redesign Network.

Duff, P. (2001). Language, literacy, content and (pop) culture: Challenges for ESL students in mainstream courses. *Canadian Modern Language Review, 58*(1), 103–132.

Echevarria, J., Vogt, M., & Short, D. (2008). *Making content comprehensible for English language learners: The SIOP model* (3rd ed.). Boston: Allyn & Bacon.

Erickson, F. (1986). Qualitative methods in research on teaching. In M.C. Wittock (Ed.), *Handbook of research on teaching* (pp. 119–161). New York: Macmillan.

Fideler, E.F., Foster, E.D., & Schwartz, S. (2000). *The urban teacher challenge: Teacher supply and demand in the great city schools.* Belmont, MA; Washington, DC: Recruiting New Teachers; Council of the Great City Schools, The Council of Great City Colleges of Education.

Fredricks, J.A., Blumenfeld, P.C., & Paris, A.H. (2004). School engagement: Potential of the concept, and state of the evidence. *Review of Educational Research, 74*(1), 59–109. doi:10.3102/00346543074001059

Freeman, D., & Freeman, Y. (1988). *Sheltered English instruction.* Washington, DC: U.S. Department of Education.

Futrell, M.H., Gomez, J., & Bedden, D. (2003). Teaching the children of a new America: The challenge of diversity. *Phi Delta Kappan, 84*(5), 381–385.

Gándara, P., Maxwell-Jolly, J., & Driscoll, A. (2005). *Listening to teachers of English learners.* Santa Cruz, CA: Center for the Future of Teaching and Learning. Retrieved October 1, 2007, from lmri.ucsb.edu/publications/05_listening-to-teachers.pdf

Genesee, F., Lindholm-Leary, K., Saunders, W.M., & Christian, D. (2006). *Educating English language learners: A synthesis of research evidence.* New York: Cambridge University Press.

Holmes, J. (1978). Sociolinguistic competence in the classroom. In J.C. Richards (Ed.), *Understanding second and foreign language learning: Issues and approaches* (pp. 134–162). Rowley, MA: Newbury House.

Lemke, J.L. (1985). *Using language in the classroom.* Geelong, VIC, Australia: Deakin University Press.

Long, M.H. (2006). *Problems in SLA.* Mahwah, NJ: Erlbaum.

Marks, H.M. (2000). Student engagement in instructional activity: Patterns in the elementary, middle, and high school years. *American Educational Research Journal, 37*(1), 153–184.

Mehan, H. (1979). *Learning lessons.* Cambridge, MA: Harvard University Press.

Olsen, L. (1997). *Made in America: Immigrant students in our public schools.* New York: The New Press.

Roderick, M., & Engle, M. (2001). The grasshopper and the ant: Motivational responses of low-achieving students to high-stakes testing. *Educational Evaluation and Policy Analysis, 23*(3), 197–228. doi:10.3102/01623737023003197

Ruiz, N.T. (1995). The social construction of ability and disability: II. Optimal and at risk lessons in a bilingual special education classroom. *Journal of Learning Disabilities, 28*(8), 491–502. doi:10.1177/002221949502800804

Ruiz-de-Velasco, J., Fix, M., & Clewell, B.C. (2000). *Overlooked and underserved: Immigrant students in U.S. secondary schools.* Washington, DC: The Urban Institute.

Short, D. (1993). *Integrating language and culture in middle school American history classes. Educational Practice Report: 8.* Washington, DC: Center for Applied Logistics.

Skinner, E.A., & Belmont, M.J. (1993). Motivation in the classroom: Reciprocal effects of teacher behavior and student engagement across the school year. *Journal of Educational Psychology, 85*(4), 571–581. doi:10.1037/0022-0663.85.4.571

Snow, C., Cancino, H., Gonzalez, P., & Shriberg, E. (1987). *Second language learners' formal definitions: An oral language correlate of school literacy* (Technical Report No. 5). Los Angeles, CA: University of California Center for Language Education and Research.

Suárez-Orozco, C., & Suárez-Orozco, M. (2002). *Children of immigration.* Cambridge, MA: Harvard University Press.

Valdés, G. (2001). *Learning and not learning English: Latino students in American schools.* New York: Teachers College Press.

Willingham, W.W., Pollack, J.M., & Lewis, C. (2002). Grades and test scores: Accounting for observed differences. *Journal of Educational Measurement, 39*(1), 1–37. doi:10.1111/j.1745-3984.2002.tb01133.x

Zhao, Y. (2002, August 5). Wave of pupils lacking English strains schools. *New York Times*, pp. A1, A11.

CHAPTER 8

Supporting the Writing Development of High School ELLs With Guided Writing: Success Stories From One Classroom

Kathleen A.J. Mohr and Eric S. Mohr

In 2007, the results of the 2005 National Assessment of Educational Progress (NAEP) measurement were released, and they confirmed what many had suspected. Despite efforts to increase academic achievement, high school students in public schools throughout the United States continue to perform poorly in reading and mathematics. Of the students tested in the 12th grade, 27% performed below the basic level in reading, and 39% performed below the basic level in mathematics (National Center for Education Statistics [NCES], 2008). This lack of skills evidenced by 12th graders is a concern for educators and employers. Of equal or greater concern is the achievement gap that continues between white and minority high school students. For example, results of 2007 NAEP writing assessment demonstrated that African American and Hispanic 12th graders continue to achieve far less than their Caucasian counterparts (Salahu-Din, Persky, & Miller, 2008).

The challenge to improve student achievement in general and minority student achievement in particular is made more complex by the rising percentage of English language learners (ELLs) in secondary school. Teachers should prepare to welcome these students who are at various stages of English language development, and they must know how to accelerate their language, literacy, and content area achievement. Teachers at this level are also presented with the challenge of ensuring that once these students are in high school, they find a reason to remain there. Of the students identified as having difficulty speaking English in eighth grade on the 2000 U.S. Census, only 18% graduated from high school four years later (NCES, 2004). To reverse this trend, especially at such a critical stage, it is important to identify successful instructional interventions that recognize the characteristics and needs of older ELLs. In the following section, we take a look inside one classroom to explore how instruction can support ELLs' writing.

A Teacher's Challenge: Teaching ELLs With Little Training or Preparation

Just as the school year was about to start in August of 2006, Eric (the second author of this chapter) learned that his teaching assignment included the 12th-grade Sheltered Instruction (SI) English class. Eric had taught English composition and literature successfully for more than two decades; however, he had limited experience teaching ELLs. Furthermore, similar to many teachers who find themselves teaching ELLs with little training or preparation, he also learned that there were few instructional resources for this class. Eric willingly had taken on last-minute teaching assignments in the past, but this particular assignment provided a unique challenge. Eric needed to accelerate the students' language and literacy achievement while developing their understanding of classic literature and guiding them toward the adult world. And because the students assigned to this class had not been able to pass the exit-level English test given during their junior year, he had only one year to help these students become success stories.

To meet this challenge, Eric sought resources outside his school district including Kathleen (the first author), a teacher educator and former English as a second language teacher. Kathleen had investigated guided writing as an instructional approach to accelerate language and literacy development among younger ELLs (Mohr, 2004). She suggested to Eric that they investigate the efficacy of this approach on the writing achievement of older students. The purpose of this chapter is to share the outcomes of that collaboration. We begin with an overview of guided writing for ELLs. Then we turn to the implementation of this approach in Eric's SI English classroom with an emphasis on sharing students' success stories. We conclude with recommendations for supporting the writing development of high school ELLs.

Guided Writing for ELLs

The guided writing approach described here is similar in some ways to other approaches to supported writing. These approaches include the language experience approach (Hall, 1999), guided writing (Meeks & Austin, 2003; Smith & Bean, 1980), interactive writing (Button, Johnson, & Ferguson, 1996; Collom, 1996; McCarrier, Pinnell, & Fountas, 2000), modeled writing, and the Picture Word Inductive Model (Calhoun, 1999; Wood & Tinajero, 2002). In these approaches, teachers and students engage in shared writing experiences and use the written product as a meaningful context to examine a variety of linguistic elements.

In addition to these features, guided writing for ELLs (Mohr, 2004) includes a brief, teacher-directed lesson that incorporates a context-based discussion (Saunders & Goldenberg, 1999), modeled writing, and sentence dictation that ELLs can use to "launch" a writing assignment. Informed by the understanding that second language listening, speaking, reading, and writing skills develop in a mutually reinforcing manner (August, 2002; Echevarria, Short, & Powers, 2006), this approach is designed to be conversational in nature. Thus, it provides many opportunities for students to share ideas, make comments, or ask questions. At the same time it provides students with models of various written genres to scaffold students' construction of more extensive written compositions. The entire guided writing sequence takes only 30 minutes but can be shortened or extended as needed and includes the following steps:

1. Picture/text talk: The teacher conducts a discussion of a picture or text, allowing for rehearsal of English vocabulary, the sharing of thoughts and ideas, and the generation of questions and related sentences. This instructional conversation allows for student input and encourages the use of listening and speaking skills.

2. Vocabulary brainstorming and word web: The teacher elicits and records 8–10 key vocabulary words that were generated during the picture/text talk. The teacher may ask the students to repeat the pronunciation of these words and use them in sample sentences. The teacher may also select a few of the words to feature in a word web, showing students how key terms are related to other words. For example, the word *friend* is related to the words *friendship, friendly, unfriendly,* and *befriend* because the common base word can be combined with other morphemes to communicate separate but related meanings.

3. Modeled sentence writing: After the oral discussion and focus on keywords, the students are encouraged to generate two or three sentences related to the picture or text. The teacher records these on chart paper or an overhead transparency. The teacher writes down a composite of the student-generated sentences, helping to refine these initial sentences so that they serve as a platform for further writing. As the teacher writes, he or she can highlight pronunciation, grammatical structures, the keywords, and spelling patterns. The students should participate in the sentence generation as much as possible, spelling words, clarifying word endings, and so forth. The teacher can use think-aloud comments to address various mechanical and orthographical elements, such as plural endings, compound words, or the need for a capital letter. The composite sentences should be read several times by the students. Repeated readings of the jointly drafted sentences promote some ownership of the shared text and oral reading fluency.

4. Minilesson: The sentences can then provide a context for a lesson on an element of the English language. For example, the teacher can point out key prepositional phrases, transition words, or the derivation and spelling of words.

5. Language analysis: The sentences also may provide an opportunity for a brief analysis of similarities and differences between English and students' first languages. For example, the teacher can demonstrate how to attend to cognates or point out spelling patterns particular to English such as *ng* used after short, single vowels.

6. Rereading: The next step is a shared rereading of the sentences. This brings the parts back to a whole and allows students to develop reading fluency (Hastings-Gongora, 1993). Students are encouraged to be able to read the sentences successfully and in collaboration with their peers.

7. Sentence dictation: Following a listen, repeat, write, and check the sentence format, students apply what they know (and remember) to record the dictated sentences. This is when the students write the sentences that the teacher dictates, which have been removed from sight. The teacher repeats the sentences in word phrases slowly and distinctly so that students can attend to their spelling and mechanics. To scaffold student success, the teacher can use prompts to helps students use what they know while concentrating on their writing.

8. Adding more: Then students write additional sentences related to the topic. Students are challenged to write their own ideas that build upon the shared beginning. Because some students write faster than others, allowing students to illustrate their work is one way to manage this difference and extend the activity, if necessary. This is an important step because it allows the students to use words and pictures to show what they know about the instructional topic. It also provides the teacher with examples of individually generated sentences that can be used as diagnostic tools to target future instruction and practice.

9. Individual instruction: If time allows, individual students read back the sentences to the teacher who identifies and responds to students' needs. At this point, reminders about vocabulary, mechanics, and spelling patterns can be addressed with individual students.

The guided writing approach as described here largely targets word-level items for students in the earlier stages of English language development. The process may be modified according to students' needs and teaching goals. For example, attention to concerns beyond the word level, such as paragraph and essay organization, can be addressed through the use of carefully constructed graphic organizers (Merkley & Jefferies, 2000/2001). The use of graphic organizers helps transition students from producing single sentences to composing organized paragraphs with stronger topic sentences to cohesive compositions.

In the following section, we turn to the implementation of the guided writing approach for ELLs in Eric's 12th-grade SI English class. We begin with a description of the school, the classroom, and the students.

Implementing the Guided Writing Approach in a High School Classroom

The School

Eric's high school is located in a suburban Dallas, Texas, school district that is among the fastest growing school districts in the United States. In addition to Eric's high school, there are three additional campuses in the district that house 1,800 students each with two more campuses planned. Eric's high school has the typical population diversity of a north Texas suburban high school, with small percentages of Asian, Asian Indian, and European students. Its next two largest groups are Hispanics (19.4%, $n = 313$; immigrant and resident) and African Americans (14%, $n = 210$). The Caucasian population is approximately 62% ($n = 999$). Because of the influx of immigrants and Spanish-speaking residents, the need for SI English classes is steady with one class currently offered at each of the four grade levels. Along with the growth that results from being a suburb of a major metropolitan area like Dallas comes the diversity of job opportunities for the parents of these students, including everything from restaurant service and home and freeway construction to medical and high-tech positions.

The Classroom

The 12th-grade English curriculum consists of literary analysis of various classic texts (e.g., *Oedipus Rex*, *Beowulf*, *The Canterbury Tales*, *The Tragedy of Macbeth*), vocabulary and grammar instruction, and writing assignments designed to prepare students for the demands of college writing. The goal of the SI English class is to provide access to this content while addressing students' language and literacy learning needs. All English classes including the sheltered classes meet on a block schedule, 90 minutes at a time.

In Eric's English literature and composition classes, he routinely employed the following sequence of activities: warm-up activity (e.g., responding to a topic from the previous class meeting or a schoolwide activity), vocabulary or grammar instruction, reading, and concluding writing activity. Eric followed this daily instructional routine in the SI English class with the addition of Kathleen's biweekly one-hour classroom visits. During these visits, which took place from September to May, Kathleen taught guided writing lessons and worked with the students as they wrote. Although Eric lacked appropriate language and literacy instructional materials for the SI English class, Eric's classroom like all classrooms in the school contained an instructor's computer and printer, video projector, and a document camera. Two portable banks of laptops were also available for classroom research projects on a first-come, first-served basis.

The Students

At the start of the school year, there were five students in Eric's SI English class. Early in the first semester, one student left the class to join a different program. Another student joined the class at the beginning of the second semester but stayed only briefly before her family relocated to the Midwest. A few weeks into the second semester, one student was dismissed from the school because he was 19 and had a poor attendance record. In this chapter, we focus on the learning experiences of four students: Valeria, Juan, Chun, and Sergio, all of whom were at least 18 years of age during the school year and who were the mainstays of SI English IV. All student names are self-selected pseudonyms.

- Valeria had lived in the United States for about six years after immigrating with her parents and a brother and sister. She entered the U.S. school system as a middle school student. Four older siblings remained behind in Mexico. Her family plans to stay in the United States, and she would like to work in a bank. Valeria was talkative and social, often serving as a translator in class to help clear up confusions. However, Valeria was concerned about being able to pass the Texas Assessment of Knowledge and Skills (TAKS) exit-level tests so that she could graduate with her classmates.

- Juan is the middle of seven children. He emigrated with two brothers from Mexico and now lives in Texas with his uncle's family. He has not been back to Mexico since he and his brothers arrived nearly four years ago. Juan had completed 10 years of schooling in Mexico, yet he was placed in eighth grade when he entered U.S. schools. Juan worked late hours during the school year as a dishwasher in a restaurant. Although quite fatigued some days in class, he was a diligent student with a kind disposition.

- Chun arrived in the United States two years prior to this project, after 16 years of schooling in Taiwan. Although college educated, her mother did not work outside the home, but her father owned a computer company. She has two younger sisters. With her father's resources as the president of a computer company, she received a great deal of support to become more proficient in English. Chun passed all of her exit-level TAKS tests for graduation but still struggled with her oral proficiency. Although she maintained nearly perfect attendance and the highest grade-point average in the group, she was incredibly shy and withdrawn in class, barely speaking beyond a whisper and never volunteering any oral responses. Her goals included attending college to become an accountant and returning to Taiwan after her postsecondary education.

- Sergio, the son of an immigrant family from Mexico, had lived in the United States for five years prior to this project. During this year, Sergio was tested for learning disabilities and was subsequently exempted from his exit-level TAKS tests. Despite being the least proficient of the students, Sergio kept up with his work to remain eligible to play sports because he was a talented soccer player whose team went to the state 4-A championship. His father was a flea market vendor and his mother cleaned houses.

All four students were reading four to eight years below grade level, and although the particulars of the students' early school histories were unknown, as shown in Table 8.1, two of the students were in their 14th and 18th years of schooling. All were of legal age to drop out of school and seek full-time employment, but all remained in school and worked toward obtaining their high school diplomas.

Writing samples produced by the students over the course of the first few days of school provided evidence of the students' struggles to write as seen in Figure 8.1, which shows a sample of Chun's writing. In addition, all four students wrote negatively about their abilities as learners. For example, Valeria commented, "I am not a really intelligent student. I'm in the middle of knowing." Sergio wrote, "Sometimes I act stupid, but I start change because I have to put attention the classes so I can play soccer." These initial writing samples demonstrated how much work needed to be accomplished if these students were to complete high school.

To learn more about the students' writing skills, Kathleen administered two writing assessments. These were the Written Language Assessment (WLA; Grill & Kirwin, 1989), in which a student is asked to produce expressive, instructive, and creative writing samples and the story construction task on the Test of Written Language (TOWL-3; Hammill & Larsen, 1996), in which a student is asked to write a narrative related to a picture prompt. Assessment results shown in Table 8.2 demonstrate the students' low levels of writing achievement. Further analysis of students' writing samples in response to the three

Table 8.1. Students' Background Information

Student	Gender	Age	Country of origin	First language	Years in U.S. schools	Years of schooling in first language
Valeria	Female	18	Guanajuato, Mexico	Spanish	7 years	5 years
Juan	Male	19	Guanajuato, Mexico	Spanish	4 years	10 years
Chun	Female	19	Taiwan	Mandarin Chinese	2 years	16 years
Sergio	Male	18	Chihuahua, Mexico	Spanish	6 years	6 years

Figure 8.1. Chun's Response to the First Writing Task

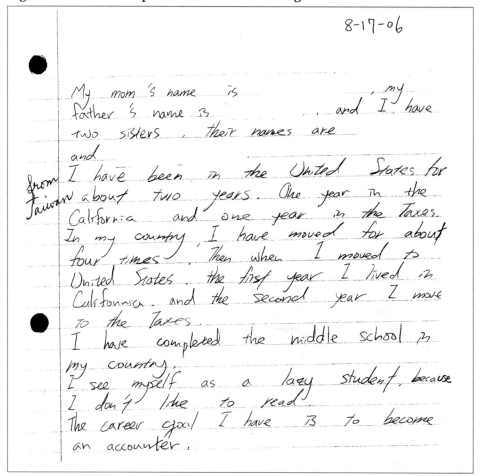

written prompts on the WLA showed that students wrote minimally. For example, when asked to write about how to talk to a child about the danger of fire, an instructive writing essay prompt on the WLA, Sergio produced the response shown in Figure 8.2.

Additionally, writing samples did not have identifiable text structures. For example, when asked to compose a narrative in response to a picture of astronauts working in space, Valeria provided the brief description shown in Figure 8.3.

Students' responses lacked well-formed paragraphs and sufficient details necessary to convey meaning. Other salient aspects of the students' writing

Table 8.2. Pre- and Post-TOWL-3 and WLA Results

Student	TOWL-3 quotient scores		TOWL-3 percentile scores		WLA quotient scores		WLA percentile scores	
	Pre	Post	Pre	Post	Pre	Post	Pre	Post
Valeria	70	104	2	61	82	112	11	79
Juan	70	102	2	55	70	105	2	62
Chun	98	109	45	73	60	94	1	34
Sergio	61	79	< 1	8	65	100	1	50

Figure 8.2. Sergio's Written Response

Write how you would tell a little kid about the danger of fire. You may write on both sides of the page.

no TO Play with fire because is
dangerous he can burn The house or
when his Mon is cooking not To get
close To The Fire because he can get
burn in his figuers leg's ect.

were the frequency of run-on sentences, minimal punctuation, inconsistent capitalization, and lack of conventional spelling.

Furthermore, it was evident from in-class writing samples and the writing assessments that the students viewed the act of writing as completing an assigned task. They seldom wrote to communicate their ideas or tell their stories. In addition to addressing writing skills, Kathleen and Eric wanted to plan opportunities for these students to take ownership of their writing and to build upon and share their background experiences. To do so, however, Kathleen and Eric needed to know much more about the students. First, they asked the students to complete the English Language Learner Information Survey shown in Figure 8.4, in which the students provided information about their families and early experiences.

Figure 8.3. Valeria's Narrative Response

> One day the people where on the moon, they were trying to find probably the planet or minerals for humans benefit. eventhoue it seems like they are exploring for gold or other things because of their tools, a shevel and pix. factory next to it that provided petroleum for the tractor, pipelines, factor was set up in there.

Next, Kathleen instituted a pen pal exchange between Eric's students and the students in her preservice course on literacy development for linguistically diverse learners. This exchange allowed Eric's students the opportunity to generate and respond in writing to friendly questions about day-to-day activities. Kathleen also requested that the pen pals share in writing their respective plans for the future.

The survey results and the students' letters written during the pen pal exchange revealed some valuable details about their lives. It was not uncommon for the students to be separated from close family members such as parents and siblings. Their parents had worked a variety of physically demanding jobs, and students' schooling had been interrupted before and since coming to the United States. They all had hopes for future schooling or employment. In many ways, these students were representative of ELLs in high schools throughout the United States. They were very different individuals with diverse backgrounds and experiences. All, however, needed greater English language competency to graduate and successfully move beyond high school. The following summarizes the implementation of the guided writing approach in Eric's classroom.

The Guided Writing Approach

Kathleen and Eric generated the following set of guidelines to help them meet their goals of increasing the quantity and quality of the students' writing:

- Select topics that are interesting and meaningful to the students and encourage them to share and build on their background experiences as they write.

Figure 8.4. English Language Learner Information Survey

1. Name: _____

2. Birthdate: _____

3. Where were you born? (City/State/Country): _____

4. Number of years/months in the U.S.: _____

5. Language(s) spoken at home: _____

6. Number of years of schooling outside the U.S.: _____

7. Number of years of schooling in the U.S.: _____

8. Why did your family come to the U.S.? _____

_____

9. Do you currently live with your father? _____ With your mother? _____

10. Other relatives living in your house: _____

11. How many brothers do you have? Number: _____ Ages: _____

12. How many sisters do you have? Number: _____ Ages: _____

13. What is your father's current occupation? _____

14. What other jobs has your father done? _____

15. How many years of schooling has your father completed? _____

16. What is your mother's occupation? _____

17. What other jobs has your mother done? _____

18. How many years of schooling has your mother completed? _____

19. What are the occupations of other wage earners living with you? _____

_____

20. Who is the person you most want to be like? _____

21. What kind of job would you like to have in the future? _____

22. When was the last time you were in your native country? _____

23. How long did you stay during your last visit to your home country? _____

24. Do you plan to return to your country of origin? (circle one)   Yes   No
    If yes, when? _____

- Scaffold students' access to the broad, 12th-grade literature curriculum, and provide students with opportunities to read authentic examples of the genres they will be expected to write.
- Explicitly teach students about text structures and the language used to organize texts such as transitional adverbs (e.g., *therefore, consequently*).
- Show students how to form simple, compound, and complex sentences.
- Target weak writing mechanics that were evident in the students' early writing. These students' writing evidenced missing pronouns, incorrect use of prepositions, shifting verb tenses, and insufficient punctuation and capitalization.

Following are overviews of guided writing lessons that were representative of the many lessons implemented over the course of the school year. We provide examples of lessons that addressed both text-level and word-level skills. To demonstrate students' growth over time, we share lessons and lesson outcomes from various times during the school year.

Kathleen and Eric planned the first guided writing lesson to support the students as they composed a draft of a three-paragraph composition in which they shared information about their families. Kathleen and Eric planned this lesson for two reasons. First, they wanted students to build on background knowledge as they wrote. Second, they wanted to encourage and support students to write well-formed paragraphs.

Kathleen began this lesson with a picture talk. As she displayed a family reunion photograph, she shared some reflections about growing up in a poor rural mining community in Pennsylvania. She also told the students some unique features about her childhood—her father was a coal miner and a mink rancher. She recalled in particular her parents' insistence that she receive a good education to help her move beyond their economically depressed area. After some initial hesitation, the students began to share information about their families including some ways in which their respective families were special. The students then shared their ideas about what they might include as they wrote about their families. This discussion provided Kathleen with the opportunity to teach a minilesson on several aspects of language in context, an important component of the guided writing approach.

First, Kathleen and the students generated a vocabulary list of words necessary to identify family members' parents (*grandparents, nieces, nephews*). Next, they completed a *family* word web in which they listed related words (*families, familiar, familial, familiarize, family-friendly,* and *family-oriented),* and Kathleen pointed out how related words are formed in English. As students talked about their siblings, Kathleen pointed out the use of the suffix *–er* to form the comparative *(older, younger)* and the use of *–er* to form a noun from a verb *(play—player, teach—teacher).* She also addressed the pronunciation of *y* at the end of polysyllabic words (e.g., *family, friendly, especially).* Finally, because all the students struggled with conventional spelling, she reminded students about the targeted suffixes and the spelling of *wh-* words *(whether, where, what)* and *w-* words *(were, was, watch).*

Next, Kathleen and the students generated a topic sentence for the first paragraph: "Whether large or small, families are special in many ways." This was followed by the sentence starter "In my family there are...." The students completed their paragraphs by describing family members and demonstrating what made their families unique. Once their first drafts were ready, Eric and Kathleen responded with questions, asking for details and elaboration. In addition, because the students wrote their ideas as one long paragraph, Eric and Kathleen had the students use colored markers to identify related sentences and divide their sentences into separate paragraphs. During subsequent revisions, the students reorganized their sentences and clustered them into three separate paragraphs.

All the students successfully wrote three paragraphs as they added to modeled sentences. Furthermore, there was evidence that students applied skills addressed in the minilesson as they wrote. For example, in Figure 8.5, Valeria correctly spelled *wh-* words.

In addition to implementing lessons that encouraged students to build upon and share background experiences, Kathleen and Eric implemented several guided writing lessons with a word-level focus at the beginning of the year. For example, past-tense verbs caused many problems for these writers. For this lesson Kathleen and Eric selected a brief article on the life and work of Mexican artist Diego Rivera. After Kathleen and the students read the article, Kathleen led a text talk about some of the artist's accomplishments. The text talk was followed by a review of the *–ed* past-tense marker and its various pronunciations in English (e.g., *played, missed, landed),* a typical challenge for ELLs. Then students reread the text and used highlighters to identify past-tense verbs.

Next, Eric used the article to help students notice the author's use of transitional words and phrases so that students would consider using these devices in their writing. The students then worked together to complete the cloze paragraph

Figure 8.5. Valeria's Revision

> Something that I don't like about one person of my family, which is my brother. I love him alot. but the thing I don't like about him, is that he overprotects me. when ever he finds out I am dating somcone he gets mad and angry specially if he dosent like him for me. what he would do, is that he'll go after him.

shown in Figure 8.6 that contained additional examples of transitional words and phrases and in which they needed to supply past-tense verb forms.

By midyear, Kathleen and Eric were eager to move the students to writing longer compositions that contained multiple paragraphs. To do so, Kathleen selected a one-page article from *Time* (Sachs, 2006) about author Mitch Albom and his popular book *For One More Day*. In this book, the main character has the opportunity to spend one more day with a loved one who has died. After students read and discussed the article with Kathleen, she asked them to consider with whom they would like to spend one special day and to write about it. To help them write more and attend to organization, Kathleen gave the students the following questions to scaffold their writing of four related paragraphs:

Paragraph 1: With whom would you want to spend one special day?

Why would you select this person to be with for a day?

Paragraph 2: What would you want to do with this person and why did you select this activity?

When and where would you like to spend this special day?

Paragraph 3: What would you like to talk about on this special day together?

Paragraph 4: What would you want as a result of this special time together?

Figure 8.6. Cloze Exercise

Last week was a busy time. I _____ many things.

First of all, I _____,

and then _____ .

At school, we _____ .

Fortunately, I _____ .

Unfortunately, _____ .

At home, my family and I _____ .

We also _____ .

Perhaps most importantly, last week _____ .

Now, I can _____ .

Students chose to write about spending a day with a grandmother, a sports hero, a favorite singer, or a best friend. Again with the support of the written scaffolds, all the students produced a four-paragraph essay including Juan, a very reluctant writer, whose essay is shown in Figure 8.7.

In addition to writing about personal topics, Eric's students needed to respond in writing to several works of literature that comprised the 12th-grade curriculum. During the first half of the school year, using adapted versions, the students read and wrote about *Beowulf* and *Dr. Jekyll and Mr. Hyde*; Eric's second-semester goals were for student to read an adapted version of *The Tragedy of Macbeth* and understand the literary term *tragedy* as the downfall of an important person. In addition, Eric wanted his students to write a five-paragraph analytical essay in response to the question How do we know that *The Tragedy of Macbeth* is a genuine tragedy? A requirement was for students to use evidence from each of the five acts in the play to support their responses. Over the course of several weeks, as the students read and discussed the play, Kathleen and Eric continued to conduct guided writing lessons.

The goal of the first guided writing lesson in this unit was to generate sentence models that students could use to begin their analytical essays. Kathleen began this lesson with vocabulary brainstorming and building a word web related to the word *tragedy*. The students first consulted their dictionaries for the definition and then generated a list of synonyms (*catastrophe, disaster, calamity*).

Figure 8.7. Juan's "Someone Special" Essay

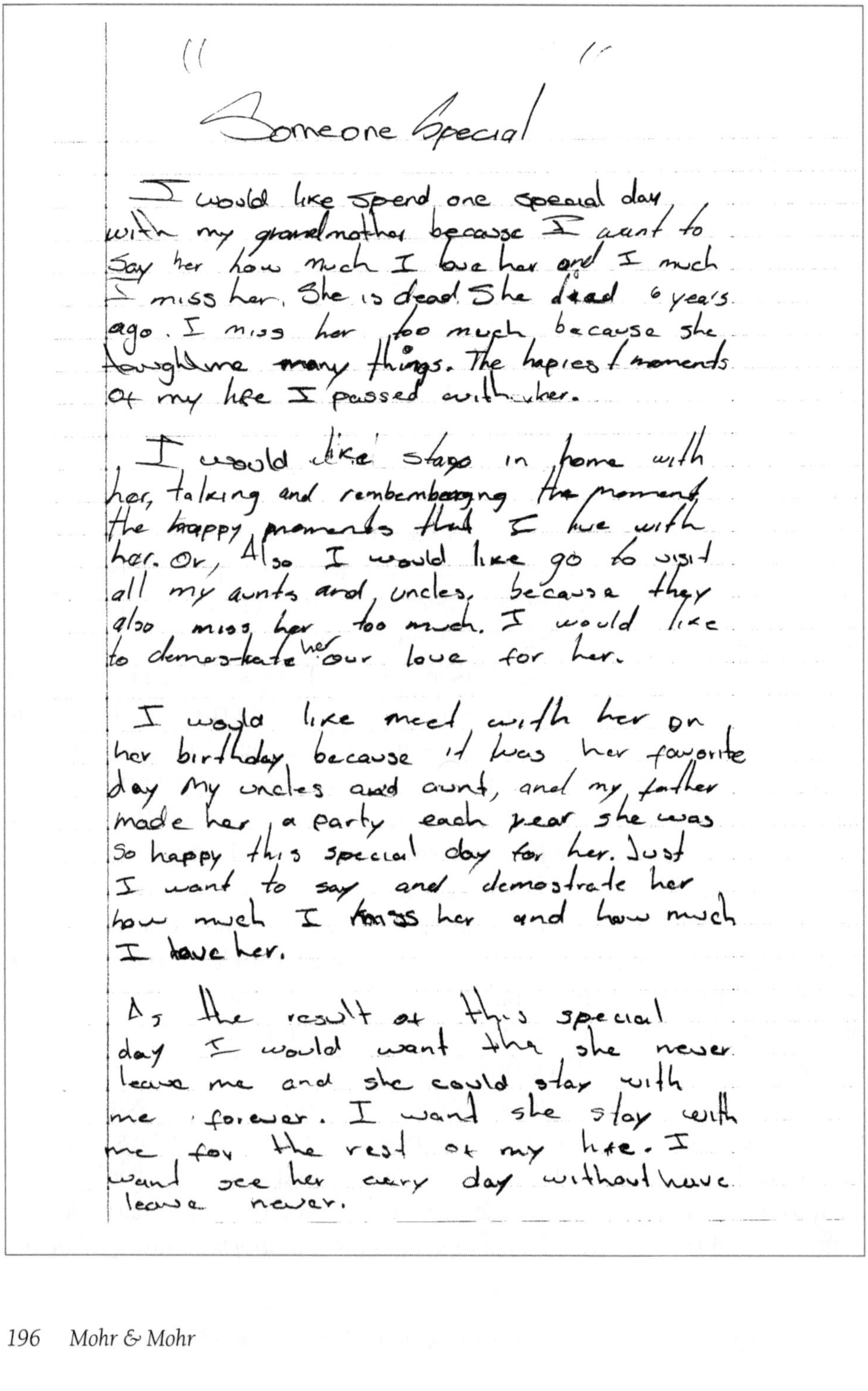

"Someone Special"

I would like spend one special day, with my grandmother because I want to Say her how much I love her and I much I miss her. She is dead. She dead 6 year's ago. I miss her too much because she taughtme many things. The hapiest moments of my life I passed with her.

I would like stay in home with her, talking and remembering the moments the happy moments that I live with her. Or, Also I would like go to visit all my aunts and, uncles, because they also miss her too much. I would like to demostrate her our love for her.

I would like meet with her on her birthday because it was her favorite day My uncles and aunt, and my father made her a party each year she was So happy this special day for her. Just I want to say and demostrate her how much I miss her and how much I love her.

As the result of this special day I would want that she never leave me and she could stay with me forever. I want she stay with me for the rest of my life. I want see her every day without have leave never.

Next, using current-day examples, Kathleen and students differentiated between the use of the word *tragedy* to refer to natural disasters (e.g., Hurricane Katrina, the Southeast Asian tsunami) or accidental deaths and *tragedy* as the downfall of an important person (e.g., Saddam Hussein). Kathleen then introduced the students to the sentence models used in *The Important Book* (Brown, 1949). Using these sentence models and the dictionary definition of *tragedy*, Kathleen and the students generated the following sentences to begin their essay.

> The important thing to know about *The Tragedy of Macbeth* is that it is mainly a tragedy. A dictionary definition of the word "tragedy" is the downfall of a great person. Some people think that a tragedy is any disaster or catastrophe. However, there are important differences.

Subsequent guided writing lessons were devoted to helping students brainstorm, draft, revise, and edit their essays. These lessons typically began with a brief text talk about one of the five acts of the play. During these lessons, Eric or Kathleen and the students generated topic sentences demonstrating to the students how to use transitional devices and include other academic language as they drafted, revised, and edited their essays. It was challenging work for these students, and they relied heavily on the modeled writing constructed in class. However, their confidence improved as they experienced the writing process. Their discussions of the play's events were lively and inquisitive; they made many comparisons to movie characters and celebrities. As their paragraphs grew and the essays developed, students were proud of how much they knew and could write about the topic.

Results of the Guided Writing Approach

Excerpts from Chun's essay shown in Figure 8.8 demonstrate that students accomplished many of the goals that Kathleen and Eric had set for this class. The essay has a clear purpose and structure, transitional devices necessary to lead the reader through the argument, and examples and details. Chun also produced few errors in spelling and mechanics. It is also interesting to note that although writing a five-paragraph analytical essay is a routine requirement for high school students, Eric's students revealed that it was the first time they had been expected to do so. They were proud that they were able to produce work that was comparable to their peers in the grade-level English classes.

Figure 8.8. Excerpts from Chun's *Macbeth* Essay

The important thing to know about The Tragedy of Macbeth is that it is mainly a tragedy. The dictionary definition of a tragedy is the downfall of a great person. Some people think that a tragedy is any disaster or catastrophe. However, there are important differences. A catastrophe or calamity can be unfortunate, but such events are natural disasters, such as Hurricane Katrina or the 2005 tsunami in Southeast Asia. Rather, a tragedy includes a series of conflicts in the life of a person of high position, and the decisions that the tragedy hero makes create problems for him/herself and others. These choices lead to a sad or pitiful conclusion for a person who had the chance to be great. Shakespeare's play Macbeth is just such a fine example of what a tragedy looks like and how it works.

In Act I and II, we see that Mabeth is a ~~good~~ example of a ~~tragedy~~ tragic hero ~~because~~ Mabeth is an ~~important~~ person who unlawfully wants to be ~~the~~ King of Scotland and ~~murders~~ murders King Duncan to have ~~the~~ throne. For example, we see that Mabeth is an ~~go~~ important person because he won the ~~war~~ against the Vikings, and then he also ~~be~~ named the Thane of Cawdor. Moreover, we ~~see~~ that Mabeth unlawfully desires to the King because he sent a letter explaining this to his wife.

(continued)

Figure 8.8. Excerpts from Chun's *Macbeth* Essay (continued)

> In Arts IV and V, we see Macbeth also concludes the play as a good example of a tragic hero because he must pay a penalty for all of the murders he has committed. For example, Macbeth talks to the witches about his future and his life as king. He also finds out that Macduff is a danger to him. Next, Macbeth's soldiers go to Macduff's home to kill everyone there, but Macduff has run away. Then, Lady Macbeth kills herself to end the troubles in her mind. Finally, Macbeth chooses to fight Macduff anyway, proving that he has courage, but he is killed by Macduff at the end of story. As we have seen, Macbeth ends the play as a tragic hero who most pay for his bad choices.

In May, Kathleen and Eric readministered the initial writing assessments. Each student made impressive gains in writing. As seen in Table 8.2 (see page 189), student assessment scores were well below average at the beginning of the school year; however, all scores were within the average range in May. Much of this improvement was related to the increased word productivity and complexity in their writing. Students wrote more and took more semantic and syntactic risks, as summarized in Table 8.3.

As graduation neared, Eric asked the students to submit a final personal essay about successes they experienced during their senior year. They all mentioned their writing growth. For example, Juan wrote, "I think now I can write better than when I start this year. I know that because I pass the TAKS, and I have better grades in the essays than at the beginning of the year." Sergio commented, "I pass all my classes to play soccer in school and speak better English." Chun recognized the challenge of reading "the whole story of Macbeth and... getting prepared for college." In addition to sharing her successes, Valeria also revealed her frustration about not passing the English Language Arts TAKS by two points. She would have to retake it later in June.

Table 8.3. Pre- and Post-WLA Subscores for Productivity, Word Complexity, and Readability

Student	Productivity—Scaled scores and percentiles				Word Complexity—Scaled scores and percentiles				Readability—Scaled scores and percentiles			
	Pre		Post		Pre		Post		Pre		Post	
	SS	P	SS	P	SS	P	SS	P	SS	P	SS	P
Valeria	5	5	13	84	4	2	13	84	11	63	13	84
Juan	2	0.4	13	84	2	0.4	11	63	11	63	0	50
Chun	2	0.4	10	50	1	0.1	7	16	3	1	9	37
Sergio	3	1	10	50	1	0.1	12	75	9	37	12	75

Note. SS = scaled score; P = percentile

> My three greatest successes were learning more words, and their definitions, write 5 paragraph essays, and the main one which...was the [math] TAKS. Hopefully I'll get my most important goal in June [ELA TAKS] and hopefully all of this could help me later to get a good job.

Recommendations for Supporting the Writing Development of ELLs

More attention needs to be given to how to implement effective practices to support the writing development of ELLs, especially high school students who face high-stakes testing requirements with such dire consequences as not completing a high school diploma. Such students need to make accelerated progress (Cummins, 2000; Mohr, 2004), which requires teachers and researchers to collaborate on innovative and motivational methods for developing language and literacy skills (Gibbons, 2002). In addition, having access to appropriate resources allows such collaborations to focus on students' learning, rather than on finding suitable materials. Although we acknowledge that what these students accomplished was only limited, contextualized success, we believe that some insights gained from our experiences using the guided writing approach with older ELLs will be helpful to other teachers. We have found the following to be beneficial when implementing guided writing with ELLs:

- Use a block schedule format for sheltered classes so that students have the necessary time to learn and apply listening, speaking, reading, and writing skills in an interrelated manner.

- Maintain a small class size to build "esprit de corps" among the students, stronger relationships with the teacher, and ensure more opportunities for student talk (August & Shanahan, 2006).

- Know students well enough to help them make connections between their personal and school lives and future plans. Encourage students to build on their background knowledge and share their personal experiences and goals and plans for their life after high school in their writing.

- Set high standards for students' writing in terms of structural complexity and sentence variety and carefully scaffold students' attempts to meet these high standards.

- Analyze each writing task and use thoughtfully constructed graphic organizers to help students talk about the organization of a text or written piece. Use sentence starters and cloze techniques to model written rhetorical structures and help students acquire academic language that can be used as they read and write (Faltis & Coulter, 2008).

- Use formal and informal assessment results to inform teaching practice rather than rely on a predetermined sequence to teach grammar and mechanics.

Much more work needs to be done to determine best practices that promote ELLs' writing development. Making their writing achievement a priority is imperative to making their journeys through high school and beyond successful ones.

REFLECTION QUESTIONS

1. What does your school or school district do to support ELLs' writing development? How do you meet the needs of ELLs who are several years behind in their reading and writing proficiencies?

2. How are modeled, guided, and interactive writing alike and different? How might each be used appropriately with ELLs?

3. Which aspect of process writing (i.e., brainstorming, planning, drafting, revising, editing, and publishing) do you find most challenging for your ELLs? What supports do you have or might you put in place to assist your students as they write?

4. What kinds of informal or formal writing assessments do you use with your students? How do these assessments help you identify your students' writing strengths and needs?

5. Which writing prompts or topics have you found to be especially productive or successful with ELLs? Did you use a graphic organizer with ELLs to support their writing efforts? What characterizes an appropriate topic or organizer for writing tasks among ELLs?

REFERENCES

August, D. (2002). *Transitional programs for English language learners: Contextual factors and effective programming* (Report No. 58). Baltimore: Center for Research on Education of Students Placed at Risk.

August, D., & Shanahan, T. (Eds.). (2006). *Developing literacy in second-language learners: Report of the National Literacy Panel on Language-Minority Children and Youth*. Mahwah, NJ: Erlbaum.

Button, K., Johnson, M.J., & Ferguson, P. (1996). Interactive writing in a primary classroom. *The Reading Teacher, 49*(6), 446–454.

Brown, M.W. (1949). *The important book*. New York: Harper.

Calhoun, E.F. (1999). *Teaching beginning reading and writing with the Picture Word Inductive Model*. Alexandria, VA: Association for Supervision and Curriculum Development.

Collom, S. (1996). *Sharing the pen: Interactive writing with young children*. Fresno, CA: California State University and San Joaquin Valley Writing Project.

Cummins, J. (2000). *Language, power, and pedagogy: Bilingual children in the crossfire*. Buffalo, NY: Multilingual Matters.

Echevarria, J., Short, D., & Powers, K. (2006). School reform and standards-based education: How do teachers help English language learners? *The Journal of Educational Research, 99*(4), 195–211. doi:10.3200/JOER.99.4.195-211

Faltis, C.J., & Coulter, C.A. (2008). *Teaching English learners and immigrant students in secondary schools*. Upper Saddle River, NJ: Pearson Merrill Prentice Hall.

Gibbons, P. (2002). *Scaffolding language, scaffolding learning: Teaching second language learners in the mainstream classroom*. Portsmouth, NH: Heinemann.

Grill, J.J., & Kirwin, M.M. (1989). *Written language assessment (WLA)*. Novata, CA: Academic Therapy Publications.

Hall, M. (1999). Focus on language experience learning and teaching. In O.G. Nelson & W.M. Linek (Eds.), *Practical classroom applications of language experience: Looking back, looking forward* (pp. 12–18). Boston: Allyn & Bacon.

Hammill, D.D., & Larsen, S.C. (1996). *Test of written language: Examiner's manual* (3rd ed.). Austin, TX: Pro-ed.

Hastings-Gongora, B. (1993). The effects of reading aloud on vocabulary development: Teacher insights. *Bilingual Research Journal, 17*(1/2), 135–138.

McCarrier, A., Pinnell, G.S., & Fountas, I.C. (2000). *Interactive writing: How language and literacy come together, K–2*. Portsmouth, NH: Heinemann.

Meeks, L.L., & Austin, C.J. (2003). *Literacy in the secondary English classroom: Strategies for teaching the way kids learn*. Boston: Allyn & Bacon.

Merkley, D., & Jefferies, D. (2000/2001). Guidelines for implementing a graphic organizer. *The Reading Teacher, 54*(4), 350–357.

Mohr, K.A.J. (2004). English as an accelerated language: A call to action for reading teachers. *The Reading Teacher, 58*(1), 18–26. doi:10.1598/RT.58.1.2

National Center for Education Statistics. (2004). *The condition of education, 2004*. Washington, DC: Author. Retrieved August 30, 2007, from http://nces.ed.gov/programs/coe

National Center for Education Statistics. (2008). *National Assessment of Educational Progress (NAEP), 1999, 2002, and 2007 writing assessments*. Washington, DC: Author. Retrieved April 16, 2009, from http://nces.ed.gov/nationsreportcard/writing/moreabout.asp.

Sachs, A. (2006, October). Life and death. *Time*, p. F17.

Salahu-Din, D., Persky, H., & Miller, J. (2008). *The nation's report card: Writing 2007* (NCES 2008-468). Washington, DC: U.S. Department of Education.

Saunders, W.M., & Goldenberg, C. (1999). Effects of instructional conversations and literature logs on limited- and fluent-English proficient students' story comprehension and thematic understanding. *The Elementary School Journal, 99*(4), 277–301. doi:10.1086/461927

Smith, C.C., & Bean, T.W. (1980). The guided writing procedure: Integrating content and reading and writing improvement. *Reading World, 19*(3), 290–293.

Wood, K.D., & Tinajero, J. (2002). Using pictures to teach content to second language learners: Research into practice. *Middle School Journal, 33*(5), 47–51.

Improving Teaching and Learning in Multilingual Classrooms

Collaborating With "Hard-to-Reach" Parents in an ELL Population: One Teacher's Exploration

Trini Lewis and Esmeralda Ramos

Parent–teacher conferences are important forums for discussing children's progress and provide parents and teachers with opportunities for collaboration. Nonetheless, concerns about the traditional parent–teacher conference format persist within the teaching profession. For example, during our respective careers, we struggled with the brief time periods allotted by our school districts for these meetings. Trini (first author), a professor and former classroom teacher, and Esmeralda (second author), a first-grade teacher, found the time limitations of 15–20 minutes per family inhibited our ability to fully discuss topics or to develop better relationships with our students' parents or guardians. Researchers have also noted problems with the traditional conference format and claim that it is not conducive to promoting collaboration between parents or guardians and teachers. For example, Swap (1993) observes that because parent–teacher conferences are bound by tradition to occur over several days and to last for approximately 15 minutes, authentic dialogue and effective problem solving is compromised. Swap asked, "In what other circumstance would one allow only 15 minutes to share a significant amount of information about a situation of deep mutual concern with a virtual stranger?" (p. 20).

In addition to our concerns about time constraints, we developed concerns about our communication skills. We knew that an unspoken professional expectation was that we were to conduct successful conferences. We encountered instances of awkwardness, however, when parents raised unexpected topics or questioned our professional judgment. In such instances, we thought we lost

One Classroom, Many Learners: Best Literacy Practices for Today's Multilingual Classrooms edited by Julie Coppola and Elizabeth V. Primas. © 2009 by the International Reading Association.

control of the discussion because our identity as experts was challenged. And, from time to time, we observed and discussed these situations with our colleagues who had similar encounters.

Finally, and most important, over the years, we found that the traditional conference format did not lead to collaborations with "hard-to-reach" parents whose children were English language learners (ELLs). These were the parents who resisted attending our conference sessions or who, when they did attend, resisted implementing our suggestions for improving their children's progress. However, this resistance was often related to misunderstanding the importance of attending parent–teacher conferences and the active role parents can play in their children's schooling. For example, many of the parents had limited formal schooling in their country of origin and were unfamiliar with the expectations for parental involvement in U.S. schools.

Our experiences with and concerns about parent–teacher conferences occurred independently and during different time periods in our careers. Yet, our mutual interest in improving collaborations with hard-to-reach parents brought us together when Esmeralda first served as a master teacher/mentor for one of Trini's student teachers. A year later, Esmeralda enrolled in a master's program with a dual-language development emphasis that Trini coordinates and took Trini's course on biliteracy assessment. As a result of various course sessions, we came to know each other better and found that we shared a belief that parents had many opportunities to be involved in their children's learning.

We also realized, however, that hard-to-reach parents appeared uninvolved in their children's education and, as a result, were not contacted by us or other teachers as often as the more involved and amenable parents. We knew our communication patterns with such parents were contrary to our professional knowledge about what we knew was in the best interests for promoting students' progress. Additionally, we had personal experiences that served as examples for improvement, yet we were unable to resolve the issue in our classroom practice and sought solutions. For example, Esmeralda observed her two aunts, who were teachers in Mexico, develop close relationships with all of their students' families. Her aunts were invited frequently to celebrations, such as birthday parties, and developed a great familiarity with their students' families. When Esmeralda's aunts met with parents to discuss their children's progress, they not only focused on the individual student but also included inquiries and comments about other family members, demonstrating a sincere interest in the family's overall well-being. Moreover, these teachers became highly respected and trusted members in the community.

With her aunts as her role models, Esmeralda also developed excellent relationships with a majority of her students' families. For example, parents attended schoolwide events and volunteered for various classroom-related activities, such as attending field trips. However, as much effort as Esmeralda put forth, challenges persisted in collaborating with hard-to-reach parents. Over the course of our conversations, we continued to share our past experiences and new ideas about collaboration, and as a result, Esmeralda expressed an interest in piloting new communication strategies with her students' parents drawn from Trini's research on parent–teacher conferences (Lewis, 2003).

In this chapter we share Esmeralda's experiences as one teacher's effort to improve collaboration with hard-to-reach parents in a school with a high ELL population. We highlight conferences as the focal environment for promoting collaboration because they are the most common form of parental involvement and can be the most problematic for parents and teachers. We begin with a review of the literature on parental involvement and parent–teacher conferences, and then we discuss the effective communication strategies Esmeralda employed. We then examine Esmeralda's interactions with parents with a particular focus on her interactions with one hard-to-reach parent whose daughter's literacy progress at the beginning of the school year was significantly below the first-grade level, and we conclude with a discussion of the significance of our findings and the implications for practice.

What Does the Literature Tell Us About Parental Involvement and Parent–Teacher Conferences in ELL Settings?

It isn't surprising that teachers such as Esmeralda find themselves underprepared for collaborating with parents, and especially with those who are traditionally viewed as "hard to reach." Although Simich-Dudgeon (1993) notes that "there is an urgent need to train teachers to recognize the importance of parental participation and student outcomes, and to gain the cross-cultural skills needed to make this partnership work" (p. 189), few colleges and universities offer course work on parental involvement beyond the early childhood education level.

To improve our knowledge about collaboration with such parents, we reviewed several important studies that offered new insights for guiding our work. For example, Lopez, Scribner, and Mahitivanichcha (2001) find that schools were successful in promoting parental involvement in migrant populations when they met the needs of parents in multiple ways on a daily and ongoing basis. Other research by Carreon, Drake, and Barton (2005) in high-poverty, urban communities with large ELL populations suggests that parents' presence in their children's schooling needs to be understood within formal school spaces as well as informal spaces created by the parents themselves. The authors reported that principals and teachers lacked an awareness of how parents felt about their roles in schools. Carreon and colleagues conclude

> If schools continue, even with the best intentions, to implement parental participation programs without listening to parents voice their particular needs and hopes, these programs will remain stagnant and do little to reduce the marked distance between the home and the school. (p. 494)

Research by Hidalgo (1998) and Valdes (1996) also found similar results in urban schools with high ELL populations. Other research conducted by Mattingly, Prislin, McKenzie, Rodriguez, and Kayzar (2002) poses questions about the effectiveness of parental involvement programs in promoting parents' participation in their children's education and improving children's learning outcomes. According to Mattingly and colleagues, a gap exists between popular support and scientific evidence. In evaluating 41 parental involvement programs in grades K–12, the researchers found insufficient data to suggest that the parental involvement programs were effective for improving student achievement or changing parent, teacher, and student behavior. The researchers criticized a majority of the programs for "changing parent behavior—especially in the areas of parenting and supporting home learning—rather than changing teacher practices or school structures" (p. 571).

The authors' findings hold important implications for ELL populations in schools where parental involvement efforts routinely focus on what parents can learn from schools—but not always what schools can learn from parents. Given the lack of attention to parental involvement in university course work, we were also not surprised to find that the literature on parent–teacher conferences contained an abundance of opinion pieces but few investigations—and even less research on ELL populations. Nonetheless, two contrasting perspectives about parent–teacher conferences are vividly depicted in practitioner and research-based articles. In the following sections, we present these two major perspectives on parent–teacher conferences. Although the literature is not entirely specific to parent–teacher conferences and ELLs, the findings are applicable to ELL populations.

Parent–Teacher Conferences Are Forums Plagued With Strife

The first perspective on parent–teacher conferences depicts conferences as tense encounters. In fact, parent–teacher conflict is thought to be so common that many practitioner publications routinely provide tips for teachers on how to improve communication when meeting with parents. However, because much of the advice isn't grounded in research, questions remain about the efficacy of the suggestions offered in this body of literature.

Popular periodicals also attempt to shed light on the problem of parent–teacher conflict. For example, *Time* magazine (Gibbs et al., 2005) devoted an entire issue to examining problematic parent–teacher interactions. And, to make light of the strife, *The New York Times* annually publishes a cartoon bank of illustrations lampooning adversarial aspects in parent–teacher relationships (Mankoff, 2006).

The studies on parental involvement indicate even more troublesome issues for urban school populations, particularly when parents are foreign born or are unfamiliar with school culture (Delgado-Gaitan, 1990; Goldenberg, 1993; Laureau, 1989, 1996; Trueba, 1989; Valdes, 1996). According to recent census data reported by the Center for Immigration Studies (Camarota, 2007), immigrants with U.S. born children under the age of 18 have a 50% higher poverty rate than natives and their children. Marzano (2004) also claims that students living at or near the poverty line are 70% less likely to experience academic success in comparison to students above the poverty line.

Moles (1993) further notes that communication problems might be inherent in the parent–teacher conference format. Moles observes, "the parent–teacher conference can be fraught with psychological barriers for disadvantaged parents. Invitations, as well as other communications to parents, are frequently couched in educational jargon, big words and lengthy prose" (p. 34). Paredes Scribner (1999) also finds that schools struggle with meaningful ways to involve culturally and linguistically diverse parents in their children's schooling. Home–school partnerships are often sought as the school infrastructure for supporting parental involvement and improving student success, but more research is needed to learn how best to guide parents in general and culturally and linguistically diverse parents in particular. Studies continue to be inconclusive and longitudinal investigations are limited, especially with respect to identifying the causal links between parental involvement and academic achievement in ELL populations.

Parent–Teacher Conferences Are Forums of Opportunity for Collaboration

The second perspective on parent–teacher conferences presented in the seminal work of Bronfenbrenner (1979) suggests that, despite differences between families and schools, there are many commonalities leading to substantial benefits for improving children's development. Related literature on parent–teacher conferences also suggests that collaborative opportunities for parents and teachers can occur during meetings (Lightfoot, 2003; Swap, 1993). According to the National Education Association, the largest professional teacher's organization in the United States, "when teachers and parents view the educational process as a collaborative effort, the parent–teacher conference becomes a key instructional strategy that will enhance the child's growth and promote more effective learning" (Rotter, Robinson, & Fey, 1987, p. 6). Swap (1993) also reports that effective communication leads to collaboration between parents and teachers when "both teacher and parent(s) or guardian(s) have approximately equal time to share information and express views or concerns; shared expectations are developed; and problem solving and decision making, if needed, are jointly undertaken" (p. 80).

The findings from an investigation of five case studies conducted by Lewis (2003) on parent–teacher conferences with immigrant and migrant families indicate that when parents and teachers developed a mutual understanding about how to support children's progress, collaboration resulted. For example, parents and teachers informed one another about their roles and responsibilities and were comfortable with an overlap in their spheres of influence over the children. The teachers who experienced higher levels of collaboration were also those who met with parents during informal encounters throughout the school year. The encounters were often brief and unexpected, yet the teachers seized the moments as important for connecting with parents in a friendly manner, such as hallway chats before or after school.

Additionally, Lewis (2003) finds that initiating informal parent contacts was not "natural" for some of the teachers. She did find, however, that those teachers who used a parent–teacher contact record, referred to as Contacts-at-a-Glimpse (CAG), increased their interactions with parents and improved communication and collaboration during their conference sessions. The teachers completed the CAG form, an adaptation of a parent contact record originally proposed by McLoughlin (1987), on a monthly basis to identify their patterns of informal and formal contact with families. As seen in Figure 9.1, when completing the

Figure 9.1. Contacts-at-a-Glimpse Sample

Month: November

Student/ family name(s)	Monthly contact goal (if applicable)	Dates of contact	Type of contact (e.g., informal = note, phone call, message sent with child; formal = face-to-face-conference)	Reason for contact and/or topics discussed (academic/ behavioral)	Person initiating contact
Javier	1 informal and 1 formal mtg	11/7	Phone call— informal contact	To confirm conference date	Mother
Bobby	1 informal and 1 formal mtg	11/10	Briefly met with Bobby's mother as she brought him to school, 15 minutes late— informal contact	Set-up conference date	Mother
Lourdes	1 informal and 1 formal mtg	11/15	Mom came to say hello—informal contact	To inform about family issue—death in family	Mother
Marissa	1 informal and 1 formal mtg	11/17	Cell phone call— informal contact	Reminder to attend conference	Me
Claudia's mom's friend— babysitter	1 informal and 1 formal mtg	11/17	Face-to-face, came to my classroom—formal contact	To attend confer- ence because Claudia's mother couldn't attend	Me
Antonio	1 informal and 1 formal mtg	11/19	Phone call— informal contact	To schedule a conference	Me

Additional Notes:

CAG form, teachers such as Esmeralda noted the names of the families, the dates of the meetings, the types of contacts, the purpose of the contacts, and the outcomes of the contacts. At the end of each month, the information was then analyzed to identify areas of strength and weakness in contacting parents.

What We Learned From the Literature for Guiding Our Exploration

The literature we reviewed on parental involvement and parent–teacher conferences contained two important claims for improving contacts and collaboration among parents, teachers, and schools. First, if teachers in settings with high ELL populations are to involve a variety of parents in their children's learning, then parental involvement efforts such as collaboration need to consider parents' voices and needs. To achieve this goal, the literature indicates that it is imperative for teachers to improve their contacts and communication skills, especially with hard-to-reach parents. Second, the traditional parent–teacher conference format needs to be complemented with informal encounters or meetings on a consistent basis throughout the school year. The focus of such encounters also needs to be on monitoring and assessing children's progress in collaboration with their parents. We incorporated these claims as goals in our study for improving Esmeralda's collaboration with all of her students' parents and particularly with a hard-to-reach parent. Although we acknowledge that the literature refers to parent–teacher relationships, we recognize the full range of adults or older siblings invested in children's education and include such family models in our examination and discussion of the results. In the following section, we examine Esmeralda's school and classroom settings, as well as the methods she employed to improve parental involvement in her students' literacy development. To protect the privacy of some of the participants in this study, pseudonyms are used when referring to the parents and the children.

Exploring the Implementation of Communication Strategies

The School Context

The setting is a school situated in an urban school district in southern California. The school is in a residential neighborhood and at the time of the study, operated on a year-round schedule consisting of four tracks, A–D. Tracks A, B, and D began the school year in September and completed it in July. Track C began the school year in October and ended it in August. All of the tracks had approximately four periods during the year for vacation time.

The school also had 884 students enrolled in grades K–5, and a majority of the ELL students were in grades K–3 (i.e., kindergarten had 23.6%, first grade had 18.2%, and second and third grades had 18% of their students identified as ELLs). The school's student population was diverse with 77.3% Latino, 17.5% African American, 2.1% Caucasian, 1.7% Asian, 0.7% Pacific Islander, 0.5% Filipino, and 0.2% American Indian/Alaska Native. General education classes were offered, and some classrooms were designated as intensive structured English, structured English, or transitional structured English. These designations were dependent upon the number of ELLs per grade level.

The school received Title I and special education funding and offered Reading Recovery pull-out classes for those students who were struggling readers. Since 2000, the school, in conjunction with the YMCA, received private foundation grant monies to support a school-site community center. The community center provided family support services, such as extended day care, and academic and recreational activities. During 2006, the school and the community center were nationally recognized for creating an exemplary partnership, establishing a high level of parental involvement, and improving student achievement. Despite such distinction, Esmeralda and her colleagues continued to experience difficulties with involving parents in their children's schooling.

Esmeralda's classroom was designated by the school district as English only, and she provided all of her instruction to students in English. The majority of her students, however, also spoke Spanish at home with their parents. Her class consisted of 13 boys and 7 girls. Three children were classified as special needs with individual educational plans, and four children attended Reading Recovery class sessions for 30 minute periods, five days a week, on a pull-out basis throughout each semester. Esmeralda's classroom was in session during Track B, from September through July.

Improving Informal Contacts With Contacts-at-a-Glimpse

Given the effectiveness of the CAG form reported by Lewis (2003) for improving collaboration, Esmeralda was enthusiastic about piloting the CAG form during one fall semester. She used the form as a strategy for increasing monthly contacts with her students' families and to explore if the CAG form's effectiveness was replicable with the most difficult cases—the hard-to-reach parents.

In analyzing the data, we uncovered three significant patterns in Esmeralda's parent contacts. First, the contacts were initiated on a consistent basis and included the hard-to-reach parents. During the first month of completing the CAG form, Esmeralda established a monthly contact goal to ensure consistency for meeting with all of her students' parents. Consequently, she kept a count of who had been contacted and the frequency of these contacts. Her monthly goal was to make at least one informal contact with students' parents, particularly if they hadn't initiated contact with her. Prior to maintaining the CAG form, Esmeralda was unaware of exactly how many times per month she engaged in contacts with hard-to-reach parents. Second, the data indicated that Esmeralda's parent contacts represented a range of informal communication formats, such as notes she sent home with students, parents' calls to her cell phone, and parents' unannounced visits to her classroom either before or after school. The third and final pattern revealed that the contacts were for the purpose of arranging future meetings. Thus, the informal contacts served as gateways to after-school conferences and increased the probability of the hard-to-reach parents keeping their appointments.

As Esmeralda increased her informal contacts each month, an unanticipated finding emerged. The number of parents initiating contacts increased, resulting in an even balance (approximately 50%, $N = 20$) between the contacts initiated by Esmeralda and the parents. Previously, Esmeralda had initiated the majority of contacts for meetings with parents, similar to her teacher colleagues. As she used the CAG form on a monthly basis, however, the hard-to-reach parents became better about contacting Esmeralda to reschedule meetings, or when Esmeralda recontacted them, they agreed readily to another meeting date. When one hard-to-reach parent was invited to meet for a conference, she remarked to Esmeralda about being surprised that the conference was just to "keep in touch." The parent's surprise was well-founded given that previous contacts with her children's teachers had only occurred during the report card period or when there was a problem that needed to be addressed. Thus, by maintaining the CAG form and establishing a contact goal of informal encounters, Esmeralda became more mindful of contacting parents to discuss children's progress on an ongoing basis. The CAG form also helped Esmeralda understand that when a parent inquired about a child's behavior (e.g., ¿Como se comporta mi hijo?

[How does my child behave?]) the parent wanted to know about their child's academic performance as well.

Conference Outcomes: Promoting Collaboration in Students' Progress

In addition to learning whether or not the CAG form was effective for increasing informal contacts, we also wanted to know if there were differences in Esmeralda's communication patterns during her conference sessions that inhibited or promoted collaboration with families. Thus, Esmeralda audiotaped her discussions with parent volunteers so that we could closely examine the conversations in a transcript format.

Our review of the data from the CAG forms and the conference transcripts indicated a sharp contrast between Esmeralda's conference discussions during the fall parent–teacher conference week and the informal after-school conferences. For example, Esmeralda's conferences during the conference week were conducted using a conference plan. The conference plan was designed by the school district and used by teachers on a voluntary basis to guide a discussion about students' report cards. Topics included (a) children's strengths; (b) a subject area in which the child needed to grow; (c) parents' contributions; (d) classroom plans made by the teacher, noting one or two action items for supporting the child's improvement before the next parent–teacher conference; and (e) promotion or retention information.

Although the conference plan was beneficial for guiding Esmeralda's discussions, it also limited her topics to classroom learning. As a result, Esmeralda unknowingly dominated the conversations and conversational exchanges were compromised because parents made few verbal contributions. Our analysis of the discussions revealed that Esmeralda's communication pattern during the conference week sessions was a variation of a discussion framework noted by Lewis (2003). In similar fashion with the teachers studied by Lewis, Esmeralda reported information as a teacher expert and parents responded with few remarks or little elaboration, reminiscent of a traditional lawyer–client or doctor–patient interaction. Esmeralda's conference discussions typically resembled the following one with Carlo's mother, Maria.

> Esmeralda: Let's see, umm, oh, reading with fluency. It's something he can improve on or grow on. He needs to read quickly and with a voice and, ah, umm, he's getting better about that, like, um, if

the sentence has an exclamation point his voice should change. If it has a question mark, the voice should change like he's reading the way people normally talk, not in this very boring and monotone voice. You know what I mean?

Maria: Umm...

Esmeralda: And then in fluency, quickly, which fluency means reading quickly so that he doesn't have to struggle over every single word, so practice with him if you can. Okay?

Maria: Okay.

Another excerpt from the conference transcript illustrates Maria's knowledge about her son's work habits and the support she provided for completing his homework assignments.

Esmeralda: He finishes all of his work in class. I don't know if you see the same thing at home with his homework?

Maria: Yeah, he is very...he comes home and he does his homework and I help him. And if he can't get help at that time he gets frustrated. You know he goes home by himself and he gets his folder and sometimes you know when get, gets back from school sometimes I cannot pay attention to him 'cause I'm cooking and he starts getting mad and frustrated 'cause he wants to finish it right there and right now.

Similar to other parents' conference remarks, Maria's comments were directly related to an explicit question posed by Esmeralda and did not occur spontaneously. Thus, when parents' contributions emerged, Esmeralda didn't fully explore the topics beyond what was necessary for addressing the conference plan agenda items.

Our analysis of Esmeralda's conferences during the conference week indicated that her communication pattern was effective for the subset of parents, such as Maria, whose children were progressing well and who understood Esmeralda's directives for improvement. Or who knew what actions to undertake for supporting their children's literacy progress, such as reading with their children at home and helping with homework. Collaboration between Esmeralda and this subset of parents seemed to proceed without much effort. However, we were left wondering why our goal for improving collaboration wasn't as evident with the hard-to-reach families whose children typically performed at lower proficiency levels.

Revisiting Our Outcomes and Learning to Consider a Family's Needs

In light of the conference outcomes, we needed to modify Esmeralda's communication with the hard-to-reach parents who might not be as knowledgeable about supporting their children's school-related progress and whose children were at risk for retention. For this purpose, we discuss the case of Linda, whose mother, Yvonne, proved to be the most hard-to-reach parent for Esmeralda. Esmeralda developed serious concerns about Linda's progress and thought she might be a candidate for retention. Linda was the youngest of five children, and Yvonne was expecting a sixth child in the spring. Yvonne was a single parent who supported her children by babysitting in her apartment. Yvonne was born in El Salvador and came to the United States when she was 10 years old. After arriving in the United States, Yvonne attended public schools, but at the age of 16 she dropped out of high school to give birth to her first daughter, Carolina. Yvonne was conversant in English, but Esmeralda observed that Yvonne sometimes engaged in code-switching between English and Spanish.

Consistent with her routines, Esmeralda met with Yvonne at the beginning of the school year, and she followed her practice of discussing the agenda items on her conference plan. For example, Esmeralda informed Yvonne that Linda had not passed a kindergarten district benchmark test at a satisfactory level. She also explained that the test results indicated that Linda performed poorly on counting syllables and on the other subtests, such as identifying initial and final sounds. In addition, Esmeralda mentioned that Linda would be retested during the semester and if she didn't pass the test she might be at risk for retention in the first grade.

To keep Yvonne informed about Linda's progress, Esmeralda met with Yvonne every couple of weeks. However, as the weeks went by, Esmeralda's concerns increased about Linda's progress. Linda was alarmingly slow, and she appeared increasingly tired and unmotivated to do well in school. Her ability to complete homework assignments wasn't improving, and she was missing too many school days. Esmeralda was becoming increasingly frustrated with what she believed to be Yvonne's lack of interest and follow through in her daughter's education.

In an effort to improve Esmeralda's collaboration with Yvonne, we modified several of Esmeralda's communication strategies based on the results from the CAG form and transcript data. For example, Esmeralda increased her informal contacts with Yvonne to at least once a week because the previous frequency of meeting every few weeks was not effective for promoting collaboration to improve Linda's progress. The new encounters were brief and occurred when Yvonne arrived after the school day to walk Linda home. During these interactions, Esmeralda updated Yvonne on Linda's literacy progress or provided suggestions and friendly reminders about what might be done at home to support Linda's improvement, such as completing homework. From time to time, Yvonne also discussed family situations that affected Linda's school performance. Although Yvonne was from El Salvador, she had many family members living in Mexico, and Linda missed a number of school days to travel to Mexico for family emergencies.

Additionally, Esmeralda initiated an after-school conference and increased the time from 20 minutes to 1 hour. Given the limitations of the conference plan, we omitted it so that conversation could occur spontaneously. According to the transcript data, improvements resulted in the discussion between Esmeralda and Yvonne that were in sharp contrast to their previous discussions. For example, in their former conference meetings, Esmeralda did a majority of the talking and Yvonne's participation was minimal. However, after implementing the conference changes, their meetings resembled interactive conversations. Yvonne moved beyond the role of a passive listener to an active participant who asked questions and made follow-up remarks to Esmeralda's comments. Yvonne also initiated a number of topics concerning her personal experiences that provided Esmeralda with a fuller picture and understanding about Linda's home environment. The following transcript fragment, for instance, illustrates Yvonne's difficulties in learning how to read as a teenage mother.

> Yvonne: Yeah, it's hard to read. I had Carolina. It was hard for me. I learned on the street. So, I teached myself to read.
>
> Esmeralda: Wow! So then how did you learn how to read? Did you go to classes? Or did you just practice on your own?
>
> Yvonne: Reading books at home, yeah.
>
> Esmeralda: That's good. That's really good; that's a good model for your kids. And your baby.

Yvonne's discussion about her personal struggle in learning to read enhanced Esmeralda's knowledge about the assistance and resources available to Linda at home for improving her literacy development. Esmeralda commended Yvonne for her effort in learning how to read and further learned that Yvonne watched television programs to improve her reading ability.

Esmeralda: Right, but I mean at least you practice and you're able to do it on your own. That's good. That's more than most people do. People who can't read sometimes don't take the time to do it. So at least, I mean, you should be proud of yourself for being able to do that!

Yvonne: Watching so much TV and I use to read the words at the bottom.

Esmeralda: Yeah, the captions?

Yvonne: Watching TV and I was reading the words on the bottom.

Esmeralda: That's good! [laughter] You should do that for them too. I think they have that for cartoons. They have the words on underneath too. For captions...that will be a good idea. I never even thought about that!

Esmeralda also mentioned that Linda and the other children in the class would soon begin taking little books home to read aloud to their parents. In explaining the information, Esmeralda was careful to emphasize that Linda needed to read aloud on a nightly basis while pointing to each word she read on the page. Esmeralda further mentioned that it was fine for Yvonne to read the word for Linda if she didn't know it. Yvonne agreed to read with Linda before they went to sleep, and Esmeralda followed up with a comment about how the new family bedtime practice would improve Linda's reading proficiency.

Although Yvonne had a great desire to help Linda improve her literacy progress, she was not always confident about how to help her daughter. Esmeralda was aware that Yvonne lacked confidence and was keen to praise and support Yvonne's efforts for helping Linda at home. Toward the end of the conference, Yvonne poignantly commented about her great desire to help Linda by stating: "Sometimes I tell Brenda, my daughter, help me out. Help me out with her. And she goes I have homework to do. Well, help me. I got to help her so she won't end up like me."

The conference concluded with Esmeralda stating that she would contact Yvonne the following week to see how things were going. Shortly after meeting with Yvonne in November, the school recessed for a winter break.

A New Beginning: Family-Centered Strategies for Improving Literacy Progress and Parental Involvement

After returning in January, Esmeralda arranged for Linda to receive additional literacy support through the Reading Recovery program. Linda was pulled out of Esmeralda's classroom for 30 minutes per day to work with the Reading Recovery teacher. Although Linda enjoyed her Reading Recovery sessions, she fell behind in completing the Reading Recovery homework. Consequently, Esmeralda and the Reading Recovery teacher met with Yvonne to re-emphasize the importance of Linda completing all of her homework assignments. In addition to sessions with the Reading Recovery teacher, Esmeralda arranged for a third-grade student to listen to Linda read aloud for a 20-minute period during the school day.

In mid-February, Esmeralda noticed improvement in Linda's ability to return homework assignments and she was more attentive in class. Yvonne also appeared more diligent about parental involvement activities. For example, she called Esmeralda one day to ask about the date for a school event because she didn't want to miss it. By the end of the month, Esmeralda retested Linda on the kindergarten benchmark test, and the results indicated Linda had improved at a sufficient level to pass the exam and would not be retained in first grade.

Esmeralda undertook several actions to provide Linda with additional support during the school day for improving her literacy progress, such as finding a cross-age peer tutor to listen to her read aloud and recommending her for placement in the Reading Recovery program. However, Esmeralda also needed to engage Yvonne as a collaborative partner for improving Linda's literacy progress and was careful to modify her communication strategies and suggestions to better suit Yvonne's family needs and routines. As a result, Yvonne increased her involvement in Linda's literacy development, and Esmeralda improved her knowledge and skills for accessing parental involvement.

A recent meta-analytic review by Sénéchal (2006) for the National Institute for Literacy finds that parental involvement has a positive impact on kindergarten to third-grade children's reading acquisitions and that parents listening to their children read was effective for improving their literacy skills. The review also cites evidence that home teaching, such as parents using a Reading Recovery Model, had the greatest effect on improvement. However, home teaching would have involved significant training sessions that would have been difficult for Yvonne to attend, given her family's situational needs. The probability of Yvonne improving her level of involvement in Linda's literacy development would have been compromised. However, listening to Linda read on a nightly basis was reasonable for Yvonne to accomplish because it was compatible with her family life and held the most promise for implementation as a consistent family literacy practice. Yvonne's engagement in a nightly reading activity with her daughter also provided an important opportunity to increase her confidence in helping Linda. The changes Esmeralda and Yvonne implemented to support Linda's literacy development underscore the importance of parents' role construction, sense of efficacy for helping children, and the opportunities and demands for parental involvement reported by Hoover-Dempsey and Sandler (1997).

In analyzing the data from the CAG forms and the conference transcripts, it became apparent to us that Esmeralda needed to improve the connections between Linda's home and school environments to promote collaboration with Yvonne. However, as the results indicated, meeting during traditional conference sessions wasn't sufficient for promoting collaboration, and collaboration didn't occur "naturally." Instead, we needed to modify Esmeralda's communication strategies to include consistent weekly interactions and extend the conference meeting time. Such modifications provided Esmeralda and Yvonne with excellent opportunities to share their thoughts and insights concerning their complimentary roles and responsibilities in Linda's home and school life. As Williams and Chavkin (1989) observe, two-way interactions that allow for regular and frequent communication are needed for successful collaboration with parents.

A Final Look at the Effects of Improved Communication

Although Esmeralda worked at a school that was nationally recognized for a high level of parental involvement, in her classroom practice she still struggled with collaborating with hard-to-reach parents. The communication strategies she used, however, improved collaboration and approximated the close relationship her two aunts developed with all of their students' families. These strategies included the following:

- Maintaining and analyzing the data yielded from the CAG form to monitor and promote ongoing communication on a monthly basis

- Varying forms of contact between informal and formal encounters on a consistent basis to include making or returning telephone calls, sending and exchanging notes, or conveying oral messages through the child

- Expressing explicit interest in the child's home literacy and learning activities by asking probing questions during conference sessions and during informal interactions, such as the hallway chitchats before or after school

- Increasing familiarity with the child's home environment and supporting parents' interest in learning about the child's school life

- Demonstrating flexibility with the conference agenda items by sharing with parents the responsibilities for initiating and maintaining topics, asking and answering questions, and following up with comments to previous statements

A peculiar yet poignant indicator of Esmeralda's success occurred when Yvonne, who was approximately within the same age group (30s) as Esmeralda, endearingly began referring to her as "Mom" during their informal contacts and conference sessions. By no means are we suggesting that teachers and parents should or need to replicate such interaction, but we are suggesting that the results from our study indicate that our communication strategies were effective for improving home–school connections with hard-to-reach parents. In shifting her communication practices from a traditional school model to one that considered families' situational needs and personal literacy beliefs and practices, Esmeralda built upon the continuities between the children's home and school cultures. Reese and Gallimore (2000) suggest that, "wise practitioners, who are sensitive to cultural continuity and change as well as to cultural discontinuities, and who reach out to parents, will find parents reaching back" (p. 131).

REFLECTION QUESTIONS

1. In what ways does your school communicate with parents?
2. What methods of communication have been the most successful, and why?
3. What methods of communication have been the least successful, and why?
4. What information from this chapter will you use to enhance your communication patterns with parents?

REFERENCES

Bronfenbrenner, U. (1979). *The ecology of human development: Experiments by nature and design.* Cambridge, MA: Harvard University Press.

Camarota, S.A (2007, November). Immigrants in the United States, 2007. A profile of America's foreign-born population. *Backgrounder.* Washington, DC: Center for Immigration Studies.

Carreon, G.P., Drake, C., & Barton, A.C. (2005). The importance of presence: Immigrant parents' school engagement experiences. *American Educational Research Journal, 42*(3), 465–498. doi:10.3102/00028312042003465

Delgado-Gaitan, C. (1990). *Literacy for empowerment: The role of parents in children's education.* New York: Falmer.

Gibbs, N., Bower, A., August, M., Berryman, A., Thomas, C., Booth, H., et al. (2005). Parents behaving badly. *Time, 165*(8), 40–49.

Goldenberg, C.N. (1993). The home–school connection in bilingual education. In M.B. Arias & U. Casanova (Eds.), *Bilingual education: Politics, practice, research* (92nd yearbook of the Society for the Study of Education, pp. 225–250). Chicago, IL: Society for the Study of Education.

Hidalgo, N.M. (1998). Toward a definition of Latino family research paradigm. *International Journal of Qualitative Studies in Education, 11*(1), 103–120. doi:10.1080/095183998236917

Hoover-Dempsey, K.V., & Sandler, H.M. (1997). Why do parents become involved in their children's education? *Review of Educational Research, 67*(1), 3–42.

Laureau, A. (1989). *Home advantage: Social class and parental intervention in elementary education.* New York: Falmer.

Laureau, A. (1996). Assessing parent involvement in schooling: A critical analysis. In A. Booth & J.F. Dunn (Eds.), *Family–school links: How do they affect educational outcomes?* (pp. 57–64). Mahwah, NJ: Erlbaum.

Lewis, T. (2003, April). *Parent–teacher conferences: Is anyone listening?* Paper presented at the American Educational Research Association, Chicago, Illinois.

Lightfoot, S.L. (2003). *The essential conversation: What parents and teachers can learn from each other.* New York: Random House.

Lopez, G.R., Scribner, J.D., & Mahitivanichcha, K. (2001). Redefining parental involvement: Lessons from high-performing migrant-impacted schools. *American Educational Research Journal, 38*(2), 253–288. doi:10.3102/00028312038002253

Mankoff, R. (2006). *The complete cartoons of the New Yorker.* New York: Black Dog and Leventhal.

Marzano, R.J. (2004). *Building background knowledge for academic achievement: Research on what works in schools.* Alexandria, VA: Association for Supervision and Curriculum Development.

Mattingly, D.J., Prislin, R., McKenzie, T.L., Rodriguez, J.L., & Kayzar, B. (2002). Evaluating evaluations: The case of parent involvement programs. *Review of Educational Research, 72*(4), 549–576. doi:10.3102/00346543072004549

McLoughlin, C.S. (1987). *Parent–teacher conferencing.* Springfield, IL: CC Thomas.

Moles, O.C. (1993). Collaboration between schools and disadvantaged parents: Obstacles and openings. In N.F. Chavkin (Ed.), *Families and schools in a pluralistic society* (pp. 21–49). Albany, NY: State University of New York Press.

Paredes Scribner, A. (1999). Using student advocacy assessment practices. In P. Reyes, J.D, Scribner, & A. Paredes Scribner (Eds.), *Lessons from high-performing Hispanic schools: Creating learning communities* (pp. 169–187). New York: Teachers College Press.

Reese, L., & Gallimore, R. (2000). Immigrant Latinos' cultural model of literacy development. *American Journal of Education, 108*(2), 103–134. doi:10.1086/444236

Rotter, J.C., Robinson, E.H., III, & Fey, M.A. (1987). *Parent–teacher conferencing.* Washington, DC: National Education Association.

Sénéchal, M. (2006). *The effect of family literacy interventions on children's acquisition of reading: From kindergarten to grade 3.* Washington, DC: National Institute for Literacy.

Simich-Dudgeon, C. (1993). Increasing student achievement through teacher knowledge about parent involvement. In N.F. Chavkin (Ed.), *Families and schools in a pluralistic society* (pp. 189–203). Albany, NY: State University of New York Press.

Swap, S.M. (1993). *Developing home–school partnerships: From concepts to practice.* New York: Teachers College Press.

Trueba, H.T. (1989). *Raising silent voices: Educating linguistic minorities for the 21st century.* New York: Newbury House.

Valdes, G. (1996). *Con respeto: Bridging the distances between culturally diverse families and schools.* New York: Teachers College Press.

Williams, D.L., Jr., & Chavkin, N.F. (1989). Essential elements of strong parent involvement programs. *Educational Leadership, 47*(2), 18–20.

CHAPTER 10

My Language, My Culture: Helping Teachers Connect Home and School for English Literacy Learning

Patricia Ruggiano Schmidt, Brenda Gangemi, Grete O. Kelsey, Charles LaBarbera, Sharlene McKenzie, Carol Melchior, Barbara Merrick, Roseann Sunser, and Meg Williams

Following are some of the initial comments and concerns voiced by teachers as they embarked on a yearlong, inservice program that focused on connecting home, school, and community for culturally and linguistically diverse students.

> Connecting home languages and cultures sounds like an interesting but difficult idea.
>
> Visiting in the homes and neighborhoods won't be safe, and it's intimidating.
>
> Connecting the curriculum with language and culture will be too time-consuming.
>
> It is not my responsibility to make such connections with the curriculum.

The teachers were encouraged to participate in this professional development opportunity when two parochial elementary schools merged to form Cathedral Academy at Pompei (CAP), a pre-K to sixth-grade school located in Syracuse, New York. The school's mission was to ensure the academic and social achievement of children living in poverty and those learning English. During its first year, CAP enrolled 160 students from a variety of socioeconomic, linguistic, and cultural backgrounds. Forty-eight percent of the students were African American or recent arrivals from Sudan, Nigeria, and Ghana. Almost 38% of the student body was of European American origins, and 8% were Vietnamese, 5% Latino, and 1% Native American Haudenosaunee. English language learners

(ELLs) made up 17.5% of the student population at CAP, and home languages spoken included Dinka, Arabic, Vietnamese, and Spanish. Free or partial tuition was awarded to children in high-need situations through Father Champlin's Guardian Angel Society, a local Roman Catholic–affiliated organization.

The teaching staff of the newly formed school, 13 full-time and three part-time teachers with an average 15 years of teaching experience, found that they needed information about and guidance to work with ELLs, their students from diverse cultural and economic backgrounds, and their parents. The staff requested help from nearby Le Moyne College. Patricia, a literacy professor, responded by creating and facilitating an inservice program in which the teachers studied culturally responsive teaching strategies to promote home, school, and community connections for their students' English literacy development. In this chapter, we—Patricia, Brenda, Grete, Charles, Sharlene, Carol, Barbara, Roseann, and Meg—share our experiences with culturally responsive teaching and demonstrate how such teaching may help students learn English in U.S. schools. We begin with a brief overview of research related to culturally responsive teaching. Next, we present the key components of the inservice program. Then we turn our attention to the inservice program outcomes. We conclude with our reflections on the inservice program and our plans for continuing our efforts to connect home and school for CAP students and their families.

Culturally Responsive Teaching for English Language Learning

Within 20 years, 40% of K–12 students in the United States will speak languages other than English in their homes (Gunderson, 2009). These students are considered underrepresented in education, however, because they often do not have the opportunities provided to students in mainstream, middle class socioeconomic groups. They are new to the United States and have possibly experienced racial, ethnic, or linguistic discrimination. Students from underrepresented groups are more likely to attend impoverished schools, live in high-crime areas, and have a significant impact on urban schools (Gunderson, 2009; Nieto, 1996, 1999; Schmidt, 1998a). Their standardized test scores are low, and their school drop-out rates are high (Gunderson, 2009). Furthermore, they are in classrooms with teachers who have not been prepared to address issues of second language learning (Coppola, 2009; Finkbeiner, 2006; Schmidt & Ma, 2006). As a result, ELLs generally receive few opportunities to build upon or share their prior knowledge and experiences during English literacy instruction. Frequently, this is the result of teachers' lack of knowledge about the students, their homes, and communities (Coppola, 2009; Igoa, 1995; Schmidt & Finkbeiner, 2006). Yet, even in those cases when teachers are motivated to learn more about their students, they lack information, understanding, and concrete examples of effective strategies for teaching students from different languages and cultures (Schmidt, 1998a; Schmidt & Ma, 2006). There appear to be several reasons for this problem.

First, 90% of teachers are from European American, middle class backgrounds, similar to the backgrounds of their professors in teacher education programs (Nieto, 1999; Sleeter, 2001). Unfortunately, in many cases their opportunities for personal experiences with people from other languages and cultures are limited, so they may not have had significant relationships with people from different ethnic, cultural, and language backgrounds. Consequently, teachers and professors may rely on stereotypes in the media to determine how to respond to diverse groups of people (Pattnaik, 1997; Sleeter, 2001).

Second, school curriculum, methods, and materials usually reflect only European American or white culture and ignore the backgrounds and experiences of students and families from lower socioeconomic levels and differing ethnic and cultural backgrounds (Gunderson, 2009; Igoa, 1995; Nieto, 1999; Schmidt, 1998a).

Third, many teacher education programs do not adequately prepare educators for culturally responsive (Au, 1993) or "culturally relevant pedagogy" (Ladson-Billings, 1995), a term directly related to making strong home, school, and community connections (Rodriguez-Brown, 2009; Schmidt, 1998a). Consequently, this disconnect has become a problem whose influence has been linked to poor English language development and high drop-out rates among students from urban poverty areas in the United States (Goldenberg, 1987; Nieto, 1999). Therefore, it seems that the time has come for successful teacher preservice and inservice programs that demonstrate how to connect home, school, and community with culturally relevant or culturally responsive pedagogy for English language learning.

The ABCs of Cultural Understanding and Communication

When educators reach out to connect with family members and utilize their knowledge and resources for learning, there is often a narrowing of the academic gap and an increase in positive attitudes toward school (Goldenberg, 1987; Rodriguez-Brown, 2009; Schmidt, 2005). Due to many educators' lack of knowledge and understanding of the literacies related to particular cultures, they frequently are unable to make these connections. For instance, Moll's (1992) "funds of knowledge" demonstrated that many Latino students have mechanical abilities involving literacy skills related to their community's needs, and these skills go unrecognized in schools. Similarly, cultural conflict and struggles related to home and school disconnects seem to be common occurrences for children from Asian backgrounds, yet they are not addressed in school (Pang & Cheng, 1998; Schmidt, 1998a). When family knowledge, traditions, and students' life experiences are ignored, English language learning is deterred (Cummins, 1986; Gunderson, 2007).

To counteract this cultural disconnect, Patricia developed a model for in-service and preservice programs known as the ABCs of Cultural Understanding and Communication (Schmidt, 1998b). Adaptations of the ABCs model are currently part of teacher education programs in the United States and Europe (Schmidt & Finkbeiner, 2006). The model's roots are in successful teacher education programs that incorporate reading, writing, listening, and speaking to create consciousness-raising experiences. These experiences help teachers gain knowledge of self and others through autobiographies, biographies, reflection on diversity issues, and cross-cultural analysis. In addition, teachers are encouraged to know their students' families personally, so information can be shared easily. They work with families on community projects and meet in places of worship, homes, stores, parks, and community centers to discuss school and other community issues (Cochran-Smith, 1995; Florio-Ruane, 1994; Noordhoff & Kleinfield, 1993; Rodriguez-Brown, 2009; Schmidt, 1999, 2000, 2005; Spindler & Spindler, 1987). There are five steps to completing the ABCs model:

1. Teachers write autobiographies, starting with earliest memories (Banks & Banks, 1995). Family, religion education, celebrations, victories, challenges, and so forth may be included. The autobiography is a personal, private piece of writing that may or may not be shared.

2. Teachers interview family members from different linguistic and cultural backgrounds to discover how they see their children's education in relation to culture and family. Interpreters are called upon when needed (Spradley, 1979).

3. Teachers compare and contrast the similarities and differences among themselves and their students (Spindler & Spindler, 1987).

4. Teachers analyze differences to explore areas of personal discomfort and admiration and discuss differences in small groups (Schmidt, 1998b).

5. After experiencing the first four steps of the ABCs model, teachers begin to adapt lessons and units that make connections to students' homes and communities for academic and social learning.

When educators experience these five steps, they begin to see ways to develop collaborative relationships with families, community members, and colleagues in an atmosphere of mutual respect. They learn that families and communities have a wealth of knowledge to share and that information helps in the creation of meaningful lessons and units of study (Coppola, 2009; Igoa, 1995; McCaleb, 1994; Schmidt & Ma, 2006). When teachers draw upon the five-step process, students in their classrooms have the opportunity to gain self-respect, which empowers and motivates learning (Cummins, 1986).

In the following section we turn to the key components of the CAP inservice program, in which teachers studied and implemented culturally responsive strategies to promote connections between home, school, and community.

The CAP Inservice Program

The inservice program was planned to address the teachers' desire to better know and support all their students and their families, but for the purposes of this chapter, we focus specifically on the training and outcomes related to ELLs. Patricia prepared an outline of course objectives based upon the ABC's model as shown in Table 10.1. The specific objectives of the inservice program were to

- Strengthen connections between home, classroom, and community through the study of cultural differences
- Strengthen and implement old skills and learn new skills for successful parent/family/teacher formal and informal meetings
- Create and teach culturally responsive lessons that include reading, writing, listening, speaking, and viewing

Teachers were enthusiastic about the inservice opportunity, but as noted in the opening of the chapter, they expressed doubts about its potential

Table 10.1. Course Objectives for ABC's of Cultural Understanding and Communication

- Complete reading of *The ABC's of Cultural Understanding and Communication* (Schmidt, 1998b) and discuss meaning of the adage "Know thyself and understand others." Complete cultural analyses between and among participants.

- Practice how to begin to talk...to share...to listen to families.

- Analyze home/school/community connections for literacy development. Study related research to determine what other teachers, classrooms, and schools have accomplished.

- Study the community and learn about the realities of cultural funds of knowledge.

- Connect with community leaders and community power.

- Examine parent conferences, curriculum nights, e-mail, newsletters, phone calls, home visits, and meetings on neutral ground.

- Discuss family/teacher dialogue for collaboration.

- Discuss motivation and culturally relevant pedagogy.

- Discuss culturally relevant pedagogy and academic achievement using reading, writing, listening, speaking, and viewing.

- Plan for culturally relevant pedagogy with families and community.

- Implement and assess culturally relevant lessons.

effectiveness. Nine of the 16 CAP faculty members decided to participate. Patricia and the teachers met after school for two hours per week for 10 weeks during the first half of the school year. Charles, the principal, also attended several of the weekly meetings. Le Moyne College provided teacher stipends, copies of all professional books for each participant, and classroom materials.

During these meetings, teachers were encouraged to share personal reflections related to beliefs and attitudes concerning cultural, linguistic, economic, and ethnic differences. Reading, viewing, and responding to the course materials listed in Table 10.2 also provided many opportunities for participants to reflect upon the role of these differences in schooling. Teachers analyzed multicultural children's literature for use in their classrooms, and throughout the 10 weeks teachers routinely shared ideas about how they might implement strategies to strengthen connections between home, school, and community in their classrooms.

In addition to these activities, the teachers completed the major tasks that form the core of the ABCs model. First, each teacher wrote an autobiography. The purpose was for each teacher to consider his or her own background and experiences as the context for working with people with similar and different personal histories. Autobiographies were private, but several teachers shared their stories with Patricia or with one another. Next, teachers scheduled

Table 10.2. Course Materials

Free videotapes from Southern Poverty Law Center, Montgomery, AL	Books	Youth literature
Guggenheim, C. (1995). *The shadow of hate: A history of intolerance in America* [video]. Montgomery, AL: Teaching Tolerance. Hudson, T., & Houston, S. (2000). *A place at the table* [video]. Montgomery, AL: Teaching Tolerance. McGovern, M. (1997). *Starting small: Teaching children tolerance* [video]. Montgomery, AL: Teaching Tolerance.	Edwards, P.A. (1999). *A path to follow: Learning to listen to parents.* Portsmouth, NH: Heinemann. International Reading Association. (2000). *Making a difference means making it different: Honoring children's rights to excellent reading instruction (Position statement).* Newark, DE: Author. Mason, P., & Schumm, J. (Eds.). (2003). *Promising practices for urban education.* Newark, DE: International Reading Association. Schmidt, P.R. (1998). *Cultural conflict and struggle: Literacy learning in a kindergarten program.* New York: Peter Lang. Schmidt, P.R., & Ma, W. (2006). *50 literacy strategies for culturally responsive teaching.* Thousand Oaks, CA: Corwin.	Teachers had weekly opportunities to borrow fiction and nonfiction multicultural youth literature from the Le Moyne College youth literature collection. Several titles were purchased for the school.

interviews with family members of the children in their classrooms and wrote family biographies. Some teachers found this part of the inservice program difficult and expressed fear and anxiety about visiting homes and meeting in unknown neighborhoods. Neutral ground was an option, so interviews took place at a laundromat, park, restaurant, or coffee shop. Family members were asked to talk about their goals for their children and their children's interests and needs in school. As a result, the teachers learned about the lives of the children and their families as interviewees revealed life histories. When the teachers met to share their interview results, there were two important outcomes: They noted ways that family or community members might contribute to the curriculum, and they began to identify ways to build on students' language and culture in their classrooms and throughout the school. As the 10-week inservice sessions drew to an end, teachers turned their attention to planning and implementing culturally responsive classroom lessons or unit of study.

Researchers suggest that successful professional development requires reflection, time, and encouragement (Fullan, 2004; Goodlad, 1998) for the adaptation and implementation of new instructional practices. Therefore, the inservice program continued during the second semester with scheduled monthly support sessions. During these sessions, teachers along with their principal analyzed classroom lessons, home and school communications, and revisited the professional titles first discussed in the fall meetings. In addition, Patricia modeled culturally responsive teaching strategies in teachers' classrooms. By the end of the inservice program, all the teachers had planned and implemented lessons designed to bring home- and community-based knowledge into their classrooms. Some lessons focused on making or strengthening connections between the school and students' homes and the community, while other lessons focused on acknowledging and celebrating similarities and differences in language, culture, and ethnicity among the students. Still other lessons provided students with opportunities to build on home language and cultural knowledge as they learned a language or literacy-related skill. All lessons included teacher modeling and authentic opportunities to integrate reading, writing, listening, and speaking. In the following section, we provide selected examples of the culturally responsive strategies teachers used.

Culturally Responsive Teaching Strategies

Building Home–Community–School Connections. Carol, a kindergarten teacher, planned a unit to bring parents and community members into her classroom and to provide her Sudanese, Vietnamese, African American, and European American kindergarten students with the opportunity to explore the community that surrounded their school. This unit began with a walk through the neighborhood to visit community helpers and small businesses. The students made stops at local stores, the hospital, the fire station, and a food pantry. At each stop, business owners or community helpers explained their work. Back in the classroom, the kindergartners made an eight-foot model of their community with the school in the center as seen in Figure 10.1. Carol invited parents to help the students build replicas of their homes to add to the community model (see Figure 10.2). At the conclusion of the unit, several of the business owners and community helpers joined the kindergarten class for a community soup prepared and served by the students.

Pleased with the success of the community unit, Carol invited further parental involvement through parent classroom visits in which parents shared stories and cultural artifacts with the kindergarten class.

Brenda, the physical education teacher, planned a schoolwide effort to strengthen connections between home and school. She created a unit entitled The Olympics: My World and Our Place in It. Each grade level was divided into two countries that represented the student population at CAP. Students researched their assigned countries, created country flags as seen in Figure 10.3, and practiced making short speeches in English about each country. Next

Figure 10.1. Creating a Community Model

Figure 10.2. Kindergartners Displaying Their Home Models Built With Parents' Help

Brenda and the students selected games and teams, and each team chose a country to represent. In their "parade of nations" and in the ensuing games, Ecuador, Egypt, Ghana, Ireland, Italy, Japan, Mexico, Nigeria, Norway, Poland, Puerto Rico, Sudan, the United States, and Vietnam were represented.

Several of the classroom teachers participated in this schoolwide effort by displaying world maps in their classrooms. For example, Carol hung a laminated world map in her kindergarten classroom and referred to it regularly when talking about students' countries of origin.

Celebrating Similarities and Differences. Several of the teachers tried a culturally responsive strategy for building classroom community: identifying and celebrating similarities and differences among students. Barbara's first-grade class consisted of students from European American, Sudanese, Vietnamese, African American, and Latino backgrounds, and she wanted to acknowledge the ways that the students were the same and different. Barbara began her lesson by reading and discussing *Angel Child, Dragon Child* by Michele Maria Surat, the story of a young Vietnamese girl and her struggles to adjust to her new life and make friends in America. Next she paired students from different backgrounds to work together to discuss the following questions:

Figure 10.3. Students Displaying Country Flags During the Olympics Unit

- What is the same about us? What is different?
- What are some things you like to do?
- Where were you born?
- What do you like to do with your family?
- What do you like to do in school?
- What is your favorite color, food, and book?

After observing the students and listening to their conversations, Barbara gave them crayons and colored pencils that featured colors to help show different ethnicities and to draw pictures of their partners as seen in Figure 10.4. Then each student wrote and read a sentence about his or her partner.

As the students talked, drew, wrote, and laughed together, Barbara heard one student say, "Our eyes are the same color, but our hair is a different color. I was born in Egypt. You were born in Syracuse." Furthermore, to her surprise, she heard students teaching each other words from their languages, thus giving her the courage to do the same in the classroom. As Barbara stated, "I could hear Arabic, Dinka, Spanish, and English in my classroom. After that activity,

Figure 10.4. Students Sharing Similarities and Differences With Drawings

the students knew we needed to know how to speak about something in four different languages."

Grete, the sixth-grade teacher, also wanted to work on building a classroom community that appreciated the diversity evident among her 16 students of European American, Sudanese, African American, Vietnamese, and biracial backgrounds, most of whom were ELLs. During the beginning weeks of the inservice program, Grete asked her students to work with a partner to complete a Venn diagram in which they listed similarities and differences. Grete was surprised to find that few students mentioned skin color, language, or country of origin. Rather, food, television, and sports were major topics among the sixth graders. Greta wanted her students to feel proud of language, culture, and physical appearance and to know that diversity and multiple perspectives can enrich a democratic society. So she began using some strategies discussed in the inservice program to promote the appreciation of differences. For example, she routinely used the diverse languages in her classroom to teach English, encouraging students to supply an equivalent word or explain an idea in their home languages. In discussions about family events, Grete asked her students to compare and contrast how life events were celebrated by families from different cultures. When Grete decided to repeat the Venn diagram activity in March, she saw that this time students did not hesitate to include differences in cultural background, skin color, and language as seen in Figure 10.5.

Meg, the language arts and English as a second language teacher, used the same strategy with small groups of ELLs. She adapted her lessons according to each group's level of language development. For example, students who were in the earliest stages of learning English asked a partner, "What do you like?" They then drew pictures of the response and with Meg's help labeled each response. For those students with stronger English skills, Meg modeled how to form interview questions. Then the students brainstormed a list of questions, conducted interviews with a partner, and recorded and illustrated their partners' responses. The final products created by both groups of students were displayed to demonstrate the similarities and differences among the students who were from Sudan, Nigeria, and Vietnam.

Language and Literacy Development. Teachers tried a variety of strategies that build on home language knowledge and skills for oral and written language

Figure 10.5. Completed Venn Diagram Showing Students' Diversity

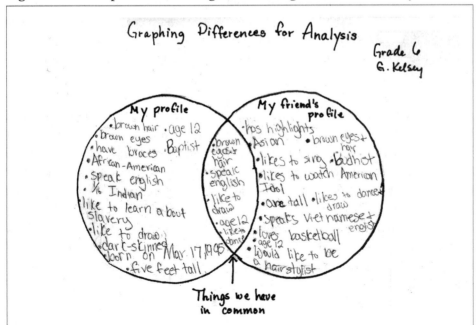

development. For example, in Carol's kindergarten classroom, students brought objects from home related to their families and created a class museum. The objects were labeled in English and each student's home language if the student spoke a language other than English. The students learned the English labels for each item. In addition, the students who spoke Arabic or Vietnamese taught their classmates the equivalent words for their items. The students from Sudan, with the help of their parents, created an Arabic-to-English poster to display next to the class museum.

Meg found that "name games," a recognition of the many different names that students bring to the classroom from all over the world, motivated English language learning. During one small-group lesson, she asked each student to write his or her name on a 9" x 10" sheet of white, unlined paper. Then the students decorated their names and drew pictures of favorite items. For example, Bak (all student names are pseudonyms), a third-grade Sudanese student, wrote his name and then drew a scene with camels in the desert and a man in traditional clothing standing next to them. Just above the scene, he included the cartoon character SpongeBob SquarePants. Nyon, a second grader from Vietnam, drew himself playing basketball. The students then shared their names and described their drawings to Meg and the other students in their group. An acrostic name game was another means of increasing written and spoken English vocabulary for those students with stronger English skills. They first wrote their names and then associated each letter with a verb or an adjective, using a word bank and an online dictionary as resources and then provided an illustration of their poems, which were displayed in the classroom.

Sharlene, the K–6 technology teacher, planned an integrated technology and literacy lesson for second and third graders that built on a major concern for many of her students and their families. Sharlene noted that students and families from tropical or desert climates feared winter and cold weather, so Sharlene planned a way to promote discussion about the weather and establish a safe place for the students to express fears. Sharlene began by asking students to create shapes such as circles and rectangles using Microsoft WordArt and Microsoft Paint. Next, the students used the shapes to create weather designs such as autumn trees, houses, and snowscapes. Working with Sharlene, each class composed a group poem about weather. One student started the verse and then classmates added, edited, or restated subsequent lines until the poem was considered complete. Each student typed the poem individualizing the font, style, and color of the title, and imported his or her picture to illustrate the poem. In Figure 10.6 and Figure 10.7, students from Sudan and Vietnam share their perspectives on fall and winter seasons.

In another literacy-related lesson, Meg showed her students how to properly address envelopes so they could write a letter to friends and family members. One student wrote to her grandmother in Egypt and received an answer, which was a memorable experience.

Rosann, the media specialist, also incorporated culturally responsive teaching in her library classes. She completed a unit on heroes and heroines with her

Figure 10.6. ELL Student's Fall Poem

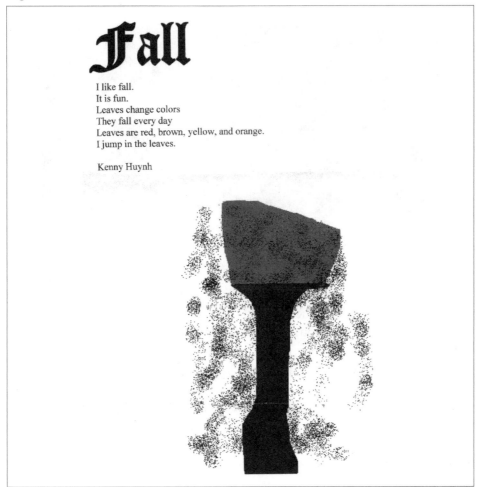

Figure 10.7. ELL Student's Winter Poem

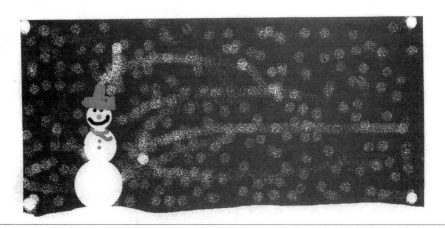

Dangerous Winter

Winter is a dangerous season.
Blizzards are snow storm that trap you inside.
They blow so much snow into your face that you cannot see.
You can get trap in the snow and get sick.
The snow can stop your car from running and you may have to wait for it to warm.

Tiir Ayol

fourth-grade Vietnamese, African American, Sudanese, European American, and Latino students. First, the students defined the word *hero* and generated a list of the characteristics of heroes and heroines using their own words. Next, they matched their definitions with dictionary definitions and compiled a list of famous and not-so-famous heroes and heroines. Nurses, soldiers, parents, siblings, doctors, firefighters, bus drivers, grandparents, police, and superheroes were included. Next, Roseann read portions of *Seven Brave Women* by Betsy Hearne, and she and the students compared the women's accomplishments with the accomplishments of their heroes. Finally, students responded to the reading and discussions by composing a written piece in which they identified a person who had touched their lives and the qualities that made him or her heroic, as seen in Figure 10.8.

In addition to implementing culturally responsive teaching strategies, teachers also reported in interviews, conducted by Patricia, and in anonymous surveys, new learning in two areas as a result of their participation in the inservice program. These areas were communicating with parents and making connections between students' and families' background knowledge and experiences and their required curriculum.

Figure 10.8. Darius's Hero

Heroes and Heroines

NAME: DATE:

A Hero Who Has Touched Your Life

Think about a hero or heroine who has touched your life—perhaps it is a parent, grandparent, big brother, sister, or teacher.

On this sheet of paper:

1. List the qualities that make him or her heroic.

2. Write a paragraph about that person. Write at least seven (7) sentences.

My hero is my big brother, because he heps mo when I have a bad day. He cookes for me when I am hongry. He is realy fun. He make me feel better when I am hurt. When I am sick he takes care of me. I love him, He gives me piggy back rides when my leg horts. He tells my mom when I need her. He do every thing when I need help. I Love Him very much.

Communicating With Parents

In their interviews, teachers commented on their new abilities to communicate with parents. For example, Grete noted that she made new friends with her students' parents.

> I really "talk with" my parents. We are open and honest with each other. We depend on each other for this communication. After getting to know one parent using the ABCs Model, I gained the confidence to reach out and talk with other parents from diverse ethnic, linguistic, and cultural backgrounds.

Meg stated, "I am excited about learning from students; I now think more carefully about what I say and do with families and their children." According to Roseann, "I have practiced reaching out to the families of the children. I know my interest in them will encourage them to read and learn." Barbara pointed out the reciprocal nature of her conversations with parents, "I need these relationships with family and community members. And they need me, so we can share for the children's education."

Teachers reported that knowing that they can communicate with parents helps them as they teach. For example, Brenda said,

> My students and their families are great resources for my classes. I feel that I have gained a certain amount of freedom in the way I teach, because I can ask questions that I might not have asked in the past.

Others described talking to parents as essential to classroom success. For example, Carol explained, "My many face-to-face meetings with parents helped in the sharing of information that would promote the children's academic and social achievement." Sharlene learned,

> Face-to-face communication with parents spells success for student projects and any class assignments. Notes are paper versions of automated operators. Personal contact has meaning and presents a caring attitude on the part of the teacher.

In their surveys, teachers also reported that they gained confidence in their abilities to talk with parents from different economic, linguistic, ethnic, and cultural backgrounds. One teacher wrote, "I have actually gotten to know more parents than I ever thought possible." Another stated,

Now I know that the face-to-face meeting on neutral ground shows the parents that I respect them and want to learn from them so that I can better teach their children. This has to be one of my best years!

Still another wrote that as a result of her participation in the inservice program,

I am more confident. I know most of [the] families, and I'm not afraid to share with them even when I don't know their languages. I can make myself understood. They know I am trying and want the best for their children.

One teacher noted that meeting with parents was both challenging and motivating.

This meeting with parents away from school was out of my comfort zone! But, making contact with families makes me more excited about teaching because I know what will motivate [my students].

Finally, another teacher shared that she learned that despite many hardships parents want to communicate with teachers and offer what they know and can do.

Family members come to class even though they don't know a lot of English. They love to share their pictures, their clothes, their work, even those who had horrible struggles in their native lands. They still miss their countries.

Making Connections

In their interviews and surveys, teachers expressed both the value of connecting with the immediate neighborhood and family members to enrich classroom learning and their ability to build on students' home and community experiences as they taught their required curriculum. For example, Carol described the responses to the unit that she taught to connect with the community and students' families.

Walking through the school's neighborhood to meet community members brought the children great joy. They saw similarities and differences among people. They saw the community as a center of daily activity and relationships, and they were part of the greater whole. Family and community members were welcomed into the classroom to share their expertise and personal stories.

Brenda was so pleased with the success of the Olympics unit implemented to connect with her students and their families that she planned to repeat the unit in the coming year with the addition of culturally authentic games and the use of languages other than English. Survey comments about what teachers learned were equally positive. For example, one teacher wrote,

> I never realized how important it was to connect with families and communities for teaching and learning. It is paramount to the success of this school and to education in general. I plan differently. I think about the unit to teach and then I think about how I will include my students' experiences in it to make it real. Drawing upon students' backgrounds and languages validates who they are and makes them want to learn.

Other teachers shared similar thoughts as seen in the following comments:

> I have learned that connecting with families and communities is essential. I have learned the importance of being patient with my students from other languages and cultures. I didn't realize what I could do to help them understand and now I know that I can include lots of activities that will help everyone in my class.

> I now invite parents in to share anything they'd like to share when it fits the curriculum and that's easy. I try to discover what they might be able to share and then I invite them.

> I think I am learning how to bring the world into my classroom. I am embracing my children's cultures through multicultural literature and planning lessons that connect their lives to what they are supposed to learn in the curriculum. It really seems natural and it's not too time consuming.

In the following section, we consider what led to these positive outcomes, and we share our plans for continuing our work in this area.

Reflections on Preparing Culturally Responsive Teachers

The inservice program appeared to be successful for several reasons. First, there was a capable faculty and staff who were aware of the need for change (Chenoweth, 2007). Most CAP educators realized that they needed to better understand the students, their families, and the local community. They agreed that this was important for their students' academic and social success. There was also strong school leadership, another important factor in school change.

As the principal, Charles led the way by attending the inservice sessions, and he routinely encouraged teachers to communicate in personal ways and plan parent-friendly programs. Charles also established a community meeting room next to his office where parents could meet to discuss problems related to work, clothing, food, shelter, and health. Additionally, he reached out to the local community to start mentoring and tutoring programs and enlisted 30 adults to work one hour per week with students having academic or social difficulties.

Second, the inservice program encouraged teachers to adapt the new ideas to their particular classrooms. Not only did teachers learn strategies that systematically connected students' prior knowledge with a new culture and language but also they witnessed their own successful implementations. Associating reading, writing, listening, and speaking across the curriculum became visible, common practice. The positive results have been documented in numerous studies over the years (Au, 1993; Izzo & Schmidt, 2006; Quintero & Huerta-Macias, 1995; Schmidt, 2000).

Third, the teachers received a small stipend for their involvement. This monetary recognition demonstrated that they were respected as professionals for their knowledge and experience.

Fourth, the teachers had the desire to make their classrooms better learning environments for all students. One could sense a strong moral obligation that signaled change, something that researchers study when learning about change agents in education (Fullan, 1999; Goodlad, 1998).

Finally, though not all teachers participated in the program, the impact of the inservice was visible throughout the school. For example, the winter and spring concerts featured music from most of the world's continents, and parents and other family members filled the gymnasium during these events. The science fair attracted 300 family and community members. In the early spring, the teachers organized an after-school literacy event for students and their families. Uno Unobagha, a noted children's author from Nigeria, read and talked about her book *Gramma, How Do You Say I Love You?* Unobagha returned for a full-day program two months later and read and sang from her award-winning book *Off to the Sweet Shores of Africa: And Other Talking Drum Rhyme.* She also presented the needlework from Nigerian clothing. Parents and community members joined in this literacy celebration as well.

Next Steps

Another positive outcome of the inservice program is the plans to continue the work begun during the first year of the school's existence. First, Patricia will be included on the agenda of regular faculty meetings. During the first 15 minutes of each meeting, she or a classroom teacher will present literature and culturally responsive strategies related to English language learning. The teachers and principal also plan monthly after-school social programs that involve families, students, and teachers and address academic content areas. A "Featured Teacher" who volunteers to show student work will be celebrated in the program. Patricia, Charles, and several faculty members plan to pursue funding to support a school-based community center to serve the literacy and learning needs of the neighborhood. The goal is to establish a comfortable place where families may receive help with educational needs, including tutoring for those struggling with English literacy.

In conclusion, this inservice program was a successful endeavor, but more information must be gathered and analyzed. Student achievement data are another means for evaluating the results of this program. Patricia and the teachers will compare results on state standardized tests to see if ELLs at CAP are outperforming students in other schools that have not had this type of inservice experience. However, as educators we know that this one statistical measure cannot alone determine success. And that is to ensure that students become contributing members of society. Students and their families from diverse linguistic and cultural backgrounds need teachers who recognize their gifts and talents brought from other lands. In doing so, the teachers promote an appreciation of the many cultures and experiences that have made the United States so unique. Cathedral Academy at Pompei is doing just that.

REFLECTION QUESTIONS

1. Have you ever thought about your own family background? How many languages and cultures are part of who you are? What makes your family unique, and why? Describe the cultural differences in your family? What makes you similar to some of your neighbors? What makes you different?

2. Think about inviting a parent to the next inservice program at your school. Other teachers may wish to do the same. This will demonstrate your trust in the parent and he or she may learn new education information that is helpful to you and the family.

3. How do you include the families and community members of your students in your classrooms? In what ways might they could they contribute to your curriculum?

4. What are some steps you will take to incorporate into your curriculum the cultural and linguistic differences you find in your classroom?

REFERENCES

Au, K.H. (1993). *Literacy instruction in multicultural settings*. Fort Worth, TX: Harcourt Brace.

Banks, J., & Banks, C.A. (1995). *Handbook of research on multicultural education*. New York: Macmillan.

Chenoweth, K. (2007). *It's being done: Academic success in unexpected schools*. Cambridge, MA: Harvard Education Press.

Cochran-Smith, M. (1995). Uncertain allies: Understanding the boundaries of race and teaching. *Harvard Educational Review, 65*(4), 541–570.

Coppola, J. (2009). *Teaching English language learners K–3: Promoting language and literacy development*. Norwood, MA: Christopher-Gordon.

Cummins, J. (1986). Empowering minority students: A framework for intervention. *Harvard Educational Review, 56*(1), 18–36.

Finkbeiner, C. (2006). Constructing third space: The principles of reciprocity and cooperation. In P. Ruggiano Schmidt & C. Finkbeiner (Eds.), *ABC's of cultural understanding and communication: National and international adaptations* (pp. 19–42). Greenwich, CT: Information Age.

Florio-Ruane, S. (1994). The future teachers' autobiography club: Preparing educators to support learning in culturally diverse classrooms. *English Education, 26*(1), 52–56.

Fullan, M. (1999). *Change forces: The sequel*. Philadelphia: Falmer.

Fullan, M. (2004). *Leading in a culture of change: Personal action guide and workbook*. San Francisco: Jossey-Bass.

Goldenberg, C.N. (1987). Low-income Hispanic parents' contributions to their first-grade children's word-recognition skills. *Anthropology & Education Quarterly, 18*(3), 149–179. doi:10.1525/aeq.1987.18.3.05x1130l

Goodlad, J.I. (1998). *Educational renewal: Better teachers, better schools*. New York: Jossey-Bass.

Gunderson, L. (2007). *English-only instruction and immigrant students in secondary schools: A critical examination.* Mahwah, NJ: Erlbaum.

Gunderson, L. (2009). ESL (ELL) literacy instruction: A guidebook to theory and practice (2nd ed.). New York: Routledge.

Igoa, C. (1995). *The inner world of the immigrant child.* Mahwah, NJ: Erlbaum.

Izzo, A., & Schmidt, P.R. (2006). A successful ABC's in-service project: Supporting culturally responsive teaching. In P. R. Schmidt & C. Finkbeiner (Eds.), *ABC's of cultural understanding and communication: National and international adaptations* (pp. 161–187). Greenwich, CT: Information Age.

Ladson-Billings, G. (1995). Toward a theory of culturally relevant teaching. *American Educational Research Journal, 32*(3), 465–491.

McCaleb, S.P. (1994). *Building communities of learners: A collaboration among teachers, students, families, and community.* New York: St. Martin's.

Moll, L.C. (1992). Bilingual classroom studies and community analysis: Some recent trends. *Educational Researcher, 21*(2), 20–24.

Nieto, S. (1996). *Affirming diversity: The sociopolitical context of multicultural education.* New York: Longman.

Nieto, S. (1999). *The light in their eyes.* New York: Teachers College Press.

Noordhoff, K., & Kleinfield, J. (1993). Preparing teachers for multicultural classrooms. *Teaching and Teacher Education, 9*(1), 27–39. doi:10.1016/0742-051X(93)90013-7

Pang, V.O., & Cheng, L.L. (Eds.). (1998). *Struggling to be heard: The unmet needs of Asian Pacific American children.* Albany, NY: SUNY Press.

Pattnaik, J. (1997). Cultural stereotypes and preservice education: Moving beyond our biases. *Equity & Excellence in Education, 30*(3), 40–50. doi:10.1080/1066568970300307

Quintero, E., & Huerta-Macias, A. (1995). Bilingual children's writing: Evidence of active learning in social context. *Journal of Research in Childhood Education, 9*(2), 157–165.

Rodriguez-Brown, F. (2009). *Home-school connections: Lessons learned in a culturally and linguistically diverse community.* New York: Routledge.

Schmidt, P.R. (1998a). *Cultural conflict and struggle: Literacy learning in a kindergarten program.* New York: Peter Lang.

Schmidt, P.R. (1998b). The ABC's of cultural understanding and communication. *Equity & Excellence in Education, 31*(2), 28–38. doi:10.1080/1066568980310204

Schmidt, P.R. (1999). Know thyself and understand others. *Language Arts, 76*(4), 332–340.

Schmidt, P.R. (2000). Emphasizing differences to build cultural understandings. In V.J. Risko & K. Bromley (Eds.), *Collaboration for diverse learners: Viewpoints and practices* (pp. 210–230). Newark, DE: International Reading Association.

Schmidt, P.R. (2005). *Preparing teachers to communicate and connect with families and communities.* Greenwich, CT: Information Age.

Schmidt, P.R., & Finkbeiner, C. (2006). *ABC's of cultural understanding and communication: National and international adaptations.* Greenwich, CT: Information Age.

Schmidt, P.R., & Ma, W. (2006). *50 literacy strategies for culturally responsive teaching.* Thousand Oaks, CA: Corwin.

Sleeter, C.E. (2001). Preparing teachers for culturally diverse schools: Research and the overwhelming presence of whiteness. *Journal of Teacher Education, 52*(2), 94–106. doi:10.1177/0022487101052002002

Spindler, G.D., & Spindler, L.S. (1987). *The interpretive ethnography of education: At home and abroad.* Hillsdale, NJ: Erlbaum.

Spradley, J. (1979). *The ethnographic interview.* New York: Holt, Rinehart and Winston.

CHAPTER 11

Preparing Middle and Secondary School Teachers to Teach Reading, Language, and Content: A Look at Professional Development Programs

Margarita Calderón and Russell Wasden

There has been a growing interest in adolescent literacy, particularly as it relates to English language learners (ELLs) because these students continue to struggle to achieve levels of literacy necessary for school and life success. For example, results of the 2007 National Assessment of Education Progress demonstrated that ELLs in eighth grade continue to score far below their English proficient peers in reading (Lee, Grigg, & Donahue, 2007). In addition, disproportionately high dropout rates among ELLs (Ruiz-de-Velasco, Fix, & Clewell, 2000) and increasing numbers of ELLs who fail to meet required benchmarks on high-stakes assessments tied to high school graduation (Batalova, Fix, & Murray, 2007) compel teachers, researchers, and policymakers to turn their attention to understanding and meeting the needs of this vulnerable student population.

As schools are held increasingly accountable for the success of all students including ELLs, teachers need support in the form of effective professional development to improve teaching to meet the needs of their diverse classrooms and as a result, student achievement (Abedi, 2004; Biancarosa, 2005). One ongoing study of professional development led by Margarita, the first author, and funded by the Carnegie Corporation of New York is designed to determine how best to prepare teachers to meet the language, literacy, and content learning needs of ELLs in middle and secondary schools. The results of this study offer several conclusions about how best to prepare teachers to provide ELLs with instruction that addresses language development, reading comprehension, and content area knowledge. In this chapter, we discuss these conclusions, which include the following:

- Comprehensive professional development of content area teachers can prepare them to teach reading comprehension strategically.
- Teaching ELLs effectively in the content classroom involves a level of proficiency and flexibility that often requires substantial and intensive teacher preparation and follow-up.
- Integrated teaching of literacy, language, and content leads to improved performance on the part of ELLs and other striving readers.
- When language and reading specialists and special education teachers work with content teachers to address students' oral language and literacy learning needs, students benefit.

Current studies of adolescent literacy development with a particular focus on ELLs suggest that the design and delivery of literacy instruction and the training of teachers must consider the unique needs and the individual differences among these students (Calderón, 2007b; Short & Fitzsimmons, 2006). These needs and differences are related largely to students' early language and literacy learning opportunities. Some ELLs possess well-developed native language and literacy skills, and these are students who are likely to make more rapid progress in learning to read English. Others struggle to decode words even in their native language. Most often these students are recent arrivals to the United States, and it is not unusual to find that many of these students have had two or more years of interrupted schooling. Often refugee and migrant adolescents are among this group of students. Still other ELLs have attended school in the United States since kindergarten. These students are often referred to as long-term ELLs. Their English oral skills may sound near native-like, but these students lack the academic vocabulary, decoding, and comprehension skills necessary to extract and use information from content area texts. Due to this extreme variation among ELLs, teachers need a comprehensive approach to pre- and inservice training that focuses on how to provide accommodations, modifications, and interventions to meet individual student's needs.

Strickland and Alvermann (2004) suggest that much of the low achievement of language-minority students may be pedagogically induced or exacerbated. They remind us that the key contributing factor to the achievement gap is the differences in the quality of instruction students receive. For example, although many well-implemented bilingual and English as a second language (ESL) programs facilitate the progress of many Latino students, others provide low levels of challenge and shield students from the curriculum necessary for successful placement at the next level of schooling (Jiménez, 2004; Valdés, 2001). Jiménez also emphasizes that a business-as-usual approach to literacy instruction will result in failure for Latino students because Latino students need much higher quality language and literacy and content area instruction that includes frequent opportunities for interaction.

In reviewing the literature, we, like others (e.g., Ivey & Broaddus, 2007), found that there is very little guidance about literacy instruction for adolescent ELLs. Therefore, research that explores both the complexity of teaching these students and preparing teachers to meet these students' needs is necessary.

We begin this chapter by presenting the content of two professional development programs planned for teachers of middle and high school ELLs. The first program, Expediting Reading Comprehension for English Language Learners (ExC-ELL), was designed for science, social studies, language arts, and mathematics teachers whose classrooms enroll English-only or English-proficient students along with long-term ELLs with a wide range of language and literacy skills (Calderón, 2007a). The second professional development program, Reading Instructional Goals for Older Readers (RIGOR), was designed for ESL, reading, and special education teachers and for tutors who work with content teachers to provide targeted instructional interventions in language and literacy to groups of students who have experienced interrupted schooling and who have significant oracy and literacy needs (Calderón, 2008). We then describe the teacher-training process and follow-up support systems provided through both professional development programs. Finally, we demonstrate how participation in these professional development programs influenced teaching and learning in the Russell's (the second author) urban high school.

Professional Development for Teaching Reading, Language, and Content

Because most ELLs are in heterogeneous classrooms that also include English-only or English-proficient students, it is important to know more about how to help teachers provide effective instruction for ELLs as well as all other students in their classrooms.

In 2003, the Carnegie Corporation of New York sponsored a five-year research project called ExC-ELL (Calderón, 2007a). The purpose of the project was to develop and study the effects of a professional development model for middle and high school teachers of English, science, mathematics, and social studies who teach ELLs. The main goal of the ExC-ELL professional development program is to prepare content area teachers to provide direct and explicit vocabulary and reading comprehension instruction integrated into their subject matter lessons.

These particular focal areas were selected for two reasons. First, poor vocabulary is a serious issue for ELLs and a major obstacle to successful reading comprehension. Word knowledge correlates with reading comprehension (Nagy & Anderson, 1984). In other words, the size of a student's vocabulary bank predicts their level of reading comprehension. Unless a student knows 90–95% of the words he or she is reading, comprehension will be stifled (Samuels, 2002). Second, reading comprehension is critical in all subjects, particularly as students progress through the grades and are required to comprehend and extract information from increasingly complex texts. ESL teachers alone cannot be expected to address ELLs' vocabulary and reading comprehension needs. Rather, the vocabulary knowledge and reading and writing skills that students need in middle and high schools can be effectively taught by content teachers when they embed a vocabulary and literacy focus specific to their discipline within their teaching practice. Furthermore, the strategies commonly used by ESL teachers or by reading specialists are not necessarily the same as the strategies students need for reading a biology text, a word problem, or historical documents. Therefore, it is significantly important that all teachers in a school with ELL populations participate in professional development that is specific to their instructional goals and content curriculum demands but that also prepares them to address students' language and literacy learning needs (Calderón, 2007b).

The ExC-ELL pilot study of the professional development program for content teachers was completed in Kauai, Hawaii, middle and high schools, and currently the formal empirical study is being conducted in New York City schools. To date, data from this pilot study show that instructional practices presented in the professional development program are effective with ELLs and with all other students, particularly those reading below grade level and needing extensive vocabulary development for comprehending subject matter text. Data also suggest that a comprehensive professional development program for content teachers should prepare teachers to do the following:

- Parse content area texts to prepare students for reading success
- Build student background knowledge necessary for text comprehension
- Select vocabulary with attention to students' differing levels of English proficiency
- Teach vocabulary
- Map out teacher think-alouds to promote student metacognition
- Teach, monitor, and assess reading comprehension skills
- Teach content area writing strategies and skills
- Assess language, reading, and content
- Establish school-based Teacher Learning Communities (TLCs) to promote peer collaboration and ongoing reflection on and refinement of teaching practice

In the following section, we describe briefly each of these key elements.

What Content Teachers Need to Be Able to Do

Parse Texts and Build Student Background Knowledge. It is important for teachers to learn how to prepare students for success with a content area expository or narrative text. In the professional development program, first teachers learn to scan the selected text for the information that addresses a content standard they plan to address. Then, teachers preview the text to select, condense, and eliminate unnecessary information and segment the text for explicit instruction. The teacher writes a short summary to share with students before, during, or after the lesson introduction. To build students' background knowledge or to provide an anticipatory set of main concepts, the teacher selects graphics, films, pictures, or real objects to present to the students. Teachers may also present important text features such as title, headings, charts, and graphs.

Select Vocabulary From Texts. It also is important for teachers to select the right words to teach so that students understand what they read. In the professional development program, teachers learn how to select words to preteach. The selection of words to preteach was based on the findings of the Bilingual Cooperative Integrated Reading and Comprehension study conducted by Calderón, Hertz-Lazarowitz, and Slavin (1998) and the work of Beck, McKeown, and Kucan (2002), who developed a systematic method of selecting vocabulary to teach to students. Beck and colleagues group words into three tiers. Tier One words are those that English-proficient students already know. Tier Two words are those words that students will need to know as they read a text. These words appear frequently in written text and in the vocabulary of mature language users, and Tier Three words are rare words that students may encounter infrequently.

Teachers in the professional development program learn how to select words to preteach using the three-tier model but with the particular word-learning needs of ELLs in mind. The majority of ELLs in our New York City sites, are from Spanish-speaking backgrounds; therefore, the professional development program emphasized how to select words to preteach using the three-tier model with the particular word-learning needs of these ELLs in mind. Tier One words are those basic words for which students know the concept and label in Spanish or their native language. They need only learn the English label (e.g., *find, search, guest*). Tier One words include simple idioms that ELLs are unlikely to know (e.g., *make up your mind, let's hit the books, sit up*), and connectors and prepositions/prepositional phrases (e.g., *so, if, then, however, finally, by, of, in, along the way*).

Some Tier One words are cognates (*family/familia, preparation/preparación*); the cognates in this category consist of words that are high-frequency words in Spanish and English; they do not require substantial instruction because students know the word meanings in Spanish. False cognates also need to be pointed out by the teacher and the correct translation given. For example, *assist* is usually translated as *asistir*, but the correct translation is *atender. Attend,* however, is translated as *asistir.* Other examples of words that are false cognates are *rope/ropa, embarrased/embarasada.*

Teachers also practice selecting Tier Two words that are important for understanding a text and help ELLs build rich language. They provide precision and specificity in describing a character, concept, or a process. Tier Two words also nest definitions of Tier Three words, such as *osmosis.* It is important that teachers are prepared for this aspect of vocabulary selection. This is because if students do not know 90% of words in a question about osmosis, even if they know what the term means, they may not be able to answer the question because of the many unknown words in the question, such as *undergo, whereby, so that, conversely, hence, state, underlying.* Tier Two words for ELLs also include polysemous words, such as *trunk,* which are some of the most troublesome words for these students. ELLs typically know only one meaning of a word, and that meaning may not be relevant to the context in which it is found. Examples of these Tier Two words that are used differently across the content areas and must be taught include words such as *table, set, ring, slip, power, cell, line, run, root.*

Cognates may also be found in Tier Two words. Cognates in this tier are high-frequency words in Spanish and low-frequency words or Tier Three words in English for English speakers. Students whose first language shares cognates with English will have a head start with these words (such as *edifice/edificio, facile/fácil, coincidence/coincidencia, industrious/industrioso, and fortunate/afortunado*) because they will know both the concept and an approximation of the label in English.

Tier Three words are words unique to a specific content area. This includes, for example, words specific to mathematics (*hypotenuse, trapezoid, decimal, digit*), science (*photosynthesis, lunar, solar*), or language arts (*irony, metaphor*). Most Tier Three words are cognates because they are derived from Latin and Greek. Although students may be able to identify the word, they may not know the concept or process.

Teach Vocabulary. After words from each tier have been carefully selected, teachers learn how to teach vocabulary using strategies such as those described by Calderón and colleagues (2005) and Beck and colleagues (2002). For example, teachers learn to use a seven-step process for preteaching words that students will encounter as they learn about new concepts or themes or as they read. The seven steps with an example are as follows:

1. Teacher says the word. (Effect.)
2. Teacher states the word in context from the text. (Weather can have a big effect on your life.)
3. Teacher provides the dictionary definition(s). (An effect is the result or consequence of something. Effect can also mean influence or the power to make something happen.)
4. Teacher explains the meaning with a "student-friendly" definition. (One cup of coffee in the afternoon has a big effect on me. I can't sleep at night!)
5. Teacher asks students to repeat the word three times.
6. Teacher engages students in activities to develop word/concept knowledge. (What has had a big effect in your life recently?)
7. Teacher highlights grammar, polysemy, cognate, pronunciation, spelling, and so forth. (*Effect* is a noun. It is spelled with a double *f*. Its cognate is *efecto*.)

During the professional development sessions, teachers learn how to use cognates as tools for their Spanish-speaking students. For example, teachers learn to highlight prefixes and suffixes that are similar in both language (*manejable*, *manageable*) and to highlight those that are different (*condición*, *condition*; August, Calderón, & Carlo, 2001). Finally, teachers learn the importance of teaching vocabulary before, during, and after reading.

Model Reading Comprehension Skills and Develop Reading Comprehension. The National Reading Panel (National Institute of Child Health and Human Development, 2000), RAND Reading Study Group (2002), and many researchers have identified teaching strategies that are beneficial to developing readers. Teachers learn to apply these strategies in their content area classrooms. First, teachers learn to model through think-alouds and read-alouds how students can

- Identify the important information in the text
- Connect information within the text in meaningful ways
- Link information from the text to personal experiences
- Engage in questioning while reading
- Make inferences to fill in gaps in information explicitly stated
- Monitor their reading to be certain what they are reading make sense
- Summarize and organize information

Next, teachers learn to ask students to apply the target strategy as they read with a peer and learn how to monitor and record student performance during peer reading. Finally, teachers learn how to gradually release responsibility and move students to independent use of the strategy.

Teach Content Area Writing Strategies and Skills. Teachers learn to use the writing process to produce a range of expository and narrative written genres across the content areas. Particular attention is paid to the teaching of writing strategies and skills that will help students increase understanding of content-based readings. This includes learning how to help students compose summaries and outlines and a range of expository text structures such as compare and contrast, problem and solution, and cause and effect. During the sessions, teachers are guided through the process approach as they compose their own written pieces. Special emphasis is given to the editing stage and the mechanics of writing where the features of second language writing are highlighted. For example, Spanish is a language with a shallow orthography in which the each of the five vowel sounds is represented consistently by the same grapheme or letter. This means that native Spanish writers expect that they will write words exactly as they sound. Therefore, it is not uncommon for an ELL to write *hart* for *heart*. Some students may even write *heart* as *jart* because the *j* in Spanish is pronounced like *h* in English. Teachers also learn how cultural differences may influence student writing. For example, in some cultures, writers begin with greetings to the reader and extended elaborations before they introduce the main topic. ELLs who know this approach to writing will need to learn that topic sentences are expected at the outset as they write in English.

Assess Language, Reading, and Content. Teachers learn about the importance of engaging in ongoing student assessment. The assessment process begins as teachers select the topic, standard, text, vocabulary, and reading or writing skills to be addressed in each integrated lesson. Teachers review and critique many examples of performance assessments and rubrics and learn how to use student assessment results to inform teaching practice.

Establish Teacher Learning Communities. Teachers establish school-based peer learning communities in which they plan to meet once a week for at least 30 minutes throughout the academic year. The goal is to share successes, analyze student assessment data, plan next steps and targets, and reflect on their collective progress toward quality instruction. In addition, they plan visits to one another's classroom. The visits are most often of two types. A teacher may choose to volunteer to model the teaching of a particular strategy for his or her colleagues, or a teacher may invite a colleague to his or her classroom to observe instruction and provide the teacher with feedback on student performance or on the instructional delivery.

Ongoing Work Related to This Professional Development Program

We continue to use what we learned from the professional development program to improve teaching and learning in middle and high school content area classrooms that enroll ELLs. We have developed an observation protocol (ExC-ELL Observation Protocol; Calderón, 2007a) that captures the essential elements introduced in the professional development program, such as the steps in parsing texts and strategies for building student background knowledge. Currently, we are testing this observation protocol as a tool that can be used by teachers to (a) guide them as they plan lessons, (b) observe and record student performance, (c) guide self-reflection tool after a lesson, and (d) guide peer coaching. We also are using the observation protocol to conduct classroom research to determine the effectiveness of the professional development program.

In addition, literacy coaches, content curriculum coaches or specialists, principals, and central office administrators also participate in professional development with a focus on how to observe and coach teachers as they deliver content lessons that integrate reading, writing, and vocabulary development. These coaches and administrators learn how to use the observation protocol to guide their classroom observations and conversations with teachers about teaching practice and student achievement.

We now turn to a description of the second professional development program, RIGOR (Calderón, 2008), designed to provide training for teachers who work with ELLs in need of intensive language and literacy interventions. Participants in this professional development program include ESL, dual-language, reading, and special education teachers as well as tutors.

Pretests of the students in those New York City middle and high schools that participated in ExC-ELL showed that these schools were serving ELLs with reading abilities that ranged from preliteracy through sixth-grade levels. Data also showed that these students tested at many different levels on the state-mandated oral language proficiency tests. In other words, some students were reading at a sixth-grade level, yet they demonstrated only beginning oral language skills. Likewise, there were ELLs reading at a second-grade level who were advanced speakers of English. Furthermore, the data showed that the students fitting this low-literacy, high-oracy profile were likely to be long-term ELLs who had been in schools in the United States for five or more years. School administrators and teachers were also very concerned about the substantial number of preliterate older students. Therefore, a professional development program for ESL, dual-language, reading and special education teachers and for tutors that addressed literacy and oracy development for middle and high school students was designed to complement the professional development that content area teachers received (Calderón, 2008). Offered in English and Spanish because of the growing number of dual-language programs in New York City middle and high schools, teachers and tutors learn how to provide beginning older readers with the tools they need for decoding and literal comprehension and address vocabulary and discourse-level skill development. Because the goal is to prepare participants to support and work closely with content area teachers, participants learn how to use content area leveled readers to provide instruction in oral language, decoding, fluency, and print conventions.

Organization of the Professional Development Programs

Both ExC-ELL and RIGOR are designed as intensive five-day institutes followed by school-based, follow-up training and peer coaching. During the five-day institutes, a team of researcher–trainers led by Margarita, the first author, (a) explain and model each of the instructional strategies teachers are expected to implement, (b) ask teachers to practice the strategies during the training sessions, (c) ask teachers to discuss how each strategy may be incorporated in their particular classrooms, and (d) ask teachers to consider how the strategy will help them meet their students' needs. As the trainers model for teachers how to orchestrate the instructional activities in their classroom, teachers work in cooperative learning groups of four members to practice each instructional component. The trainers use the same instructional practices during the training that the teachers will be expected to use in their classrooms, such as providing explicit instruction, modeling, using guided practice, and using independent practice in reading comprehension strategies and skills. In the following section, we provide a brief description of how the training in one component— teaching reading comprehension strategies and skills—is conducted, and we provide information about the follow-up support that is available to teachers.

Teaching Reading Comprehension Strategies and Skills

Providing Explicit Instruction. The trainer provides background information on the strategy to be taught and models how to explain the strategy to the students. In addition, teachers learn how to share with students why it is important for them to know about the strategy and when they might use the strategy.

Using Think-Alouds. The trainer demonstrates what strategy use "looks like" in actual operation. The trainer uses a think-aloud or a demonstration of the thought processes he or she uses to perform tasks such as predicting or summarizing.

Delivering Comprehension Strategy and Skills Instruction. The trainers model whole-group reading, guided reading, triad reading, and partner reading to demonstrate ways that teachers can help students learn, practice, and apply comprehension strategies and skills. These include, for example, identifying text structure and sequencing events, identifying main ideas and supporting details, distinguishing fact and opinion, categorizing and classifying, generalizing, identifying cause and effect, and drawing conclusions.

Using Cooperative Learning. Teachers learn how to set up a context for effective student cooperation and how to help their students develop social and metacognitive skills during group work. During each day of the five-day institute, the trainers model a variety of cooperative learning activities while teachers participate in those activities as their students would. The trainers model and teachers practice using a variety of techniques that the teachers may then bring back to their classrooms to ensure student participation, such as posing a question and asking students to "put their heads together" to discuss and prepare all group members to provide an answer. The trainer models how teachers may use such techniques during whole-group and small-group activities.

Transferring Learning Into Teachers' Classrooms. The process of transfer of learning begins during the five-day institutes as teachers practice using the observation protocol to guide them as they plan their content lessons. As described earlier, TLCs are established at each participating school site, and trainers visit classrooms three or more times each year. During these site visits, trainers provide varying levels of support, depending upon teacher request or identified needs. Trainers plan lessons with teachers, model how to teach a particular strategy or skill, coteach a lesson with a classroom teacher, or observe a lesson. Trainers also demonstrate how to observe and document student progress toward desired outcomes.

In the following section, we demonstrate how participation in the professional development programs has influenced teaching and learning at Russell's urban high school.

The Influence of the Professional Development Programs in One Urban High School

Russell, the second author, teaches language arts and ESL at Gregorio Luperon High School, located in Washington Heights, one of New York City's most historically immigrant neighborhoods. This high school provides a transitional

Spanish–English bilingual program of study for a newcomer student population of approximately 400 native–Spanish-speaking ELLs. With the exception of ESL, ninth-grade classes are taught primarily in Spanish. Instruction in English increases gradually throughout the four years so that by grade 12, most classes, particularly Advanced Placement classes, are taught exclusively in English. Many students arrive at Gregorio Luperon High School with limited first and second language literacy skills, and more than 40% of the students have experienced interruptions in their formal schooling. For example, it is typical to find a 16-year-old student at this high school who has had fewer than six years of formal schooling and who reads at a third-grade level. Providing proper services to this student population was a significant challenge to faculty and administrators. However, faculty and administrator participation in professional development that targets these students' language, literacy, and content area learning needs has resulted in some important changes at Gregorio Luperon High School. These changes included increased attention to vocabulary, reading and writing across the curriculum, and increased collaboration between content and ESL teachers.

Increased Attention to Vocabulary

To improve students' oracy and literacy skills, content and ESL teachers focused instruction on concepts, words, and phrases that could make the difference between comprehension and misunderstanding of content area texts. In most classrooms throughout the school, teachers posted word walls with vocabulary words categorized into three tiers. Many of these classroom word walls displayed similar Tier One words such as sight words and similar Tier Two words such as polysemous words. Tier Three words in each classroom, however, were specific to the content area. For example, as seen in Figure 11.1, Tier Three words in Russell's ESL 4 classroom included *critical lens*, *literary element*, and *controlling idea*. Russell's students routinely used his classroom word wall as a resource to support oral and written communication. Although many of Russell's students continued to struggle with English grammar, spelling, and word choice, he found that students frequently revised their written pieces to include words from a "higher tier."

Attention to building students' vocabulary was not limited to the classroom. The assistant principal posted a larger-than-life word wall in the cafeteria that displayed the English phrases that students were bound to encounter on the

Figure 11.1. Three-Tiered Word Wall

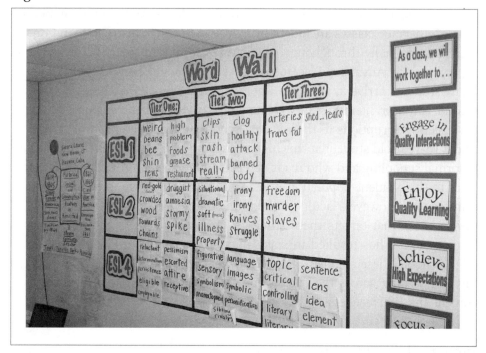

New York State Regents Examinations. As a result of the schoolwide increased attention to vocabulary, Russell found his students using new learned vocabulary not only as they read, wrote, and talked in his classroom but also as they walked through the school hallways. Russell's students also reported that knowing more about cognates helped them as they read and wrote in their science, social studies, and mathematics classes.

Reading Across the Core Subject Areas

To support vocabulary growth, teachers discovered that they needed to provide their students with longer and more complex texts than they had used previously. Many teachers reported that as a result of their participation in the professional development programs, they were able to take what they formerly considered "unmanageable" texts and make them accessible to their students who were learning English. Teachers reported success when they selected engaging text, chunked the text into manageable portions, pretaught essential vocabulary, and focused on teaching reading comprehension. The emphasis across all content areas was on ensuring that students understood more of what they read. For example, an economics teacher reported that using these strategies helped his students better understand the business section of *The New York Times*.

Schoolwide, there was clear evidence of reading growth. There was a 7% increase in the results on the standardized English language arts assessment, which contained lengthy, authentic reading passages that previously students would not have attempted to read. Teachers also reported an increase in student engagement with reading materials and motivation to read.

Writing Across the Core Subject Areas

In student work displayed throughout the school and in classrooms, there was evidence that as students read longer and more complex texts, they also wrote more. For example, science exhibits that previously consisted solely of modeling clay and other realia were now accompanied by lengthy written passages, such as explanations of photosynthesis or chemical reactions. In mathematics classes, students wrote out the processes they used to solve problems where previously they might have supplied the answer only. History teachers reported growth in the clarity and organization of students' written responses to document-based questions. In Russell's ESL class, students routinely composed PowerPoint presentations that included extended text and that they shared with their classmates as seen in Figure 11.2. There was also growth in writing from the older students who had just begun to learn to read.

Increased Collaboration Between ESL and Content Area Teachers

The TLC at Gregorio Luperon High School met two afternoons per month during the school year. This sustained, consistent time to meet provided an opportunity for teachers to continue the conversations they had begun during the five-day institutes about the importance of literacy across the curriculum for their students' success. For example, in one meeting teachers brainstormed lists of vocabulary words to teach that could be used across all content areas. Thus words such as *average, basic*, or *industrial* first encountered in history class could be reinforced in another subject area leading to increased student comprehension. In some meetings, teachers shared lesson plans and instructional

Figure 11.2. Students Demonstrating Their Writing Abilities With a PowerPoint Presentation

techniques. Other meetings were devoted to analyzing student work. Overall, teachers reported that the opportunities to meet regularly were crucial for learning about how to best meet their students' needs and for establishing consistency in teaching practices throughout their school.

Principles for Quality Instruction of Adolescent ELLs

Our analysis of student achievement and classroom observation data collected from all participating New York City middle and high schools, including Gregorio Luperon High School, is ongoing. This ongoing analysis provides important information about the support that teachers need to transfer new knowledge and teaching practices into their classrooms and how these teaching practices influence student learning. In particular, data results highlight areas that must be addressed in the design of the professional development programs, such as continuing to strengthen the level of follow-up support provided to teachers and schools. Our experiences to date, however, as developers, trainers, and teachers with both professional development programs suggest some principles for quality instruction for adolescent ELLs.

- The key elements of reading development (e.g., phonological knowledge, fluency, vocabulary, and comprehension) are the same for English-only or English-proficient students reading below grade level and ELLs in secondary schools. The instructional strategies recommended for teaching reading to ELLs are effective for all learners.
- ELLs should have opportunities every day to learn about and practice using new words and reading comprehension strategies in each content area classroom. Students also need daily opportunities to learn about and practice content-specific writing, such as formulating and solving mathematics problems, producing summaries of historical events, or explaining scientific processes.
- When all teachers—ESL, reading, special education, and content area—work together, more students achieve. ESL, reading, and special education teachers must work in tandem with content teachers to accelerate students' learning and application of new words and reading and writing strategies.
- Professional development designs should provide teachers with tools such as an observation protocol to help them reflect upon their teaching practices and determine how teaching practices influence student learning.

Educating ELLs for success in a complex world requires powerful learning by a whole school—not just the ESL teachers. Comprehensive learning, lesson study, and observation protocols can help educators change the culture of a school so that all students and teachers can improve their learning on a continuous basis.

REFLECTION QUESTIONS

1. What steps can you take to provide your ELLs with more opportunities to learn vocabulary as you teach in the content areas?

2. Consider one of your content area reading selections in light of the guidelines for selecting words to teach for ELLs presented in this chapter. What words might you select to teach after reading this chapter that you might not have selected previously?

3. What steps can you take to provide your ELLs with more opportunities to learn about and apply reading comprehension strategies as they read in the content areas?

4. The teachers in these professional development programs had many opportunities to collaborate with their colleagues. What steps can you take to increase opportunities to collaborate at your grade level and throughout your school?

REFERENCES

Abedi, J. (2004). The No Child Left Behind Act and English language learners: Assessment and accountability issues. *Educational Researcher, 33*(1), 4–14.

August, D., Calderón, M.E., & Carlo, M. (2001). Transfer of reading skills from Spanish to English: A study of young learners. *National Association of Bilingual Education Journal, 24*(4), 11–42.

Batalova, J., Fix, M., & Murray, J. (2007). *Measures of change: The demography and literacy of adolescent English learners: A report to the Carnegie Corporation of New York.* Washington, DC: Migration Policy Institute.

Beck, I.L., McKeown, M.G., & Kucan, L. (2002). *Bringing words to life: Robust vocabulary instruction.* New York: Guilford.

Biancarosa, G. (2005). After third grade. *Educational Leadership, (63)*2, 16–22.

Calderón, M.E. (2007a). *Teaching reading to English language learners, grades 6–12.* Thousand Oaks, CA: Corwin.

Calderón, M.E. (2007b). What do we mean by "quality instruction" for adolescent English language learners? *Voices in Urban Education, 15,* 29–36.

Calderón, M.E. (2008). *Reading instructional goals for older readers: RIGOR reading series in Spanish and English for English language learners in grades 4–12.* Pelham, NY: Benchmark Education.

Calderón, M.E., August, D., Slavin, R.E., Madden, N.A., Durán, D.A., & Cheung, A. (2005). Bringing words to life for ELLs. In E.H. Hiebert & M.L. Kamil (Eds.), *Teaching and learning vocabulary: Bringing research to practice* (pp. 115–136). Mahwah, NJ: Erlbaum.

Calderón, M.E., Hertz-Lazarowitz, R., & Slavin, R.E. (1998). Effects of bilingual cooperative integrated reading and composition on students making the transition from Spanish to English reading. *The Elementary School Journal, 99*(2), 153–165. doi:10.1086/461920

Ivey, G., & Broaddus, K. (2007). A formative experiment investigating literacy engagement among adolescent Latina/o students just beginning to read, write, and speak English. *Reading Research Quarterly, 42*(4), 512–545. doi:10.1598/RRQ.42.4.4

Jiménez, R.T. (2004). Reconceptualizing the literacy learning of Latino students. In D.S. Strickland & D.E. Alvermann (Eds.), *Bridging the literacy achievement gap grades 4–12.* New York: Teachers College Press.

Lee, J., Grigg, W., & Donahue, P. (2007). *The nation's report card: Reading 2007.* Washington, DC: National Center for Education Statistics. Retrieved April 28, 2009, from nces.ed.gov/pubsearch/pubsinfo.asp?pubid=2007496.

Nagy, W.E., & Anderson, R.C. (1984). How many words are there in printed school English? *Reading Research Quarterly, 19*(3), 304–330. doi:10.2307/747823

National Institute of Child Health and Human Development. (2000). *Report of the National Reading Panel. Teaching children to read: An evidence-based assessment of the scientific research literature on reading and its implications for reading instruction* (NIH Publication No. 00-4769). Washington, DC: U.S. Government Printing Office.

RAND Reading Study Group. (2002). *Reading for understanding: Toward an R&D program in reading comprehension.* Santa Monica, CA: RAND.

Ruiz-de-Velasco, J., & Fix, M., & Clewell, B. (2000). *Overlooked and underserved: Immigrant students in U.S. secondary schools.* Washington, DC: Urban Institute.

Samuels, S.J. (2002). Reading fluency: Its development and assessment. In A.E. Farstrup & S.J. Samuels (Eds.), *What research has to say about reading instruction* (3rd ed., pp. 166–183). Newark, DE: International Reading Association.

Short, D., & Fitzsimmons, S. (2006). *Double the work: Challenges and solutions to acquiring language and academic literacy for adolescent English language learners.* Washington, DC: Alliance for Excellent Education.

Strickland, D.S., & Alvermann, D.E. (Eds.). (2004). *Bridging the literacy achievement gap grades 4–12.* New York: Teachers College Press.

Valdés, G. (2001). *Learning and not learning English.* New York: Teachers College Press.

AUTHOR INDEX

SUBJECT INDEX

Note. Page numbers followed by *f* or *t* indicate figures or tables, respectively.

PHONICS AWARENESS SKILLS, 16
PHONOLOGICAL LEARNING, 33–35
PICTURE/TEXT TALK, 182
PICTURE WORD CARDS, 49
PICTURE WORD INDUCTIVE MODEL, 182
POETRY: ABCs model, 241–242, 241f–242f; integrating with science instruction, 149–151
POLAND, 236
PORTUGUESE LANGUAGE, 74
PRE-LAS ORAL, 46
PRIMARY GRADES. *See* ELEMENTARY GRADES
PROFESSIONAL DEVELOPMENT: CAP inservice program, 227–250, 232t, 233t; collaborating with family members, 207–226, 231; current studies of, 251–253; ExC-ELL program, 253–260; influence of, 262–266; literature circles and, 108–109; principles for quality instruction, 266–267; RIGOR program, 253, 260–262; teaching without preparation and, 181
PUERTO RICO, 166, 236

Q–R

QUALITATIVE READING INVENTORY, 45, 46, 47
QUESTIONER ROLE (LITERATURE CIRCLES), 92
READERS THEATRE SCRIPTS, 68
READING DEVELOPMENT. *See also* LITERATURE CIRCLES: ExC-ELL program, 258; influences of professional development, 264–265; Personal Readers for, 35–36; reinforcing natural language, 51–52; repeated reading, 35–36; RIGOR program, 261–262; word hunts, 35–36
READING INSTRUCTIONAL GOALS FOR OLDER READERS (RIGOR): about, 253, 260–261; reading comprehension, 261–262
READING INVENTORY FOR LITERACY ASSESSMENT, 15
READING RECOVERY PROGRAM, 222
THE RED ROSE BOX (WOODS), 100
REMEMBERING (TYPE OF THINKING), 132, 133
REPEATED READING, PERSONAL READERS FOR, 35–36
REREADING IN GUIDED WRITING, 183
RESEARCH ON LEARNING: basis of second language learning, 42–43; cognition, 42; on professional development, 234
RESEARCHER ROLE (LITERATURE CIRCLES), 92, 110
RESPONSE (CLASSROOM INTERACTION), 163–172
RHYMING (PHONOLOGICAL LEARNING), 33
RIGOR. *See* READING INSTRUCTIONAL GOALS FOR OLDER READERS (RIGOR)
RUSSIAN LANGUAGE, 99

S

SADAKO AND THE THOUSAND PAPER CRANES (COERR), 100
SCAFFOLDED READING EXPERIENCES (SREs): assessing effects of, 135–137; balancing challenging and easy reading, 126; defined, 4–5; development of, 121–123; fostering deep understanding, 131–135; fostering higher order thinking, 131–135; frequency of, 123–124; guided writing and, 194–195; how much to provide, 124; how often to differentiate activities, 125–126; implementation challenges/decisions, 123–130; involving students in constructing, 129–130; literature circles and, 93–94, 96, 109–115; possible components, 122t; tailoring tasks to ensure success, 127–129
SCENE SETTER ROLE (LITERATURE CIRCLES), 92, 110
SCHOOL–COMMUNITY CONNECTION, 234–236, 235f, 245–246
SCIENCE FOR ALL PROJECT, 146
SCIENCE INSTRUCTION: academic language and literacy, 142–144; classroom portrait, 151–153; current approaches for ELLs, 144–147; differentiated instruction, 148–149, 151–156; grouping students, 147–149; integrated, 153–155; ongoing challenges, 156; raising achievement in, 156–157; "risk factors," 157; role in language development, 140–160; whole-group instruction, 148
SEATTLE UNIVERSITY, 98
SECOND LANGUAGE LEARNING. *See* ENGLISH AS A SECOND LANGUAGE (ESL)
SECONDARY SCHOOLS: organizing classroom instruction, 161–179; professional development, 251–269; scaffolding reading experiences, 121–139; science instruction, 140–160; supporting writing development, 180–203
SEVEN BRAVE WOMEN (HEARNE), 242
SHELTERED INSTRUCTION (SI) MODEL: defined, 165; guided writing in, 181–201
SHOE SHINE GIRL (BULLA), 109
SI MODEL. *See* SHELTERED INSTRUCTION (SI) MODEL
SIGHT WORDS: for literacy assessment, 16; for word study development, 32
SIGN OF THE BEAVER (SPEARE), 100
SING DOWN THE MOON (O'DELL), 100, 103, 106
SOCIAL LANGUAGE, 96
SOMALI-SPEAKING BACKGROUND, 13
SORTING ACTIVITIES: developmental word study, 26–31, 28t, 30f; transitional reading stage, 31–32